How to Stop Destroying Your Relationships

By Albert Ellis

Anger: How to Live With It and Without It

How to Control Your Anxiety: Before It Controls You

How to Stubbornly Refuse to Make Yourself Miserable:
About Anything – Yes, Anything!

How to Control Your Anger: Before It Controls You
With Raymond Chip Tafrate

How to Keep People From Pushing Your Buttons
With Arthur Lange

How to Stop Destroying Your Relationships
With Robert A. Harper

How to Stop Destroying Your Relationships:
A Guide to Enjoyable Dating, Mating, and Relating

Albert Ellis, Ph.D.
and
Robert A. Harper, Ph.D.

ROBINSON

ROBINSON

First published in the US in 2001 by Citadel Press Books,
an imprint of Kensington Publishing Corp.

First published in Great Britain in 2019 by Robinson

1 3 5 7 9 10 8 6 4 2

A CIP catalogue record for this book
is available from the British Library.

ISBN:978-1-47214-280-1

Printed and bound in Great Britain by CPI Group (UK) Ltd, Croydon CR0 4YY

Papers used by Robinson are from well-managed forests
and other responsible sources.

MIX
Paper from
responsible sources
FSC® C104740

Robinson
An imprint of
Little, Brown Book Group
Carmelite House
50 Victoria Embankment
London EC4Y 0DZ

An Hachette UK Company
www.hachette.co.uk

www.littlebrown.co.uk

To Janet L. Wolfe and Mimi Harper,
who have rationally tolerated us as their mates for lo,
these many years.
Affectionately and lovingly,

A.E.
R.A.H.

Contents

Contents

Foreword

When Drs. Ellis and Harper wrote *How to Stop Destroying Your Relationships*, published in 2001, they had considered simply revising their 1961 publication, *A Guide to Successful Marriage*. However, because of the many changes intimate relationships have undergone since the 1960s, the authors had the wisdom not to do that, but chose instead to write a different book that reflected the evolution of relationships. In the '60s, intimate relationships typically resulted in marriage, marriage was between a man and a woman, people generally did not live together prior to marriage, and marriages commonly lasted longer than they do now. When *A Guide to Successful Marriage* was written, gender roles were rigid, women were socialized to believe that their "job" was to be wives and mothers rather than equal partners in the workplace, and same-sex or mixed-race couples were not very common, nor were they accepted by the culture. Obviously a new book needed to reflect—and this one does—the immense changes that have transpired since the 1960s while at the same time maintaining the core REBT concepts that contribute so significantly to successful dating and mating.

Albert Ellis and Robert Harper met in 1950 at the American Association of Marital and Family Therapy and maintained a relationship until Harper's death in 2004. Harper became one of Ellis's first collaborators and a longstanding staunch supporter. They both worked in the field of sex and marriage for many years and wrote several books together; equally important, they were both "outlaws," united in their distaste for puritanical ideas, particularly in the field of marriage and sex. Their combined years of extensive experience as clinicians and scholars more than qualified them to publish a self-help book for couples who want to learn how to relate more effectively with each other. The authors' stated goal is to help couples relate more "interestingly" and "enjoyably" (p. 2)—and what couple wouldn't want that? In their no-nonsense, down-to-earth manner, the authors systematically describe, through verbatim transcripts, case studies, and numerous exercises, how couples can work on themselves to have a positive impact on their relationships.

I recently reread *How to Stop Destroying Your Relationships* and was impressed with the relevance of the concepts for contemporary couples of "all makes and models." Having personally worked for many years with couples in private practice, what I have seen all too often is what Ellis and Harper emphasize in this book, that it takes two people to make a couple. But when couples have problems, they tend to blame the relationship or their partner instead of looking at all the elements that make up the whole. This is best exemplified when the partners are unwilling to change or the therapist is unsuccessful in helping them "own" their problems: partners who don't look at how *each* contributes to relationship problems take their problems into the next relationship. For instance, if each fails to see that demands about how the partner *should* behave contribute to the problems in the relationship and as a result the relationship ends, each may enter a new relationship only to fall into the same pattern of making demands of the new partner. As Ellis and Harper point out in their book, blaming others is easier than taking a look at one's own issues. If this example applies to you, this book will help you break out of your old patterns and get on a new and improved track.

When you look at the contents of this book, you see that Ellis and Harper pinpoint pertinent issues that all types of couples face throughout the course of a relationship. It would be a very rare but lucky couple who don't have some issues with communication, sex, money, in-laws, and perhaps the decision whether or not to have children. The book's emphasis on building a deep and long-lasting relationship is undoubtedly of value to every couple; thus it is as relevant today as ever. Despite new challenges that may have arisen since 2001, Ellis and Harper's main contention still applies: the key to a successful relationship is to understand that it cannot change until the individuals recognize how their beliefs affect their emotions and behaviors, and in turn, the relationship. This concept is the cornerstone of REBT and hasn't changed since the inception of the theory in the 1950s; it transcends time and has retained its relevance.

As a therapist, I was especially pleased to note once again that chapter 3 addresses the importance of having realistic views about a relationship. So often, couples set themselves up for disappointment and perhaps failure by clinging to the myth of romantic love as the "key" to success. If they buy into this myth, they believe that "love will conquer all," that they must "always satisfy each other's needs," and that "if they love each other, they will never disagree" (because to disagree would mean there was something drastically wrong with the relationship). If your goal as a reader is to have realistic expectations about your relationship and relate more successfully with your partner, the exercises at the end of that chapter should be particularly helpful.

Readers who wish to use this self-help book to improve their relationships will find it works in many ways. First, the book is easy and entertaining to read. It is apparent that Ellis and Harper had great senses of humor, were authentic as therapists, and knew what they were talking about. Second, they use short case examples and session transcripts to help the reader understand the concepts. There is not a lot of jargon or "psychological babble" to put readers off—it is a straightforward read with ideas that make sense. Third, as mentioned, the exercises at the end of each chapter are thought-provoking and enlightening. As a way of communicating and working through issues that are or could become problematic, both partners can complete these exercises individually, then discuss your responses.

If you want to work on your relationships, this comprehensive book can be very empowering. You first need to accept Ellis and Harper's contention that it is only *partly* true that another person's behavior upsets you and recognize that you largely disturb *yourself* about your partner's actions. Once you have achieved this, you can begin to realize that while you might not be able to change the other person, you can change how you think about the other's behavior and thus reduce the strong negative emotions and behaviors that impede good communication and problem solving. By conscientiously completing the exercises in each chapter you can learn basic REBT concepts and recognize your own behaviors that contribute to or sabotage good relationships. Ellis and Harper have shared information that from experience they know works! It is up to you to apply the concepts to your own relationships. Meeting this challenge may take some persistence, but little in life is accomplished without effort—and this definitely applies to relationships. Does it make sense to think a relationship can thrive if you never give it a tune up? Of course not! This self-help book will give you lots of insight into how to stop destroying your relationships. So start reading, apply the ideas, and enjoy your "new and improved" relationship.

Ann Vernon, Ph.D.
President, Albert Ellis Institute

Preface

Do we have the right to pen a *new* book on dating, mating, and relating? Well, yes—in fact, we do. Both of us have worked for decades in the sex/marriage/family (SMF) field—teaching, counseling, writing, and speaking. Both of us are pioneers in liberal and democratic approaches to SMF problems, sometimes to our detriment. Largely because of our full-time business as psychologists we have never undertaken a revision of our 1961 book, *A Guide to Successful Marriage*. For all its usefulness and continued popularity, changes in the four decades since the book appeared have made a revision seem inadequate. Instead, we decided to produce a new and different book on how two people can intimately relate, mainly—though it may sound odd—for their own sheer enjoyment.

In this book, we use the word "intimate" to refer simply to a "close personal relationship," not to indicate a sexual relationship. You and your partner may have a close relationship though nothing erotic has ever occurred between you, while another couple, even if they copulate extensively, may never develop real intimacy. We will focus on your achieving and maintaining intimacy in a close relationship, whether you are married or single, having sex or not, heterosexual or homosexual. The close relationships we will look at are those in which people are married or living together in an intimate, and not merely sexual, relationship. We will show you how when a close personal relationship of yours falters or fails, the relationship itself is rarely entirely to blame. We shall explore not only the nature of your problems, but ways of alleviating them.

As we try to be in our relationship therapy, so in this book we will strive to be even-handed and nonjudgmental in our approach. We will look at several types of couples: young and older, gay and straight; and show how overcoming difficulties in close personal relationships is similar to handling individual problems. So try to learn from the variety of couples presented. Don't pass over those that seem foreign to you, as the relationship and its problems might be closer to your own than you expect.

What we emphasize first and foremost is choice. Our mission is to help two (or more) people to relate more interestingly and enjoyably to one another—but only *if they so choose.* You are free to decide to relate to other people or not at all. No one *must* learn to function well in couplehood, but we have found that an overwhelming majority of people do want to learn how to do so.

While couples and families normally live with other people, couples are the main focus of this book. However, in many instances, close personal relationships include more than two people, so we have included chapters on getting along together and with others, including friends, in-laws, and children. We look closely at couples, remembering that we are not dealing with a mystical "relationship" but with two interacting *individuals.* The individual is key to the relationship, because only by working on him or herself does each individual improve his or her interaction.

Fun is a great ingredient in a close relationship, so we even try, while endorsing this concept, to have some fun ourselves. In our rational emotive behavior therapy (REBT) philosophy, long-term enjoyment of life is what makes sense. We hope you find such long-term satisfaction and your own sparkling happy couple in the process.

Cheers,

Albert Ellis, Ph.D.
Albert Ellis Institute
New York City

Robert A. Harper, Ph.D.
Washington, D.C.

1

Getting Relationships Together by Getting Yourself Together

Newborn infants often panic when a newspaper or a paper bag is rustled near their ears. To them, with their near-zero experience with the non-uterine world, any sudden change in the messages impinging on their senses may represent a great threat. As experiences increase, so may real or imagined dangers. Some dangers lessen or disappear, but others increase. As the eight-year-old shows when he or she hides in the closet at a thunderclap, experience does not necessarily teach one how to deal with fear.

How can you learn to live a relatively unpanicked life? How can you tolerate the frustrations of coupling? Not easily! Most of us learn to face crackling paper and even thunder without fear, but we tend to pick up other disturbances that interrupt our individual happiness and render us undelightful to another person who wants to keep closely relating.

Before you contemplate and get involved in couplehood, you had better keep two things in the back of your mind. First, you must make substantial headway in accepting and coping with your own life. Second, be sure to look for long-term satisfactions—not just immediate gratifications.

We emphasize coupling when we deal with happiness-seeking

not because we believe that true and lasting enjoyment cannot be achieved by solitary individuals—both history and current observation prove that it can be—but because humans try, and often try repeatedly, to be in happily intimate relationships. Also, our long experience as scientists, educators, and clinicians indicates that most of us can use all the help we can get in learning how to couple happily.

We developed the Rational Emotive Behavior Therapy (REBT) theory of human behavior in the mid-1950s. This theory holds that people are born with strong tendencies to act both well (self-helpfully) and badly (self-defeatingly), but that they have considerable choice in the way they react. You, as a human, are born with two conflicting tendencies: a tendency to needlessly (and, hence, neurotically) disturb yourself, and a tendency to seek enjoyable, non-disturbed thoughts, feelings, and behaviors. REBT tries to help you to enhance the positive second tendency and to reduce the strength and persistence of the first, which is often reinforced by yourself and by others.

Before we get to the major principles of REBT and how to apply them to your life, let us present some basic facts about humans and human behavior.

First off, all human behavior (thinking, perceiving, feeling, and acting) derives from individuals. No proof has ever been uncovered of a collective unconscious, let alone a collective conscious. Also, there is no such thing as a mystical couple merged into one being. Therefore, you have to make efforts at changing a relationship first within yourself. Then you have to *agree* with your partner that you will do or not do certain things to improve your relationship, and vice versa. But whatever middle ground you come to as a couple, your actions or inactions (and the attitudes behind them) still belong to you (Individual A) and to your partner (Individual B) separately.

Keeping that in mind, know that you can only directly change yourself. Even if you are a therapist, all you can do is try to make change seem attractive and interesting and possible for someone else—it's up to the individual whether or not s/he makes the change.

If you think you can change Individual B or that s/he automatically *should* change (because, after all, look how wonderfully changed *you* are), trouble will likely ensue!

Individuals function more effectively and enjoyably when they learn to reduce their tendency—either instilled early on or possibly innate—to rate themselves. Contrary to many other psychotherapists and educators, we have long contended that self-esteem is something to shun rather than to embrace and enhance. By all means take satisfaction in your behavior—your thoughts, feelings, perceptions, and actions—and rate or have your behavior rated by others as "good" or "bad." But rating your personhood, your totality, your self is bound to be incomplete and inaccurate. Is a "good person" always "good" and therefore a "good" hockey player, orator, or electronic troubleshooter all at once? *Self*-ratings can have distracting and disturbing effects. If you are focused on "How am I as a person?" or *"Am* I what others rate me to be?" you are probably reducing the effectiveness of what you are *doing* to that degree. Self-rating leads to self-cremating.

The next principle is a tough one to understand and difficult to act on in your daily life, as most of us have been immersed in the process of rating the total person (ourselves and others) since infancy. "She's a good baby." "I'm a bad person." Many of the efforts of REBT are directed toward helping people overcome their tendencies to rate themselves and others as persons, and instead only to evaluate actions. By rating people's actions, separate from their personhood, we can learn to live more happily.

Let's step back for a moment to examine the ABCs of REBT. *A* stands for the activating events or adversities in your life—the phone is ringing, your jury duty notice has arrived, or your life raft has developed a leak. *B* is your beliefs or belief system, or how you filter the *A*'s. *C* is for consequences (emotional and behavioral) and is a result of how you used *B* to deal with *A*. Like most people, you probably thought that A (adversities) produces C (consequences) directly and naturally. But that isn't necessarily the case. REBT teaches you to understand that your Bs largely effect your Cs. Let us illustrate.

Charlene, an intelligent and energetic fifteen-year-old, sought therapy because, in her words: "I have just squarely faced the fact that I am a lesbian, and naturally it blows my mind. What a shit I am for letting myself be attracted to *women*. I've known about my lesbianism for a long time, but I kept telling myself that it would blow over—it was a phase I was going through. Now I'm looking at it—I'm a total goddamned dyke. And it's terrible, and I hate it! I am miserable. I don't want to live, but my mother, who doesn't know what's eating me but knows something is, made me come to see you. I know it won't do a damned bit of good. I want to fucking well die." Dr. Harper had several REBT sessions with Charlene. Here is an excerpt from one of their sessions.

R.A.H.: Charlene, of course, you have the right to die, but dying is an irrevocable decision. Since you have gone to the trouble of coming here, let's look at some of the assumptions you are making. While it's possible that you may not be lesbian, let's assume for the time being that you are. Why do you think being a lesbian makes you a shit?

Charlene: Well, doesn't it? Anybody who wants to be normal and get married and have kids and be respected in the community and ends up a lesbian ends up a shit. Ask anybody—except maybe another lesbian.

R.A.H.: Your exception tells me that you don't necessarily believe that a lesbian *must* be and *must* feel herself to be a shit. So you grant the possibility that a lesbian does not *have* to rate herself negatively and go around feeling miserable.

Charlene: Yeah, but this is all theoretical crud. The *fact* is that I'm a lesbian and I don't want to be and I think I'm a shit and I'd rather die than go on this way.

R.A.H.: Please understand that I fully accept you as a person who has an undeniable right to feel however you choose to feel. That's the concept: *choice*. And by this I mean a *practical* choice, not just some way-out theoretical choice.

Charlene: You mean I can choose whether to be a lesbian or not?

R.A.H.: What you can choose is whether or not to act on it. But for now let's assume that you are a lesbian, and we are challenging your assumption that this makes you a shit. Because you understandably want results and not a philosophical discussion at this point, close your eyes, please. Now think, "I am a lesbian," and tell me what you are feeling.

Charlene: What I've already told you: shitty, terrible, miserable, like dying.

R.A.H.: Okay. Keeping your eyes closed, think, "I am a lesbian," but see if you can *feel* any differently about it.

Charlene: Oh, come on. You're treating me like a stupid child.

R.A.H.: It probably seems that way to you, but *I* think I am accepting you as a full person who has developed some heavy self-downing ways and could use a little help in easing up on it. So what have you got to lose? Please close your eyes again and think, "I am a lesbian." Now see if you can feel less miserable about it.

Charlene (after several silent minutes and with eyes still closed): Well, maybe now I feel like yeah, I'm a lesbian, but maybe it's not the end of the world. I suppose I don't have to die, but I still see a pretty shitty life for myself compared with what I'd thought I would be: a beautiful and brilliant young physician who is also a perfect wife and mother to a perfect husband and three perfect children. To say the least, I feel disappointed. *(She opens her eyes and gives a rather sickly smile.)*

R.A.H.: Splendid! You have quickly moved from *despair* to feeling *disappointment.* There is a world of difference: In despair, as you know, all hope is gone; in disappointment, no matter how crushed and discouraged you feel, hope creeps back in. Tell me, how did you change your feelings?

Charlene: I'm not sure, but I think the way you reacted to me showed me that it was at least worth *trying* to feel differently about being a lesbian. As I tried I thought about how *you* weren't treating me like a shit—so maybe I wasn't entirely a shit. But I also thought about a number of people who are lesbians and who don't despair about it. They're not blowing their brains out or jumping in front of a train.

R.A.H.: Very good again! You realize that your self-acceptance was encouraged by my unconditional acceptance of you as a person, but that was not the whole reason your self-feelings started to change. You began to think of some other people and their behavior, which cast some doubt on your earlier conviction that lesbianism and shithood are synonymous. Are you also starting to see how what you think and what you *feel* are so mixed up in each other that it becomes hard to distinguish one from the other?

Charlene: Yeah, I suppose if I *think* I'm a shit for being a lesbian, I'm going to *feel* like a shit. Which, by the way, I still do. I just don't feel all's necessarily lost.

R.A.H.: That is progress. None of us completely transforms his/her behavior in one easy lesson. To change even the simplest thoughts, feelings, and actions often takes long, hard, and persistent work. But that's life—and it's not awful.

Through her comments about thinking and feeling, Charlene indicated she was already beginning to understand the fundamentals of the ABCs of REBT: namely, that her beliefs about lesbianism and not the activating event of her "discovery" of her sexual disposition led to her feelings (consequences). Dr. Harper indicated to her, however, this fine beginning did not mean that Charlene would not have a long and difficult learning process ahead. While she saw this, she also saw that it might work, so we continued working on the ABCs of her feelings and on her understanding and challenging her self-rating process.

By gradually learning to make better judgments about her thoughts, feelings, actions, and perceptions—her behavior—*instead* of making judgments about her total self or personhood, Charlene chose this solution to the problem of self-downing. No person can be shown to be, as a person, good or bad. Either way is an unprovable assumption. However, you will feel miserable if you assume that you *are* bad (at the core no damned good), and you'll feel much better if you assume that you're okay—that is, a satisfactory human being. Why not make the assumption that makes you feel better?

"*But,*" Charlene said at first (like many of our clients do), "it is no assumption that I am a shitty person. I really am." Over and over again we had to help her see that she was accepting an arbitrary and unprovable judgment as indisputable and unchangeable, and that was a *choice* she was making. She could, as I kept pointing out, learn to dispute such a nonsensical and destructive judgment of herself and gradually (with diligent persistence) substitute a more positive self-rating.

As REBT therapists we are never wholly satisfied with what we call the inelegant, but workable, solution chosen by Charlene. Why? Because we are quite aware that positive self-evaluations are readily reversible. If you become convinced you are a good person for any reason except "because I exist," that reason can be snatched away, and you can be left again with the old conviction that you are somehow inadequate, unacceptable, undesirable, inferior, or "bad" because you were not able to achieve whatever you had decided you *had* to achieve to be "good."

We believe, however, that if you work hard at challenging your self-downing judgments, substituting positive judgments, and deciding, "I am good only because I am alive and not because of the worthy things I do," you are likely to end up close to what we call the elegant therapeutic solution. That solution (like all things human, imperfectly stated and imperfectly executed by anyone) is to not rate your self or essence or personhood *at all*. Instead, you must learn to rate only what you think, feel, and *do*. You, of course, are responsible for your actions. But ideally you should rate only your *actions* and not your *youness* or *self*.

Learning not to rate yourself as a person means learning not to rate the personhood of others. Because this concept probably goes against the way most of you have been brought up, and it is possibly contrary to your biological nature, none of you is likely to become perfect at not judging others as persons any more than you are going to overcome the tendencies to rate your total selves. But if you become more conscious of how you are rating yourself and others, you can make a lot of progress—progress that will definitely help you in couplehood.

Is this all you have to know about REBT and how to get it all together for a happy and functional union? Not really! But it is not a bad beginning. What we've covered so far is not easy. It will take a lot of hard work on your part to successfully apply this chapter.

But this hard work will definitely pay off whether you are in or out of couplehood. Whether or not you take our advice is your choice, but if you take it, you may learn how to live more effectively and enjoyably. At the end of this chapter, you'll find a few exercises that will start you off on the hard—but very rewarding—work of achieving unconditional self-acceptance (USA) and other thoughts, feelings, and behaviors that will help you in your dating, relating, and mating goals.

EXERCISES TO KEEP YOU EMOTIONALLY FIT

It is easy to read about—and even to think about—what you're doing badly. We wrote this book to give you insight into how you and your mate are defeating yourselves and what you can do about changing. Insight, however, is not enough. Some of the most brilliant insights you have, and often keep having, can sound great. Utterly real. Quite convincing. But, as I, Dr. Ellis, discovered when I was a card-carrying psychoanalyst, some of these insights can be pretty useless.

One of my clients, a twenty-five-year-old teacher named Carol, who I saw in the 1950s, insisted that she had "good, healthy relations" with her mother, father, and younger brother and couldn't understand why she was so hostile toward her boyfriend, Don. I soon found out that she was intensely jealous of her mother, terribly hurt by her father's favoring her brother, and exceptionally angry at her boyfriend for ignoring her demands for more affection. Carol was thrilled with these important insights and was sure that they explained her hostility. She thought that these revelations would cure her. Well, they didn't. For the next few months, Carol's rage against Don escalated and he threatened to break up with her. Carol was distraught about this—and about the dismal failure of her insights into her hidden feelings to help her.

Fortunately, I was becoming skeptical myself at that time about the virtues of psychoanalytic revelations. So I went back to the details of Carol's two-year relationship with Don, and soon helped her gain a different kind of insight. Carol had with Don—as she had had all her life with other relatives and friends—an overwhelming Irrational Belief. "I absolutely *need* significant people's approval. Without it, I am a thoroughly unlovable, worthless person!" While that shook Carol up, it still didn't quite change her.

REBT—which I was then formulating but hadn't quite developed—tries to help people with a number of non-psychoanalytic insights. Let's take a few moments to review these insights and how they relate to Carol's situation.

As we have already noted, people rarely just *get* emotionally upset. They also actively *make* themselves anxious, depressed, and hostile with their beliefs (Bs) *about* the unfortunate adversities (A's) that happen to them. So Carol was *believing*, "I absolutely *need* greater affection than Don usually expresses—or else I am a thoroughly unlovable, worthless person!" When she did not get—or *thought* she did not get—what she "needed" from Don, she felt worthless. Noting this feeling and believing that Don's neglect *made* her feel inadequate (which is a common belief of self-downing people), Carol defensively turned some of her self-hatred against Don. No matter when Carol started to believe her IB about direfully needing people's affection, she was still holding it *in the present*, though it seemed to have originated in her childhood and adolescence. But she *still* strongly believed it—both consciously and unconsciously. She could have originally held it and later given it up, which would have meant she would *no longer* have been affected by it at the time she was. But that was not the case.

So, with my help Carol began to have insights into her early *and* her remaining need for significant people's expression of affection. What she did not yet see—and what it took me another year to show her as I kept developing REBT—was that insight by itself is not enough. The only way to correct her hostility toward Don was through hard and persistent *work and practice*—yes, work, and yes, practice. She had to *change* her IBs. When she began to do that, she started to feel much less angry and much more loving toward Don.

Actually, as she gave up her dire *need* for Don's affection, she realized that he probably would never fulfill her *preference* for affection, so she *un*angrily broke up with him. Eventually she found another—more loving—partner, whom she eventually married.

This book looks at the principles and practices of REBT as they relate to dating, mating, and relating. But we also include a number of exercises for relevant homework. As Daniel Goleman and other psychologists have emphasized, humans have academic or intellectual intelligence, but they also have emotional and practical intelligence. In REBT terms, they can think, can think about their thinking, and think about thinking about their thinking. This enables them to observe, analyze, and change their IBs, their disturbed feelings, and their dysfunctional behaviors. REBT shows them how.

As a human, you have emotional intelligence—which includes self-awareness, self-control, persistence, self-motivation, and social deftness. As you can see, self-awareness includes a good deal of thinking and thinking about thinking—and so do the other aspects of emotional intelligence. But therapy requires a considerable amount of work and practice—of pushing yourself, pushing yourself, and pushing yourself. And it also involves a lot of time and effort when you're not "on the couch"—a lot of homework—to get results. If you want to use it to change yourself in the process and make yourself—yes, *make* yourself—less disturbed and more fulfilled, you had better do your homework.

Remember, you don't *have* to do your homework. You don't *have* to do anything. You don't *have* to change and you don't necessarily *have* to work in order to change. But you preferably should. Not for our sake, but for your own and for the sake of those you want to relate to intimately.

The exercises in this chapter are designed to put you in touch with your feelings. Your feelings keep you alive and happy, even your negative feelings. When something goes wrong in your life—some adversity (A), such as failure, rejection, or discomfort—you want to feel bad, not happy or neutral. If you lose a partner, a good job, or a tennis match, you can try to be optimistic and tell yourself,

"That's great! What a fine opportunity to learn from my mistakes! That gives me something to live for!" Which is fine. By all means, learn from your errors and don't beat yourself up. But watch it. What about acknowledging your healthy *bad* feelings, such as sorrow and regret? Such as frustration and annoyance? Such as real determination to do better in the future? These healthy negative feelings motivate you to look at your failings, to work at correcting them, and to push yourself to improve. They energize and expand you. They are not too pleasant—but they help.

REBT, though highly cognitive, stresses feelings: pleasurable feelings that add to your life and unpleasant feelings that *also* add to your life. But it doesn't look at *all* feelings. Not even all "high" feelings—like narcissism and grandiosity. While these have their place—in moderation—they can also sabotage you. For example, when you insist that you run the universe and therefore can get anything you want. You know where this leads you.

But worse than these feelings are your strong negative *unhealthy* feelings. You fail at love, work, or tennis and you choose to feel panicked, depressed, enraged. *Choose?* Yes, you have considerable choice here. Panic, depression, and rage won't get you very far. Will they get you more love, better work, greater wins at tennis? Hardly.

REBT, like other major therapies, deals with your feelings— good, bad, or indifferent. But it is unique, however, in that it helps you to distinguish between healthy and unhealthy negative feelings. When something goes wrong—or you *make* it wrong—in your partnership and in your life, it is healthy to feel *healthily* sorry, regretful, frustrated, and displeased. These feelings help you acknowledge, cope with, preferably change, or at worst accept adversities (A's) that you presently can't change. *Healthy* negative feelings can be aversive and unfriendly but they are not usually self-sabotaging.

Sample Exercise 1A: Becoming Aware of Your Healthy and Unhealthy Negative Feelings

List Some of My Main Goals, Purposes, and Values

My General Relating and Mating Goals	My Specific Goals
To find a suitable love partner.	To discover more about my partner.
To win his or her favor.	To see more of him or her.
To build an ongoing relationship with him or her.	To commit to him or her.
To maintain that steady relationship.	To have satisfactory sex with him or her.
	To find enjoyable pursuits with him or her.
	To discuss important questions with him or her.
	To agree to differ at times with him or her.
	To resolve some of my main disagreements with him or her.
	To live successfully with my remaining disagreements with him or her.
	To stop criticizing him or her.
	To resolve my hostility toward him or her.
	To get along well with my partner's parents.
	To get along well with my partner's friends.

Exercise 1A

My General Relating and Mating Goals	Specific Relating and Mating Goals
_____	_____
_____	_____
_____	_____
_____	_____
_____	_____
_____	_____
_____	_____
_____	_____
_____	_____
_____	_____
_____	_____
_____	_____
_____	_____

Sample Exercise 1B: Becoming Aware of My Healthy and Unhealthy Negative Feelings When My Relating and Mating Goals Are Blocked and I Am Faced With Adversities (A's)

Adversities That Might Occur	Healthy Negative Feelings I Might Experience	Unhealthy Negative Feelings I Might Experience
I keep looking for but cannot find a suitable partner.	Disappointment	Depression; horror
I find a suitable partner but get rejected.	Sorrow; regret	Panic; depression
I get in a good relationship but it breaks up.	Real sadness; grief	Panic; depression; extreme loneliness
My partner disagrees with me on an important matter.	Disappointment; determination to reach an agreement	Anger; blaming my partner; panic
My partner severely criticizes me.	Keen disappointment; regret	Self-damning; rage at partner
My partner's mother is impossible.	Frustration; disappointment	Impatience; frustration intolerance; anger at partner for making me visit his or her mother
My partner keeps avoiding me sexually.	Frustration; disappointment	Feelings of inadequacy; rage at partner; avoiding discussing this matter

Exercise 1B

Adversities That Might Occur	Healthy Negative Feelings I Might Experience	Unhealthy Negative Feelings I Might Experience

Sample Exercise 1C: What I Can Do to Change My Unhealthy Negative Feelings to Healthy Negative Feelings When I Am Faced with Relating and Mating Blocks and Adversities (A's)

Unhealthy Negative Feelings That I Might Experience	How I Can Change My Unhealthy Negative Feelings to Healthy Negative Feelings
Depression and horror when I cannot find a suitable partner.	I can transform my depression into keen disappointment by convincing myself that it is difficult but not impossible to find a suitable partner and that if I keep undepressively looking I will probably find one. I can accept the *bad* but not *awful* reality that if I never find a suitable partner I can still be a reasonably happy person.
Panic and depression when I find a suitable partner but then get rejected.	I can make myself feel only sorrow and regret by showing myself that I *can* find another suitable partner and succeed with him or her. I can convince myself that I may have failings for this potential mate but that I am not a *total failure*. I can show myself that rejection is *bad* but it is not *the end of the world*.
Panic, depression, extreme loneliness when I get in a good relationship but it breaks up.	I can make myself feel only real sadness and grief by convincing myself that being alone is very *uncomfortable* but not *horrible;* that it is most probably temporary and not permanent; and that perhaps I can learn from this break-up and later do better in a realationship with a partner more compatible with me.

Exercise 1C

Unhealthy Negative Feelings That I Actually Experience	How I Can Change My Unhealthy Negative Feelings to Healthy Negative Feelings

2

Getting Relationships Together as a Couple: Using the ABCs of REBT in Your Relationship

Marital problems, and the ABCs that lead to them, are usually more complicated than the problems of a single person, such as Charlene, trying to find a suitable mate. Take the case of Sid and Jo, a married couple who came to see me, Dr. Ellis, because, they said, they loved each other deeply but were incessantly fighting. Sid's initial ABCs were simple. He said that Jo gave him very little sex, but that she had the gall to lie and say that she often not only initiated but had sex with Sid. Let's chart Sid's ABCs, starting with the A's and the Cs:

Adversities: Jo had sex with Sid, he claimed, about once a month. Worse, she insisted that they really had sex at least once a week. Sid saw himself as being very sexually deprived, and Jo denied this.

Consequences: Sid was angry with Jo and insisted that she was a "goddamned liar." She fought back—and they both got nowhere.

Sid—as you might well guess—fully acknowledged his anger but insisted, "Jo keeps saying she loves me, but gives me very little sex. Then she lies about it and that makes me very angry!"

"Oh, no," I objected during my first session with this couple. "She can't make you angry. Only *you* can."

"Well, she does! So there!"

Let's assume that you are right about Jo's behavior. She gives you little sex and then insists that she gives you more than she actually does. These are the As in the ABCs of REBT, your adversities.

"They damned well are!"

Jo tried to interrupt at this point, to show that Sid was wrong, but I stopped her. I explained briefly to them that even if Sid was mistaken, he *still* was needlessly upsetting himself about it and I wanted to show him how wrong he was about his "rightness" about Jo's disturbing him. So she agreed and I continued, talking mainly to Sid.

"So Jo is presenting you with your A's—your adversities. But obviously she can't *make* you angry, which is your consequence."

"She damned well can—and does!"

"No. Because if a hundred Jos deprived a hundred Sids of sex—as let's assume your Jo is doing—would all the Sids be just as angry as you are? Think, now—would they?"

"*Most* of them would be!"

"Yes, they probably would. But *all* of them—the *whole* hundred?"

"Well, no. I guess not."

"How come? What would the few unangry Sids be doing, be saying to themselves, to stop from infuriating themselves about their Jo's rotten behavior?"

"Oh, I don't know. I guess something like, 'Too bad Jo is that way about sex, and about lying about it. But she has some other good traits, too. And I still love her for *those* traits.'"

"Good! See, you nicely figured it out. You figured out that the unangry Sids could tell themselves unangry, self-pacifying beliefs (Bs) about Jo and about the adversities (A's) she is creating for them. Fine! You very clearly showed that unfortunate A's, by themselves, do not create disturbed Cs like anger. It is your Bs, along with your As, that largely lead to disturbed Cs. Do you see that?"

Sid said reluctantly, "Well, yes. I guess so."

Great! I said to myself. *Half the battle won.*

Still talking mainly to Sid, but hoping that Jo was listening, I then tried to show him that his rage at his wife, his C, stemmed largely from two different types of beliefs (Bs). He initially had Irrational Beliefs (IBs): "Jo gives me very little sex—and then lies about it. Therefore, Jo doesn't love me." But eventually, by stepping back and thinking the situation through, he was able to develop healthy, Rational Beliefs (RBs): "I don't *like* Jo's depriving me of sex—and lying about it, no less! I *wish* she would treat me better! But if she doesn't, too bad. It's not the end of the world, and I can still live with her and enjoy her other good traits. But I still *wish* that she'd change and give me more sex."

If Sid had *only* had these RBs in the first place about his adversities, he would most probably—I tried to show him—have strong negative feelings about being deprived, such as healthy feelings of disappointment and frustration, but he would not have had unhealthy feelings of rage. In REBT, we call these Healthy Consequences (HCs). Why are they healthy? Because unlike Unhealthy Consequences (UCs), these might help Sid cope with his sex deprivation and, instead of fighting nastily with Jo about it, he might find a noncombative way to encourage her to have more sex with him.

Sid and I knew, however, that he was not merely disappointed and frustrated by Jo's sexual *behavior* but also enraged at *her* for acting this "terrible" way. I asked him if he could figure out the additional IBs that led to his rage, his consequence.

"Jo has *no right* to treat me so badly—and then, to boot, lie about *not* doing so!" he said. "She *shouldn't* be that unfair! How *terrible* she is. She's a nasty, lying, *rotten person!*"

Sid was right. Almost certainly, these were his main IBs. And typically, they included, first, a basic, underlying absolutistic *should* or *must:* "Jo *absolutely must not* act the way she is acting!" Second, going along with Sid's grandiose, dogmatic demand were his "logical" conclusions: "Because she is behaving in a sexually frustrating way as she *must not*, it is *terrible* (totally wrong and inconvenient) and she is a nasty, lying *rotten person* (incapable of practically ever acting considerately and lovingly)."

Let's take a few moments to look at the IBs of REBT. When I (Dr. Ellis) first developed REBT in the mid-1950s, and after using it for a while, I discovered several types of IBs. These included:

1. Absolutistic musts, shoulds, oughts, and demands, such as "I *must* perform all important tasks well!" and "I absolutely *have to be*

approved or loved by people I care for!" —also known as "mustur-batory beliefs."

2. Core disturbing conclusions, which usually "logically" stem from or accompany these grandiose demands, such as, "If I don't do an important task well, as I absolutely must, I am an *incompetent, inadequate person!*" "If conditions are not as good for me as they *should* be and I get more frustrations than I *must* get, life is *awful* and *horrible* and I'll *never* be able to enjoy it at all!"

3. Automatic thoughts and unrealistic observations, which often stem from people's rigid musts and their core disturbing conclusions such as, "Because I absolutely *must* perform all important tasks well, and I will be an *incompetent, inadequate person* if I don't, I am sure that the paper I just wrote is one of the worst ever written and that I shall fail the course for which I wrote it" and "Because I *have to* win Jo's love and would be *totally unlovable* if I didn't, I am sure that I acted stupidly with her and that she will never have anything to do with me!"

What I came to learn through the years is that these beliefs are common, but that they work on different levels. The IBs of REBT changed and evolved throughout the next decades, basically demonstrating that people's—and couple's—absolutistic musts come first. At least, in the case of neurosis. I now assume—and most followers of REBT go along with me—that when you only have preferences and wishes, including *strong* preferences and wishes that you will tend to perform competently, that others will usually treat you nicely and fairly, and that the conditions under which you live will be good, you will rarely upset yourself when your preferences are not fulfilled. Yes, you will then rarely think, feel, and act neurotically.

However, when you strongly think and feel that you absolutely *must* perform well, *have to* be treated considerately by others, and utterly *need* your life conditions to be satisfactory, watch it—you're in trouble.

Once you consciously or unconsciously, explicitly or implicitly (tacitly) insist on any of the three basic musts—"*I* must perform well!" "*Others* must treat me nicely!" "*Conditions* must be comfortable and enjoyable!" —you then almost always create one or more accompanying core IBs that appreciably add to your insistent musts. These include:

1. *Awfulizing.* "Because *I* didn't do as well as I *must*, it's *awful* (just about as bad as it can be)!" "Because *you* don't treat me as nicely as you *absolutely should*, it's *terrible* (totally bad)!" and "Because the *conditions* under which I live are not as good as they ought to be, it's *horrible* (thoroughly unlivable)!"

2. *I can't-stand-it-itis.* "Because I did poorly, or you *treated me* poorly, or conditions dealt with me poorly—none of which *must* exist—I *can't stand* it, *can't bear* it (can't be happy *at all*)!"

3. *Damnation.* "Because I keep failing at important things, just as I *must* not, I'm *no good* and *don't deserve* a decent life!" and "Because you don't treat me as well as you *should*, you're a *rotten, damnable* person!"

4. *Allness and neverness.* "Because I failed to win your love, as I absolutely *must*, I'll *never* win the love of a worthy person!" and "Because you failed to treat me properly, as you *invariably must*, you'll *always* behave poorly and *never* be lovable!"

Over the course of our sessions, I helped Sid to see that Jo may well have been depriving him of "good sex" —his adversity (A) — and perhaps also had been exaggerating or lying about how much sex they were regularly having. But he was largely *making* himself enraged at her—his consequence (C) —by insisting, because of his belief system (B), that she absolutely *should not, must not* act the way she presumably *was* acting. So it was not his *preferences* at B ("I *wish* Jo would give me more regular sex") but his grandiose *demand* at B ("She therefore *must* give me the sex that I prefer!") that was largely creating his rage at Jo, his consequence (C).

Sid's admission that he was largely upsetting himself was great. So I briefly showed him that his self-disturbing beliefs could in fact be disputed (D) and changed back to healthy preferences. When he questioned and challenged his IBs, he came up with these disputes and answers:

Dispute: "Why has Jo *no right* to treat me so badly and then lie about doing so?"

Answer: "She has every right, as a fallible human, to do whatever she does—including depriving me sexually and then refusing to admit her poor behavior. Like all humans, she has the right to be wrong—even to me!"

Dispute: "Where is it written that Jo *shouldn't* be as unfair as she is to me?"

Answer: "It is not written anywhere—except in my head. She *should* be unfair right now—because she is that way at present. If she is really acting unfairly—as I am sure that she is—she *has* to act that way. How can she be fair when she's actually unfair. No way!"

Dispute: "Is it really *terrible* that Jo is treating me unfairly?"

Answer: "No—it's very bad and, to me, very inconvenient. But not *totally* bad. It could be worse—much worse. She could deprive me sexually *and* rob me, hurt me, even kill me."

Dispute: "How does her rotten behavior, if I see it correctly, make her a *nasty, lying, rotten person?*"

Answer: "It doesn't. She doesn't *always* act nastily, lyingly, and rottenly, as a thoroughly *rotten person* would. Even when she acts damnably she is not a subhuman, damnable *person*. She often *does* badly but she *is not* her bad behavior because she also does many good and neutral things. So I can legitimately deplore some of the things she does but not blame her *entire personhood* for doing these things."

I helped Sid with this disputing and answering and also, as I usually do, got Jo into the act. She came up with the idea that if she *always* did bad things to Sid and everyone else she would still not be a thoroughly *rotten person* because she might change and do neutral or good deeds in the future. Her point helped both of them to see that there are really no *good people* nor *bad people* but just people who *up to now* have done a number of bad acts but who might well change in the future.

As Jo put it, "I am a *process*, not a *thing*, and as a process I can always change."

"Yes," Sid jokingly added. "And you may even become too sexy for me and insist that I have much *more* sex than we are now having."

"Fat chance!" said Jo, and we all laughed.

I spent about twenty minutes of their first marital counseling session helping Sid to see that no matter how wrong and unfair Jo might be about depriving him sexually, his anger at her for doing so was largely self-created and could soon be uncreated. He agreed and Jo was particularly pleased with this part of our session. For she felt less threatened when we were talking about *Sid's* emotional problems, had little resistance to seeing how *he* largely created them, and could at least vaguely see that most of the points I was making about him could well apply to her. She began to recognize, while we were talking about Sid, that she was upsetting herself, too.

Jo's main problem—her disturbed consequence (C)—was depression mixed with guilt. Her main adversity was Sid's rage at her (his C). Her RBs were: "I hate Sid's being enraged at me. What a drag! Especially when I'm doing my best to satisfy him sexually." These RBs led to her healthy consequences (HC), feelings of disappointment and frustration.

Jo's IBs, which I quickly helped her see, especially since she had already learned some of the ABCs of REBT by listening to and participating in solving Sid's problem of anger, were: "I *absolutely must not* be angrily criticized by Sid! I *have to* please him sexually and am not doing what I have to do! How awful! He's right about my failing him and that makes me a hopeless failure!" As a consequence (C) of these IBs, Jo felt guilty and depressed.

As I did with Sid, I helped Jo to actively and forcefully dispute (D) her IBs and to show herself that: (1) there was no reason she *absolutely must not* be angrily criticized by Sid, (2) she didn't *have to* please him sexually, though that would be *preferable*, and (3) she may well have been failing Sid sexually but that didn't make her a failure. When she started to see this, she felt keenly disappointed with some of her behaviors—especially her lying to Sid that they were having more sex than they actually were having. But she was only guilty about her actions or inactions and no longer put herself down for behaving this way. She therefore lost most of her depression.

I am, however, getting ahead of my story, because I really want to show, in this chapter, how complicated some of the disturbances in marriage are; and how they interact with the other partner's upsetnesses.

It took us several sessions to figure out the following interrelationships between Sid's and Jo's disturbance; but when we did so they were most illuminating to both of them. They also showed how these kinds of problems frequently arise in marriage and lead to more and more problems.

Partners are often affected by the dysfunctional Cs (consequences) of the other partner. If Sid makes himself angry at Jo, she may easily make herself guilty about "causing" his anger. If Sid makes himself very critical of Jo, she may easily make herself very self-downing about "making" him critical. Similarly, if Jo makes herself angry at Sid, he may easily use her anger as an A (activizing event or adversity) and make himself angry at her—or he may blame himself for "creating" her anger. Each partner frequently disturbs himself or herself about the other partner's disturbed reactions.

Fortunately, however, one partner's disturbed emotions and actions importantly *contribute to*, but do not actually *make*, the other partner "crazy." Consequently, if either or both of them learn and use the ABCs of human disturbance that are described in REBT, they can, after a while, undisturb themselves about the other's disturbance. After even a longer period of time, they can get so good at doing this that either or both of them may become much less disturb*able*, and may refuse to overreact to the other's overreactions.

This is what happened, at first, in Jo's case. Though she had a long history of making herself neurotic about her relationships and about other adversities in her life, and though at first she was much more disturbed—depressed—than Sid, she soon started to do two things: She acknowledged that she, and not only Sid, made herself upset about the unfortunate things that happened in their marriage;

and, second, she saw that Sid had many self-disturbing tendencies, too—that he made himself needlessly upset about her "poor" behaviors and that she also unduly disturbed herself about his upsetness. When she worked on these problems—including somewhat similar ones that she experienced in her work as a teacher—she began to give herself unconditional acceptance, to give Sid unconditional acceptance as well, and to accept some rotten conditions—especially those in the school system in which she worked—without wailing and whining about them.

After eight sessions of REBT with her husband, Jo was confronted with the grim reality that Sid's parents, who had always hated her taking their darling boy away from them, had put up considerable money—which they could really not afford—to help Sid's sister and her husband buy a fairly luxurious home, while refusing to help Sid and her out in any way when they wanted to borrow a modest sum to make a down payment on their own new home. Normally, Jo would have made herself exceptionally angry at Sid's parents for being so unfair, as well as depressed about the fact that they did not sufficiently care for her and probably thought that she was a "worthless person" who didn't deserve to live in a reasonably nice home while her brother-in-law and sister-in-law were "good people" who deserved the very best kind of home. She would have worked on these feelings of anger and depression, ultimately forgiven Sid's father and mother, and gone on with her life.

This time, however, she only felt moderately disappointed with what had happened. She used REBT to combat her feelings of anger and depression in regard to Sid, and was successful in doing this on several occasions. So when she learned about her in-laws' "crummy" and "unfair" actions, she almost automatically said to herself, "Look, what's the use of upsetting myself about this? They always did act this way to me—probably because I took their 'nice' boy away from them. No matter. That's their nature, and they are merely showing it once again. I wish to hell they weren't that way; but damn it, they are! Tough! Sid and I will just have to find some other way to get a sizable down payment on the home that we really want, and luckily we won't be beholden to them for helping us get it. It means nothing about me or about Sid—just about them. Too bad!"

So Jo's use of REBT really paid off. Her marriage with Sid improved remarkably, including her willingness to satisfy him sexually even when she didn't feel particularly sexy herself. And just as his Cs had sparked her IBs and UCs, her RBs and HCs now encouraged healthy reactions in her husband when unfortunate adversities occurred. Their bickering largely ceased and they enjoyed being together much more than they had before they began to understand and to use the ABCs of REBT.

EXERCISES FOR CHAPTER TWO

In this chapter, we showed how Jo and Sid discovered, acknowledged, and worked to dispute some of their main IBs—particularly their self-defeating demands that led to their feelings of anger at each other and guilt about their own feelings and behaviors. Now let's do some exercises that will help you disclose your own dating, relating, and mating irrationalities, show you how to dispute them and come up with effective new philosophies.

Sample Exercise 2A: List of the Main Unfortunate Activating Events of Adversities (A's) in My Life—Particularly Those About My Dating, Relating, and Mating Problems—And My Main Unhealthy Feelings and Behaviors That Accompany Them

Unfortunate Activating Events or Adversities Now In My Life	Unhealthy Feelings and Behaviors That Often Accompany These Events
Not being able to find a suitable partner.	Depression. Horror. Withdrawing and giving up on looking. Foolishly continuing with unsuitable partner.
Getting rejected by a suitable partner.	Panic. Depression. Refusing to date or to get involved again.
Recent breakup of a previously good relationship.	Depression. Severe anxiety. Compulsively seeking a new partner. Settling for an unsuitable partner.
Present partner disagrees with me on important matters. Present partner is very critical of me.	Anger at him or her. Criticizing him or her severely. Putting myself down severely. Becoming very defensive and not acknowledging my failings. Hating my partner.
Present partner is sexually unresponsive to me.	Feeling very inadequate. Plaguing my partner for more sex. Avoiding discussing reasons for partner's avoidance.

Exercise 2A

Unfortunate Activating Events or Adversities in My Life	Unhealthy Feelings and Behaviors That Often Accompany These Adversities

Sample Exercise 2B: List of Dysfunctional or Irrational Beliefs (IBs) That I Create to Produce My Unhealthy Dating, Relating, and Mating Feelings and Behaviors (Cs) That Accompany My Adversities (A's)

Unhealthy Feelings and Behaviors	My Irrational Beliefs Creating These Unhealthy Feelings and Behaviors
Depression and withdrawal at not finding a suitable partner.	I *must* find a suitable partner or else I'm no good! I'm unable to find a suitable partner! What's the use of looking. I'd better give up!
Panic and depression after getting rejected by a suitable partner. Withdrawal.	*I* absolutely must not get rejected—or else I'm no good! No suitable person will ever accept me! I'd better become a monk or a nun!
Depression and anxiety and settling for an unsuitable partner when a previously good relationship breaks up.	I *can't* maintain a good relationship! It's *too hard* to find a suitable partner! It *must not* be that hard!
Anger at partner for "unfair" criticism. Severely criticizing partner in return.	He or she *must not* criticize me unfairly after all I do for him or her! I'll show him or her how bad s/he really is!
Anger at partner for disagreeing on an important matter. Very critical of partner.	Since I'm right about this matter, s/he *absolutely must* go along with me. How stupid s/he is for disagreeing like this!
Self-downing when partner is sexually avoidant. Avoiding discussing reasons for partner's avoidance but keep plaguing my partner for more sex.	I must be sexually repulsive if my partner avoids me. S/he *should* explain why s/he keeps avoiding me. S/he *must* try to satisfy me.

Exercise 2B

Unhealthy Feelings and Behaviors (Cs) That I Actually Experience	Irrational Beliefs (IB's) That I Create to Produce My Unhealthy Feelings and Behaviors (Cs)
_____	_____
_____	_____
_____	_____
_____	_____
_____	_____
_____	_____
_____	_____
_____	_____
_____	_____
_____	_____
_____	_____
_____	_____
_____	_____

Sample Exercise 2C: Ways of Disputing the Irrational Beliefs (IBs) That I Create to Produce My Unhealthy Dating, Relating, and Mating Feelings and Behaviors (Cs) That Accompany My Adversities (A's)

My Irrational Beliefs (IBs) About Relating and Mating	Disputing My IBs	Rational Answers to My Disputing
I *must* find a suitable partner or else I'm no good!	Why *must* I find a suitable partner, no matter how preferable it might be? How does failing to find one make *me* a failure for being alone?	I don't *have to* find what would be preferable. Failing at finding a partner never makes *me* a total failure.
I *must not* get rejected after first finding a suitable partner! If I do, I'll *never* be able to keep one!	What is the evidence that I *must* never get rejected and can *never* keep a suitable partner?	Only in my nutty head! I may find it *difficult* but not *impossible* to keep a suitable partner.
I *can't* maintain a good relationship. It *must not* be that hard—and it's *awful* that it is!	Prove that I *can't* maintain a good relationship. Why must it not be so hard to do so? How is it *awful* that it is hard to find a suitable partner?	I can only prove that I haven't *yet* maintained a good relationship, not that I *can't*. It must be hard to find one if it *is* hard—and that's highly inconvenient but not *awful*.
My partner *must* not criticize me unfairly! That proves how wholly rotten he or she is.	Where is it written that my partner *must* not criticize me unfairly? How does his or her rotten *behavior* make him or her wholly rotten?	It's not written anywhere that he or she has the right to criticize me unfairly. If my partner is *acting* badly, he or she is obviously not a wholly *rotten person*.

Sample Exercise 2C (cont.)

My Irrational Beliefs (IBs) About Relating and Mating	Disputing My IBs	Rational Answers to My Disputing My IBs
Since I'm right about this important matter with which I disagree with my partner, he or she *absolutely must* go along with me. He or she is an idiot for contradicting me! I must be sexually repulsive if my partner avoids me. He or she *should* explain why and *must* try to satisfy me!	Am I completely right about this matter? Even if I am, *must* my partner absolutely go along with me? If he or she doesn't, how does that make him or her an idiot? How does my partner's avoiding me sexually show that I am a repulsive person? Does my partner *have to* explain his or her avoiding and *have to* satisfy me sexually?	Even if I am right—and I obviously may *not* be—he or she *can* easily disagree with me. This may be quite wrong but never makes him or her a *total* idiot. My partner may avoid me sexually for many different reasons. Even if she or he finds me repulsive this doesn't prove that I am repulsive to *everyone*. He or she clearly doesn't *have to* explain the avoidance or satisfy me sexually, though that would be great!

Exercise 2C

My Irrational Beliefs (IBs) About Relating and Mating	Disputing My IBs	Rational Answers to My Disputing My IBs
_____	_____	_____
_____	_____	_____
_____	_____	_____
_____	_____	_____
_____	_____	_____
_____	_____	_____
_____	_____	_____
_____	_____	_____
_____	_____	_____
_____	_____	_____
_____	_____	_____
_____	_____	_____
_____	_____	_____

3

Starting Out With Realistic Views of Couplehood

In reading the preface, you learned that in this book we are using the term "intimacy" to refer to any close relationship between two people. Although we certainly intend to analyze the erotic component of intimacy (which is present in many close relationships), we are not limiting intimacy to sex. We are likewise not contending that intimacy cannot be achieved by more than two people. Most people seem to develop close personal relationships as couples and our focus is to help them to do so in more satisfying ways.

The first session that I (Dr. Harper) had with Heather and George several years ago brings out some things to keep in mind as you explore potential couplehood. Heather was twenty, and George was twenty-one.

Heather: We're planning to live together, and we thought it was a good idea to talk to an expert about it. I suppose I should say *I* thought so because I'm afraid George still thinks it is a *dumb* idea.

George: Not stupid—just unnecessary. We haven't even lived to-gether yet. So how can we discuss our problems sensibly with a counselor until we have experienced them? They may or may not be problems we can solve ourselves. If we can't, *then* it may be ad-visable to see a counselor.

Heather: Oh, George, you're not being honest. Last night you said that these counselor characters take huge fees to tell people what they already know or what they will find useless to learn.

George: It's true I've heard such comments from others and am inclined to believe them. But I am here, so why is it still a problem?

R.A.H.: Actually, you are both right. Heather is wise in wanting to prepare for and reduce problems you may encounter in living together and in believing that someone who has specialized in work with couples might be helpful. George is right, on the other hand, in seeing that a lot of pap is dished out in one form or another in this and other areas of psychotherapy. I think my pap-dishing is minimal, but that's up to you to decide as we go along.

Just on the basis of what you've already said, I'd like to make several points. First of all, it is evident that you already have a close personal relationship, so George's wait-and-see attitude doesn't entirely fit reality. Living together may well bring additional joys and woes, but much of the pattern of your intimacy has been already set (not set in concrete, we hope, for it is our job to de-set or un-set or even upset some of the patterns that are causing problems or that look as if they could lead to future difficulties). Second, you already have problems as a couple. It's probably safe to say that all couples (and persons, for that matter) have problems. The question is, "What are *our* problems and how can we effectively deal with them?" One problem that you demonstrated splendidly at the outset is that you are relatively inexperienced as personal problem solvers. From what you have said so far, though, I believe that an important difference in your approaches to problem-solving is that Heather seems willing to subject herself to a counseling experience that has a good chance of improving her skills in this area, while George seems more reluctant to do so.

George: I'm here. What's the problem?

R.A.H.: Yes, you are here, and for us to try to deal with couple-hood, your presence is desirable and perhaps essential. I was not giving you a hard time, but rather I wanted to point out that reluctance to look at a situation objectively in the presence of an experienced and trained third party tends to block the thinking or problem-solving process. Would you be willing to explore with

Heather and me some of the things you think may be leading you to be reluctant?

George: Well, I'm not sure. You say your fees are not so high, but they are high for Heather and me. And all I've heard from you so far sounds very theoretical. In fact, it sounds like bullshit.

R.A.H.: Bullshit it may well be. On the other hand, it may seem theoretical to you because you may be denying the existence of problems in your and Heather's relationship. If that's the case, trying to do something about problems you deny the existence of can seem intellectual or theoretical rather than realistic, personal, practical, and gutsy. I once saw a war casualty in a veterans' hospital who denied that he had lost a leg. Therefore (until we had overcome some of the denial, and he began to look at the reality of a missing leg), anything I asked him or suggested to him about adjusting to life as a person with just one leg was too nauseatingly theoretical to him.

Now your denial, George, is not so deep, complete, and intense as the veteran's. Otherwise I believe you would have refused to come here even once. If you are avoidant we can have trouble in looking at and doing something about things that Heather or I see as problems. Believe me, we will not always see things similarly, nor will I "side" with Heather. In fact, I am only on Heather's "side" now in the sense that I believe couples generally have problems, and you two in your brief interactions here have, in my opinion, already manifested some. My allegedly theoretical efforts so far have been directed toward seeing if we can begin looking and working at some of your interactional difficulties and improve your skills in the process.

George: Yeah, well, while I still think you talk too much and too theoretically, I am willing to buy into the idea that Heather and I need to improve our problem-solving skills and that *in case* we get problems we may become top-ho problem-solvers. Beyond that I won't go.

George at this point smiled at both Heather and me, and Heather walked over to George's chair to kiss him and tell him he was marvelously flexible and the light of her life and so forth. This was an excellent development—George's deciding he wanted to become a better problem-solver and Heather's immediately rewarding him, whether or not this was what she intended for changing, or at least relaxing, his problem-denial and indicating a desire to learn. Not only was the couple better able to look at and try to do something about their difficulties, they also had more positive feelings toward each other and toward undertaking problem-solving.

Neither luck nor magic, of course, provides the best explanation of how and why George and Heather got to a point where they could begin to learn to relate more effectively. As with any other kind of negotiation (labor-management, nation-to-nation, or whatever), couples need to develop means of negotiating ways of opening honest (but not devastating) interchanges. This helps them discern problems to discuss.

What are some of the important points in this interview with Heather and George? How can you use them in your own coupling effort? Let us break them down.

Nondefensiveness

People generally tend to dig in and hold fast to whatever point of view they have (often unthinkingly) arrived at—especially in those views involved with their sense of selfhood, for this influences most of their behavior. Thus, George had his sense of self-worth attached to the propositions that: (1) he (and he and Heather as a couple) had no problems, and (2) that *he* (not some fuzzy-headed counselor) would beautifully deal with any problems he and Heather would have living together. His *grandiosity* was at work.

Direct and immediate attack of George's defense of denial might, of course, strengthen it. Because we try to live by and not just promulgate REBT, I didn't tie in my own sense of self-worth with my profession. I tried to help George (and Heather) by interacting nondefensively with him, including returning geniality for persistent put-downs. This enabled George to reconsider his denial. He could even relax a little, and later "buy" my problem-solving proposition. Just as important, I provided a model of nondefensiveness for both Heather and George to start (perhaps unconsciously) to apply to their own interactions.

It is highly desirable for a therapist to contribute to the reduction of defensiveness. While couplehood has no copyright on defensiveness, close relationships tend to bring out and exaggerate many destructive tie-ins of behavior with self-esteem.

We shall say a lot more about the desirability of couples' developing nondefensiveness and about the importance of learning not to rate your *self* or *personhood,* but only rating yours and other people's *behavior,* because engagement in the personhood-rating process is deeply ingrained and is often enormously pernicious in human relationships.

Authenticity of the Therapist

Therapists are frequently taught to be "authentic" and to be "genuinely themselves" (whatever that might mean). We want to stress the importance of my congruent behavior (thoughts, feelings, perceptions, and actions) in my relating to Heather and George. I could hardly teach and model desirable interacting for them if my own thoughts, feelings, perceptions, and actions kept galloping off in different directions. For example, if I tagged myself a guru (personhood-rating), I would then believe I was deserving of deference, which would likely cause me to perceive George as a dreadful young upstart (more personhood rating) for calling my fine and beautiful wisdom "bullshit." If I were too egocentric, no matter how hard I tried to control my expression of feelings or my tone of voice, I might have come through to both George and Heather as a phony (although they might not have been immediately aware that they were reacting to me that way). Since close personal relationships demand reliability, and since problem-solving is sabotaged when phony thoughts, feelings, and actions infect the boiling pot of problems, the therapist's authenticity is important to communicate to a couple to help them enhance their own relationship.

Antiperfectionism

Perfectionism is one of the great scourges of human existence, especially in trying to effect an enjoyable relationship. Ironically, parents, teachers, and other influential people (including, alas, some therapists) tend to extol perfectionistic strivings in the young and impressionable. ["It brings out the best in us," the saying goes, "to keep striving for high and even unattainable goals and to be dissatisfied with anything less."]

Quite the contrary. Children quickly learn that it is impossible to meet adult ideals ("Why don't you get all A's?"), so they make various adaptations. One is to deny their failure to meet rigid standards; another is to avoid activities where perfect standards are demanded. (Perfectionists tend to consider only "important" goals toward which to strive, but their inconsistency is common.) Still another reaction is to internalize the perfectionist expectations and to judge your *self* an unsatisfactory human being when you (inevitably) fail to achieve ideal *performance*. (Remember Charlene in chapter one, who thought she was a shit because she was not rolling along ideally toward heterosexual heaven?) You believe that if you are not perfect in whatever you design as *the important* aspects of life, you're an indubitable turd. All your efforts either to deny your imperfection or to deny the *importance* of your undeniable failings are futile in the long run because you still subscribe to the deeply instilled belief that it is terrible not to be perfect, and if you do not function ideally, you are no good.

When perfectionism is carried into a close personal relationship, you not only continue to experience your own difficulties, you also often extend them to your partner and to the relationship itself. This *must* measure up to impossible ideals. Whether you are in a business or personal partnership, you demand that it must be the best because you deem it very important. "I, am no damned good if any of my important relationships are not the best! I, therefore, *must* guarantee that I, my partner, and our relationship all function ideally—or at least *seem* to function ideally." As a perfectionist, you often are unable to hide "horrible" imperfections from yourself, and you may try to hide them from others and consider yourself even more reprehensible for your concealing efforts. If you tie in with another perfectionist, difficulties may (or may not) multiply. We have rarely seen a couple where each person's idealistic rigidities gear with the other's and help them both to function satisfactorily.

Let's get back to Heather and George. George's denial that there were any important problems that could not be readily handled stemmed from his perfectionist perception of himself and of extensions of himself (Heather and the relationship). If he admitted to the possibility of problems—and especially to the need for help in facing and dealing with them—then the idea of a-okay George was all shot to hell, with nothing but George the nebbish left. This thinking in extremes is characteristic of perfectionists. If, for example, they put a lot of importance on grades in school, then an A-minus or a B-plus is the same as a failing grade. It was a first-step victory in the long, hard road of overcoming perfectionism for George to agree to try to learn how to improve his problem-solving skills. He could do this within the favorable ambiance of the therapy session because he was not having his defense of denial directly attacked. He was being asked simply to participate in a (to him) theoretical process of enhancing his problem-solving skills in his relationship with Heather. Since we began to get into some problems even in our first session and since George was by no means stupid, he began (he later admitted) to let some of his denial melt away.

Heather was a somewhat different story. Because I found it desirable to focus at first on George's situation, there was danger that Heather might begin to think she was an innocent and virtuous bystander. While it turned out that she had some disturbed tendencies (many of us do), she was committed to facing and trying to work out difficulties in herself and in the relationship with George. Even such a commitment, however, may itself sometimes conceal perfectionistic tendencies that need to be examined. Namely: "If George and I (Heather) work hard and do all the things the therapist says, then we'll have no more problems and will live happily ever after. After we get this magic overhaul job, we will achieve perfection."

No. A close personal relationship does not necessarily become fascinating and enjoyable when problems disappear. Problems may improve, but problems also remain. Couples who learn effectively and steadily to *cope* with problems will likely find fuller satisfaction.

EXERCISES FOR CHAPTER 3

Couplehood has many joys and disadvantages, just like any other type of relationship. Some of the main troubles with mating, particularly in a culture like our own where romantic ideals of love and marriage are prominent, are the unrealistic expectations with which two partners often get together. Disillusionment follows from illusion. As REBT notes, the road to hell is frequently paved with exaggerated or false expectations. It is not merely the hassles of mating—adversities (A's)—that lead to separation and divorce—consequences (Cs)—but the utopian and perfectionistic beliefs (Bs) about the difficulties of successful mating.

What are some of the unrealistic and illogical beliefs that you—like millions of other partners—may bring to your partnership? And what are some of the realistic, rational beliefs with which you could replace them? Let us complete this exercise by listing some of the main IBs that you may imbibe from your culture and concoct yourself that may disrupt your relationships, and then substituting some of the realistic RBs with which you could replace them.

Exercise 3A: Some Common Unrealistic and Irrational Beliefs (IBs) and Expectations That I May Hold About Mating

Circle whether you hold the following beliefs: S (Strongly), M (Moderately Strongly), or W (Weakly).

			Some Common Unrealistic and Irrational Beliefs (IBs) and Expectations That I May Hold About Mating
S	M	W	Because my partner and I really love each other, we will rarely strongly disagree with each other.
S	M	W	When my partner and I strongly disagree with each other, we will always talk out our disagreements and work hard at making compromises.
S	M	W	I can expect my partner to practically always satisfy me sexually when I desire satisfaction even if s/he is not in the mood to have sex at that time.
S	M	W	Because I generally love my partner, I will be madly in love and be excited to be with him or her at practically all times.
S	M	W	Because my partner generally loves me, s/he will be madly in love and excited to be with me at practically all times.
S	M	W	Being with my partner means having some problems but will also mean having so many pleasures and advantages that I will practically never upset myself about the difficulties of mating and will never really think about separating from him or her.
S	M	W	Because I really love my partner, I will never think of being strongly attracted to someone else, nor think about having love or sex relations with another person.
S	M	W	If my partner and I have children together, I shall only love and cherish them and never be out of sorts with and angry at them.

Exercise 3A (cont.)

<table>
<tr>
<td></td>
<td></td>
<td></td>
<td>Some Common Unrealistic and Irrational Beliefs (IBs) and Expectations That I May Hold About Mating</td>
</tr>
<tr>
<td>S</td>
<td>M</td>
<td>W</td>
<td>If my partner and I have children together, we shall put their interests first and never fight with each other to get them to do the "right" things.</td>
</tr>
<tr>
<td>S</td>
<td>M</td>
<td>W</td>
<td>I shall always cooperate with my mate's relationship with his or her family and try never to make myself angry at him or her nor at his or her family members.</td>
</tr>
<tr>
<td>S</td>
<td>M</td>
<td>W</td>
<td>Other unrealistic IBs that I hold about mating (specify):_____</td>
</tr>
</table>

_____

_____

_____

_____

_____

_____

_____

_____

Exercise 3B: Some Realistic and Rational Beliefs (RBs) and Expectations That I Will Try to Hold and Maintain About Mating

Circle whether you will work at holding the following rational beliefs: S (Strongly), M (Moderately Strongly), or W (Weakly).

			Realistic and Rational Beliefs (RBs) and Expectations I Will Work at Holding and Maintaining
S	M	W	Even though my partner and I really love each other, we can easily strongly disagree with one another.
S	M	W	When my partner and I strongly disagree with each other, we may easily and often slip, make ourselves angry, fail to talk about our disagreements, and therefore fail to work at making effective compromises.
S	M	W	I should not unrealistically expect my partner to always want to have sexual relations with me when I really want to have them.
S	M	W	I should not unrealistically expect my partner to satisfy me sexually even when s/he is not in the mood for sex.
S	M	W	Even though I generally love my partner, I will realistically expect that I will not be madly in love nor excited to be with him or her at practically all times.
S	M	W	Even though my partner generally loves me, I will not realistically expect that s/he will be madly in love nor excited to be with me at practically all times.
S	M	W	Even though I generally love my partner, I will realistically expect myself to be inconsiderate and selfish to him or her at times.

Exercise 3B (cont.)

			Realistic and Rational Beliefs (RBs) and Expectations I Will Work at Holding and Maintaining
S	M	W	Even though my partner generally loves me, I will realistically expect him or her to be inconsiderate and selfish to me at times.
S	M	W	Even though being with my partner has many pleasures and advantages, I will realistically expect that sometimes I will upset myself about the difficulties of mating and may sometimes even think of separating from him or her.
S	M	W	Even though I really love my partner, I will realistically expect to be strongly attracted to someone else and to think about having love or sexual relations with him or her.
S	M	W	If my partner and I have children together, I will realistically expect that I will be out of sorts and angry at them even though I love them.
S	M	W	If my partner and I have children together, I will realistically expect that we will sometimes put our own interests first and fight with each other to get the children to do what s/he or I feel are the "right" things.
S	M	W	I will realistically expect that I will not always cooperate with his or her relationship with his or her family and will sometimes make myself angry at his or her family members.
S	M	W	Other realistic and rational beliefs (RBs) I will work at having and maintaining in my mating relationship (specify): _____
			_____
			_____

We shall now give Exercise 3C, REBT's Famous Shame-Attacking Exercise and other emotional-evocative exercises. But first, let us say more about unconditional self-acceptance (USA) which these exercises address.

Psychotherapists—and philosophers before them—have struggled for years to find and cure the one central or core problem of disturbed people. Why? Partly because humans like to simplify complex things—and to figure out one crucial, and presumably final, answer to the difficult human condition. We probably never will find this core problem, because humans *are* complex—and so are their woes.

Of the many existent therapies, REBT is one of the simplest and tightest. It says that practically all people's neuroses—not their severe personality disorders and their psychoses—involve or are largely sparked by their absolutistic shoulds, oughts, musts, and demands. And REBT has an excellent record of helping tens of thousands of clients, as well as millions of readers, to see their musturbatory thinking, feeling, and behaving, to change it to strong preferring, and—voila!—to significantly improve.

But REBT also includes many related, more complex theories. For example: (1) Musts and demands are not *merely* cognitive but *also* emotional *and* behavioral, (2) they are not *merely* learned or innately created but *also* imbibed, practiced, *and* manufactured, (3) they are not *only* experienced and followed in childhood and adolescence but *also* reconditioned and actively reconstructed in the present, (4) they are not *simply* changed to helpful preferences by people's making a profound philosophical change but *also* modified by their using a large number of cognitive, emotive, and behavioral exercises and techniques, (5) people's absolutistic and dogmatic thinking and experiences are quite individualistic and self-destructive but *also* stem from cultural and subcultural teachings and can be harmful, and (6) human goals, purposes, experiences, and personality are again personal and individual but are *also* amazingly social and cultural.

So REBT is simple—and has its complications. It is constructivist and postmodern—and also (hopefully) scientific, practical, and efficient. Read Ellis's revised and updated edition of *Reason and Emotion in Psychotherapy* and see for yourself.

Back to self-help basics. REBT theorizes that you tend to have two major IBs when you think, feel, and act self-defeatingly: (1) self-deprecation, self-downing, or self-damning—"I *absolutely must* perform well and be approved by significant others or else *I* am, my *person* is, incompetent and worthless!" and (2) frustration intolerance (FI) or discomfort, anxiety, rage, and depression—"Conditions and other people *absolutely must be* easy, comfortable, and enjoyable, and *absolutely must not be* very frustrating and depriving, or else people and/or the world are no damned good. I *can't stand* it, and my life is *awful!*" These two IBs often interact, reinforce, and complicate each other and lead to mental and physical "horror" and pain. Moreover, when they help to create physical and emotional disturbance, we humans—including you—often have self-downing and low frustration tolerance *about* our disturbances. Result: more disturbance.

In this chapter we looked at Heather's and George's defensiveness, lack of authenticity, and perfectionism. But aren't these disturbances all related to self-downing? Intimately! In some ways they are products of, or what in REBT we actually call *derivatives* of self-deprecation. For if Heather and George and the rest of the human race were not self-downers, how would they ever be defensive, inauthentic, or perfectionistic? Not very easily.

When you are defensive—that is, when you deny your failings to yourself and others and fail to *be* "yourself"—you are scared that they will witness your flaws and (of course) down you for having them. You are *afraid of* severe criticism. So defensiveness, when you could be honest and perhaps be severely penalized, in large part *is* highly *conditional* self-acceptance instead of *unconditional* self-acceptance.

Isn't lack of authenticity pretty similar? Indeed so. When you are inauthentic you pose, pretend, posture, and put on an act. Again, you *refuse* to be "yourself," because if you were, other people would presumably down your "real" self—would down *you.* More important, you would *agree* with them that you *are* no good.

Perfectionism is in the same class—piled higher and deeper. Following it, you believe that you have to do *perfectly* well at important tasks—and be *perfectly* approved by significant others. And if not, back to self-downing you go. Other people witness your imperfections and supposedly put *you*, the person, down. And again, you fully agree.

All of the above illustrates what we touched on in chapter one. Unless you decide to commit to and work hard at achieving *un*conditional self-acceptance, you will cultivate self-downing—and be a willing victim of your partner's and other people's assaults on your personhood. Moreover, when your partner inevitably exhibits flaws and unniceties, will you really resist denigrating him or her? Not very likely.

So, how can you powerfully, consistently, and persistently avoid the pitfalls of arrogant self-aggrandizement on the one hand, and self-beration on the other hand? Answer: Think your way through the philosophy of USA, especially in your intimate relationships. Be determined to always accept yourself as a "worthy" or "good" person *whether or not* you perform important tasks and relationships well—and *whether or not* significant other people accept you. Even more elegantly, use the unique REBT solution to the problem of self-evaluation by establishing important goals and purposes and only rating your thoughts, feelings, and actions in terms of these aims, and not globally rating yourself, your essence, your being, or your person at all. We shall keep returning to this point again. But let's stop here to complete more exercises and be more specific.

Exercise 3C: REBT's Famous Shame-Attacking Exercise

I (Dr. Ellis) vaguely realized when I practiced psychoanalysis in the late 1940s and early 1950s that feelings of shame, embarrassment, and humiliation were the essence of much—no, not all—human disturbance. When you are really ashamed of something you have "foolishly" done or of some "good" thing you have thought of doing but "cowardly" refrained from executing, you are almost always criticizing your "bad" behavior. You may well be right. To dress "ridiculously" when with your partner or to "stupidly" fail to give support when he or she is in trouble *will* often bring on censure, penalties, and disruption to the relationship. So, noting this, you'd better feel moderately abashed and push yourself to act differently next time. As a social creature and a would-be partner, use caution and vigilance.

Deep-seated shame or humiliation, however, usually adds some Irrational Beliefs (IBs) to create disturbances that we described above. First, especially when your partner criticizes your "ridiculous" dress or your lack of support, you feel ashamed of *it*—your "wrong" and "dislikable" *behavior*. Good. But, simultaneously, you put *yourself* down for your "foolish" or "bad" acts and feel ashamed of *yourself*. Quite a jump! Actually, your partner may only be criticizing what you've *done*. But you take it as criticism of *you* and agree that *you* are "bad" for doing *it*. A very neurotic overgeneralization. Deadly.

Second, you often horrify yourself about the *discomfort* of the "shameful" situation. You hate the *hassles* of defending your actions, of arguing with your mate, of being scorned, of correcting your behavior, and so forth. You define these hassles as *too* hard, tell yourself you *can't stand* them, insist that they are *awful*. So, in addition to making yourself feel ego-anxiety, you also create considerable discomfort-anxiety or frustration intolerance (FI).

Noting this, when I gave REBT group marathons in the 1960s, I invented some shame-attacking exercises that members of the group could risk doing, and dare being looked down upon for performing, during the marathon. For example, asking another member for a special personal encounter, removing some of one's clothing, or taking the risk of criticizing another's participation in the marathon.

My shame-attacking exercises during the REBT marathons worked so well that I added them to my regular weekly group therapy procedures, as well as to my individual therapy sessions. Usually, I give them as homework assignments and check later to see whether they are actually carried out, what results are experienced during and after doing them, and whether the participants became significantly less ashamed in their real lives. To date, many thousands of REBT-oriented people have done these shame-attacking exercises all over the world; and so many favorable results have been reported that they have been widely incorporated into cognitive behavior therapy (CBT) and into many other kinds of active-directive treatments of anxiety, shame, shyness, and other aspects of self-downing and frustration intolerance.

Here are guidelines for your trying some shame-attacking exercises:

Pick some action that you would be ashamed to do, and especially to be observed doing by others. Make sure that you don't harm anyone else by doing this "shameful" act. Don't, for example, slap anybody in the face or really intrude on their privacy. Also, don't do anything that would harm yourself—such as walking naked in public or picking a fight with someone.

Give the matter of shame some deep thought and see that it usually consists of publicly doing something foolish or stupid, being viewed critically for doing it, and putting yourself, as a person, down for your poor behavior. So you have the *choice* of only rationally feeling ashamed—meaning, sorry or disappointed—about your "foolish" or "shameful" behavior *or* agreeing with your critics that you are less worthy as a person for behaving "shamefully." Decide that you will deliberately do the act you now think of as being "shameful" while *not* downing yourself, as a person, for doing it.

When you clearly see the difference between criticizing your "shameful" *act* and berating *yourself* for doing it, force yourself to do this act—preferably implosively, several times within a short period. If you complete the "embarrassing" act, see how you feel, and if you at first feel ashamed, work on your thoughts and feelings to minimize or eliminate the shame. If you fail to do it, work on not feeling ashamed of yourself for failing!

Before, during, and after your "shameful" act, you can think of rational coping self-statements and do your best to believe them. Such as:

"I can always fully accept *myself* even when I act foolishly and other people put me down."

"I don't like other people criticizing me and seeing me as a fool. But I never have to agree with them. I don't *need* their approval."

"My behavior is not bad in the sense of being immoral but even if it were, or were considered so, it makes me a *person who* is acting immorally and had better stop doing so. It doesn't make me a *wicked, evil person.*"

"I will most likely suffer very little reprisals for doing this 'shameful' act and can gain greatly by giving myself unconditional self-acceptance (USA)."

Preferably, do a number of "shameful" acts until you consistently begin to feel—before, during, and after doing them—sorry, regretful, and disappointed about the censure you may get, but *not* ashamed, humiliated, embarrassed, or depressed. You can feel *good* about actually doing these exercises and conquering your own self-downing while doing them because you're doing them to *help* yourself. But, at worst, make yourself feel displeased with some of the criticism you get, but not disappointed or displeased with *you*.

Exercise 3D: Rational Emotive Imagery

Since its beginning in 1955, REBT has included a number of cognitive exercises in addition to its active-directive: Disputing (D) of people's Irrational Beliefs (IBs). One of these is imagery techniques, such as positive imagery or positive visualization.

In 1971, Maxie C. Maultsby, Jr., a creative psychiatrist who had studied REBT with me for a month in New York, in 1968, combined REBT's use of imagery with a highly emotive procedure and named the combination Rational Emotive Imagery (REI). I immediately saw that REI was a valuable addition to REBT, but because Maxie's original use of it overlapped too much with REBT Disputing of IBs, I kept the imagery and the emotive aspects of it and didn't focus as much as he did, at the same time, on showing my clients how to Dispute their Irrational Beliefs. I do this separately, usually before using REI.

I have used REI thousands of times with my clients and with my workshop participants. My version follows, and you may particularly find it useful to help you and your partner work to acquire unconditional self-acceptance (USA). Here is a set of instructions that I frequently give to my clients at my famous Friday Night Workshops and on other occasions.

Close your eyes and vividly imagine one of the worst things that you fear might happen to you—such as your partner telling you how impossible you are in several important respects, saying that no good mate will ever stay with you, and that you will soon wind up being totally alone forever. Vividly imagine that this grim event is actually happening and let yourself feel very negative about it. Feel whatever you feel—such as panicked, depressed, or enraged.

Can you vividly imagine that this very bad event is actually happening? I'm sure that you can. All right, I see that you said, "Yes." Good! How do you actually feel *right now* as you vividly imagine this unfortunate event? How do you spontaneously feel?

(The person almost always replies, "Very anxious." Or, "Quite depressed." Or, "Extremely angry.")

Good. Get in touch with your feeling. Really feel it! Feel it as strongly as you can. Feel it, feel it, feel it! Are you now strongly feeling it?

(The person almost always responds, "Yes, I really do. I feel quite upset.")

Good. Now I want you to keep the same image—don't change it in any way. Keep the same image in your mind. But now work on your disturbed feeling and change it, as you are definitely able to do, to a healthy negative feeling—such as keen sorrow or regret. You can control your emotions, though often, not what happens to you. So make yourself, really make yourself, feel very sorry, very regretful about the bad things you are imagining happening to you. Only sorry and regretful about what's happening—not depressed, not self-hating. Only sorry and regretful—which you can definitely do.

(I usually wait a few minutes for the person to change her or his feeling from an unhealthy to a healthy negative emotion. You can wait for yourself to do this.)

Fine! Now what did you *do* to change your feeling? How did you change it?

(I deliberately do *not* ask the person, "What did you *tell yourself* to change your feeling?" For then they might not have really changed it but have figured out, from my leading question, that they're *supposed to* tell themselves something to change it. This makes it too easy for them to give the "right" answer, even if they don't really believe it. It also makes the REI technique too much like Disputing and answering with rational coping self-statements. It then may lose its emotive quality.)

I can tell by the person's answer whether he or she really has changed his or her unhealthy negative feeling to a healthy negative feeling. If they have, they give a rational coping self-statement that they have figured out for themselves, such as "I hate losing my *partner* but I do not hate *myself* for losing him or her." "Too bad that my partner is unfairly putting me down, but that's her or his way— which I don't agree with. He or she is a fallible human who is acting unfairly but is *not* a rotten person."

When you do REI and come up with a suitable rational coping self-statement that leads you to feel healthily rather than unhealthily negative, you repeat this at least once a day for thirty days, using the same or additional coping statements to change your disturbed feeling. If you do this properly and consistently, you soon train yourself to come up with automatic and spontaneous healthy negative feelings, instead of self-defeating ones, when you imagine very bad Activating Events or when they actually do occur.

You may have difficulty, at first, with this exercise. But if you keep doing it, you will start to see that your unhealthy negative feelings largely stem from your IBs—from the self-defeating statements that you tell yourself; and that you can always change them to healthy negative feelings by using rational coping self-statements. Then you don't *completely* control your self-sabotaging feelings, but you give yourself much more ability to call the shots on them!

4

Trying It Out Before Commitment

As we start this chapter, let's review what we have covered so far about ways to relate successfully to another individual. Although a relationship could be any kind of twosome, most people seek help on romance and erotic coupling. Why? Because our culture emphasizes romance and also because many assume (often falsely) that they can competently handle non-romantic relationships. If you are entering a business partnership, you take great care to inspect your potential partner's knowledge and skills in this field, but you may take for granted the problems that will arise from relating to him or her on a personal level. When things turn sour in this non-romantic situation, you'll probably turn to experts in your field to tell you what went wrong rather than examine how you and your partner related badly.

So while most of you may focus on romantic and erotic coupling, we shall still emphasize those problems that stem from matters other than sex and romance. Almost all of the ways we will suggest for improving close personal relationships can be applied to non-romantic and non-erotic couples, to the married and unmarried, and to straights and gays.

The toughest block to functioning effectively in couplehood is almost everyone's foolish tendency to rate self and others as total persons. REBT practitioners valiantly strive to help individuals and couples to focus on improving their *behaviors* rather than on rating their *selves* or other *people*. REBT teaches that long-term and not short-term satisfaction is the best guide to improvement; and it stresses the importance of beliefs in helping you change your ineffective functioning.

In chapter 3, with the help of Heather's and George's session, we saw how two people can begin to face, understand, and deal with some of the almost inevitable problems of couplehood, such as making themselves nondefensive, authentic, and unperfectionistic.

Now we will explore some ways that people who are tentatively living together can improve their relationship and test the possibility of a long-term commitment. In our earlier book, *A Guide to Successful Marriage*, commitment meant marriage. While it still means that to some people, our culture has changed so much in the last few decades that couples may or may not have marriage in mind even though they intend to live together permanently.

Couples who live together may do so for several reasons: (1) one or both is still legally married to someone else; (2) their relationship is nonsexual, so marriage seems inappropriate; (3) the advantages of marriage (greater community acceptance and legal and economic advantages, such as joint health insurance) are outweighed by the disadvantages (restrictions on individual freedom). This may especially be true when people decide to mate without having any children. Those who live together without intent to marry may be realistic, while some may mainly have irrational fears of being legally wed.

In addressing people today on "Living Together in Unfettered Love," we often bring out the following points. For one, "love conquers all." How many of you still believe that? Fewer, no doubt, than your parents' generation, but it is not a completely dopey idea when you take some of the absolutism away. How about, "love can help a hell of a lot?" Caring deeply for another person (which is how we're defining "love") can help you overcome some of the difficulties of mating. We say "difficulties" because most of us have never learned, even in our original families, how to relate warmly and understandingly to others. Many of us grow up in conditions where family members pretend to be warm and understanding and then pretend that they are not pretending. This *double pretend* may constitute deep-seated *denial*, because the pretender is often unaware of his or her real feelings.

How do you know if family members are unaware of their real feelings? And if you find double-pretending is indeed going on, how does that relate to our topic of living together in unfettered love? We tend to emerge from our original families with love quite fettered—in a kind of double bind of double pretend. So to unfetter ourselves, we had better first accept our possible fettering.

To reveal our pretenses about loving those we blithely suppose that we do love, we need to be skeptical of our alleged feelings and probe to see how realistic they are. We can also look for the occasional flashes of awareness that break through our denial of our pretenses. In clinical work, the evidence for pretend and double pretend, especially in matters of love, is often vague. But we can often accept pretense as a helpful working hypothesis and try to change it to nonpretense whenever we discover it.

The question is, how do people emerge from a double-bind pretend and start living in loving couplehood with other persons who may be similarly unaware of their pretending? The answer is that usually they don't. But because they have learned to pretend so well, they may stay together for quite a long time. Most of them used to get married and transmit the same patterns of pretense to their offspring, generation after generation. At least some of you in this generation are testing out living together before launching such major legal and social commitments as marriage and parenthood.

Do we approve of a couple living together before marriage? Definitely yes, but not just "before marriage." In the last two or three decades a lot of people (excluding religious and political extremists, but including some conservatives) have changed their attitudes toward unmarried couples who live together. They have gone from thinking "Let's jail them as moral criminals" to at least "Let's not talk about it or interfere." Personally, we approve of two persons living together in a close relationship even if marriage is never to be considered. That means a woman and a man, a woman and a woman, or a man and a man, as long as the two are consenting adults—consenting to living together; not necessarily consenting to sex as sexual interest and/or activity may or may not be present.

That doesn't mean that we are necessarily against two people under eighteen living together (providing it can be responsibly worked out within legal and social frameworks, as it sometimes can). Nor that we are against more than two people taking a whack at living together except that threesomes and foursomes are so much more complicated than twosomes that we highly recommend trying with two first.

Sex generally plays a role in human interaction when love is involved, and although sex and love are not interchangeable, the two can affect each other when it comes to relationships. We use the term "love" to refer to intense caring for another human. Sex (erotic desire and activity) may often interfere with or distract from deep love. How? Sometimes if you really concentrate on how much you deeply *care* for your sexual partner, you may well interfere with—not enhance—your and his or her erotic satisfaction. If so, you may focus too much on your partner's satisfaction and not enough on your own; or you may be so tender and "nice" that you may neglect powerful sex urges that would help stimulate your partner.

When we work with a couple trying to achieve a close personal relationship, each member of which has emerged from the frequent family background of phony caring, we often say, "You don't *have* to love each other, but it would probably help a hell of a lot if you learned to do so." And they say: "Yeah, sounds lovely. How do we do it?" What do we then reply?

We show people how to behave more lovingly with each other and how not to rate each other as total persons. We try to help each of them see how they can be more affectionate toward their partner and how not to focus on the "goodness" or "badness" of the other person. That is the essence of the REBT view of unconditionally accepting and therefore being able to better love each other.

We encourage people to *behave* more lovingly toward their partner rather than asking, "How can I be a great lover?" or "Why do I

have such an asshole of a partner who fails to meet my every wish?"
or "If my stupid parents had been more genuinely affectionate
wouldn't I now be a truly loving person?" If people can concentrate
on seeing how they can improve their loving behavior, they will
often make real progress.

In the all-too-usual family, the child lives with angry, depressed,
or indifferent parents who *say* they are interested and loving. They
instruct the child, "Be a nicer boy or girl. Only a bad child would
eat up all the cookies. So you know what *you* are!" Many children
learn to pretend that they do not have horrendous inner urges, such
as the urge to gobble up all the goodies in sight. But in order to
convince themselves they are not "bad children" they double-
pretend—that is, pretend that they are not pretending. Otherwise,
they may see themselves as "bad persons" for the rest of their lives.

When we say to an individual in couple therapy, "Try to behave
more lovingly toward your partner," we are not duplicating the
pathology of this kind of family scene. This is why. First, each partner is asked to describe his or her thoughts, feelings, perceptions,
and actions in a problematic couple situation. Next, both may be
asked to close their eyes and focus on that "awful" situation and to
silently let their reactions have full sway. After, they are encouraged,
while their eyes are still closed, to see if each can imagine ways of
behaving more lovingly toward the other in a similar future situation. Finally, both are asked to describe how they modified their
imagined behavior change with as little reference as possible to how
they think the other person might react to this change.

Is this imagined change still somewhat phony and superficial?
Possibly, but it is still very different from what most people experienced in developing undesirable and unloving behaviors in earlier
interactions. Part of its lingering artificiality is that both partners
may make some imaginative changes to impress the other one. But
using REBT for couples helps many couples to wipe out other stim-
uli and to focus intensively on ways of improving their own behavior. The effect of each partner's saying in front of the other how he
or she would behave more lovingly is often very positively reinforc-
ing. They remember what they said; they remember that they

thought it up themselves with no pressure from anyone else; and they are likely to try to do their damnedest to actually function that way.

REBT, however, goes even further. It also points out the harmful nature of perfectionism. It describes how couples have great difficulty in changing their habits. It helps people to give up their unrealistic expectations and to cherish even their small successes at becoming more loving.

Can these procedures that work with couples also be used to make behavioral changes not related to lovingness? Yes, they often can be. As REBT has noted since the 1950s, people not only learn to be unloving in their original families, but just about all people have strong innate or biological tendencies to disturb themselves, and thereby to disrupt their relationships.

What people need to look at and do something about is how well or badly their behavior fulfills the purpose of the relationship they want. What is that purpose? Just to have fun? It's presumably more than that or they typically would not consider living together.

Falling in love with someone causes readjustments in your life, and therefore, you and your mate should think long and hard about what you are trying to accomplish in this living-together situation. This arrangement is *not* unfettered love! So look at your behavior to see how it fits in with your purposes. Then work at improving your communication and problem-solving skills.

Sound difficult? Not exactly, but an REBT way of life *does* take extra effort. It's well worth it, though, when it increases satisfaction in living. It usually brings more love and more fun for individuals and couples alike. Totally unfettered? Hell, no—because it takes planning and problem-solving. This shatters the myth that fun should be something that just happens and that somehow the greatest joy is to have no responsibility laid on you to do anything at all. Even when you have interesting and enjoyable experiences as a result of your special efforts, you may still believe that "the ideal" is do-nothingness. One of the benefits that you can get from a close personal relationship is that both you and your partner reinforce each other in living a more rational, realistic, and satisfying life.

EXERCISES

Up to now, we have mainly been emphasizing how to be honest with yourself and your partner—that is, how to stop pretending that you *really* care and that you are *not* pretending. Great stuff! But your honesty is often blocked by your direly *needing*, instead of healthily *wanting*, your partner's (and other people's) approval and by your attaching your worth as a person to how much acceptance you get.

Pretending that you're not pretending goes, again, with defensiveness, inauthenticity, and perfectionism. Antidote? Unconditional self-acceptance, which can be marvelous *if* you work to achieve it.

Seeing through your own and your partner's possible dishonesty often requires doing things the hard way—living together to see how both of you actually react to the difficulties of everyday life as a couple.

Let's take it a step further. Suppose that you do live together or otherwise get to really know each other and that you do find, first, that you both are talented pretenders and, second, that you react badly to the rigors of Holy Couplehood. Quite annoying. Almost enraging. Now, what do you do about *that?*

Answer: Discover and dispute the second main set of IBs that lead to fury about your partner's dishonesty and difficulties and to experience frustration intolerance (FI), awfulizing, and I-can't-stand-it-itis about the "horrible" hassles of intimate living. So far, we have mainly given you exercises to combat your feelings of wormhood. Now it's time for exercises that uproot your rage and then, later on, ones to reduce your FI.

Exercise 4A: Acknowledging Your Highly Conditional Acceptance of Your Partner

   Naturally you love your partner, enjoy being with him or her, and do many caring things to show your love. But is that *all?* If you are human, you also at times hate your mate, feel disgust for her or him, would even like to kill that person. How can you honestly admit this? Examine Sample Practice Sheet 4A, give it some deep thought, then forcibly and probably painfully tackle Actual Practice Sheet 4A. Be honest about what you see!

Sample Exercise 4A: Acknowledging Your Highly Conditional Acceptance of Your Partner

Partner's Failings and Mistreatment of Me	My Disturbed Feelings and Actions About My Partner's Failings and Mistreatment of Me
Partner is very untidy.	Pissed off. Keep nagging him or her to be tidier.
Partner severely criticizes me.	Self-pity and self-downing. Defensiveness. Look for things to lambaste him or her about.
Partner is careless about money and spends too much.	Feel aghast when bills come in. Lecture partner steadily about this. Think he or she is a damned baby.
Partner is often late to appointments and makes me late.	Keep yelling at him or her. Angrily leave without her or him. Keep seething about this and spoil our outings.
Partner gives me much less sex than I want.	Angrily refuse to have any sex. Tell partner she or he is a basket case for being sexless. Feel very hurt.
Partner lies to me about important things.	Fume and froth and accuse him or her of always lying. Refuse to discuss reasons for lying, and feel there is *no* excuse except death.

Exercise 4A

My Partner's Failings and Mistreatment of Me	My Disturbed Feelings and Actions About My Partner's Failings and Mistreatment of Me

*Sample Exercise 4B: Irrational Beliefs (IBs) That Encourage My
Disturbed Feelings and Actions About My Partner's Failings and
Mistreatment of Me*

My Disturbed Feelings and Actions About My Partner's Failings and Mistreatment of Me	My Irrational Beliefs (IBs), Which Encourage My Disturbed Feelings and Actions About My Partner's Failings and Mistreatment of Me
Pissed off about his or her untidiness. Keep nagging him or her all the time. Self-pity and self-downing when partner criticizes me.	He or she *must not* be untidy! That seriously handicaps me and is unfair. She or he *must* be fair! Woe is me! After all I do for him or her! I must be an incompetent person if this criticism is correct. If my partner really loved me, he or she could never be so critical.
Feel aghast when my partner spends more than we have. Lecture him or her for being a damned baby.	S/he is dishonest and totally rotten for treating me this way! How incredibly idiotic! S/he is a baby who never faces reality! After I go out of my way to save, my partner should not get us into debt!
Keep yelling at partner for always being late to appointments. Keep seething and spoil our outings.	How can he or she be that rotten way! It's so easy to plan to be on time and there's no excuse for him or her not to be! S/he is a thoroughly disorganized and rotten person!
Angrily refuse to have any sex and tell partner s/he is a basket case when my partner gives me less sex than I want.	I'll fix his or her wagon! S/he could easily have more sex with me and is an inconsiderate, unloving, lousy person for refusing to have it!

Sample Exercise 4B (cont.)

My Disturbed Feelings and Actions About My Partner's Failings and Mistreatment of Me	My Irrational Beliefs (IBs), Which Encourage My Disturbed Feelings and Actions About My Partner's Failings and Mistreatment of Me
Fume and froth when partner lies to me about important things. Feel there is no excuse for this.	What a complete liar s/he is! A hopeless liar who can't ever tell the truth completely does me in—as a loving partner never should!

Exercise 4B

My Disturbed Feelings and Actions About My Partner's Failings and Mistreatment of Me	My Irrational Beliefs (IBs) That Encourage My Disturbed Feelings and Actions About My Partner's Failings and Mistreatment of Me
_____	_____
_____	_____
_____	_____
_____	_____
_____	_____
_____	_____
_____	_____
_____	_____
_____	_____
_____	_____
_____	_____
_____	_____
_____	_____
_____	_____
_____	_____
_____	_____

Sample Exercise 4C: Rational Coping Self-Statements to Minimize My Irrational Beliefs (IBs) About My Partner's Failings and Mistreatment of Me

My Irrational Beliefs (IBs) About My Partner's Failings and Mistreatment of Me	Rational Coping Self-Statements I Can Use to Minimize My Irrational Beliefs (IBs)
My partner *must not* be untidy! That seriously handicaps me and is unfair. S/he *must* be fair and be tidy!	My partner is a fallible human who has every right to be untidy. Yes, his/her untidiness may seriously handicap me and may be unfair. But unfairness must exist when it exists and untidiness is quite disadvantageous but not *horrible*. Let me see if I can *un*angrily help him/her to change.
Woe is me! After all I do for my partner s/he must not severely criticize me. I must be an incompetent person if this criticism is correct. If s/he really loved me this would never happen. S/he is dishonest and totally rotten for treating me this way!	No matter how well I treat my partner s/he can still easily criticize me. That may be his/her nature! This criticism never makes me an incompetent person—even if it is correct. Just a person who at times *acts* incompetently. Even if my partner really loves me, s/he can still be over-critical and usually honest about my failings. This may be rotten, but s/he is not a *rotten person*.
How incredibly idiotic it is when my partner overspends! S/he is a baby who never faces reality! After I go out of my way to save, s/he must never get us into debt!	Foolish overspending is hardly incredible but actually fairly common. My partner is acting childish in that respect but is not a total baby who never faces reality. S/he is only *sometimes* unrealistic. It's good that I go out of my way to save, but that doesn't *make* her/him a sensible spender who never gets us into debt. Too bad!—but s/he has several other good traits.

Sample Exercise 4C (cont.)

My Irrational Beliefs (IBs) About My Partner's Failings and Mistreatment of Me	Rational Coping Self-Statements I Can Use to Minimize My Irrational Beliefs (IBs)
How can s/he be this rotten way—always being late to appointments? Because it's so easy to plan to be on time, s/he has no excuse for not arranging to be! My partner is a thoroughly disorganized and rotten person!	My partner has no trouble—alas!—in acting this rotten way. That's the way s/he often is. Even though I find it easy to plan to be on time my partner seems to find it very hard to arrange this. S/he is disorganized in this respect but does many other things well and is obviously not a disorganized rotten *person.*
I'll fix my partner's wagon when s/he gives me less sex than I want. S/he could easily have more sex with me and is an inconsiderate, unloving, lousy person for refusing to have sex!	It's really silly if I try to hostilely fix my partner's wagon—because then I'll get less sex! S/he can't *easily* have more sex with me—otherwise s/he would probably have it. S/he may still be considerate and loving, but have several good reasons for refusing to have more sex. Perhaps he/she is acting rottenly *in this* respect, but is surely not a rotten lousy person.
My partner is a complete liar when s/he lies to me about important things—a hopeless liar who *can't* ever tell the truth! S/he completely does me in—as a loving partner never should!	My partner lies about some important things but is obviously not a *complete* liar who lies about *everything.* S/he most probably is *not* a hopeless liar and *can* tell the truth—but for certain reasons, chooses to do otherwise at times. S/he handicaps me somewhat by lying but hardly *completely* does me in. S/he *should* lie right now, because that is his/her present way. Loving partners *still* sometimes lie—and they, too, must right now be the way that they are. Too bad!

Exercise 4C

My Irrational Beliefs (IBs) About My Partner's Failings and Mistreatment of Me	Rational Coping Self-Statements I Can Use to Minimize My Irrational Beliefs (IBs)

5

Communicating and Problem-
Solving as a Couple

So far, we haven't shown how you and your partner can teach yourselves to focus on your own loving behavior. As with many REBT
procedures, you can do this most effectively outside of therapy, during homework time. In this chapter we'll try to give clear examples
of how couples can improve their communication and problem-
solving skills in and out of the therapy situation.

We have found that no matter how experienced couples may be
in the art of communicating, they should assume that they often do
not successfully transmit the messages they think they are transmit-
ting to each other. If you do already make such assumptions, some
of the communication exercises we recommend may at first seem a
bit kindergartenish. So it was with Jan and Ed, who I (Dr. Harper)
saw for couples therapy, and who I tried to get to listen to each
other:

Ed: You mean I am supposed to repeat after Jan what she has just
said? And then she's supposed to say to me: "Hey, Ed, do I hear you
correctly as saying you'd like me to pass the butter?"

R.A.H.: If butter-passing was an area in which the two of you had
difficulty understanding each other, we might well begin there. As I
understand the two of you, your problems are somewhat different,
so I'd like to start with this exercise to learn a little bit more about

your situation. Let's ask Jan to start with something that is really troubling her, and then the two of you can replay the other's requests back and forth.

Jan: Well, the thing that troubles me the most is: Ed, I don't think you really take me seriously as an equal.

Ed: Oh, crap! Okay, I'll play the game. Jan, I hear you saying that you don't think I really take you seriously as an equal.

Jan: Yeah, that's what I said. But I hear you interpreting that what's troubling me is a lot of crap and that this is all an idiotic game.

Ed: You heard me all right, sweet buns.

Jan: Defense rests! (She turns to me.) He apparently doesn't understand that he just proved that what troubles me is true. (I interrupt to tell Jan to talk to Ed.) Okay, can't you see that by calling my troubles "crap," and by not taking seriously what the therapist prescribed as an exercise to help us understand better what the other person is trying to communicate, *and* by calling me sweet buns, you are proving to me the very thing that troubles me most, namely— you dumb bastard that I unfortunately love—that you don't relate to me as an equal?

R.A.H.: Before we get to Ed's response, let's examine why it might well be negative. Although Jan's summary analysis was splendid, she first labeled Ed as a dumb bastard (even if she was kidding), and then asserted that she *unfortunately* loved him. She thereby made it almost certain for Ed to be distracted from her main message. Jan, please deliver your main message again in as close as you can to the same words as you used before. (Jan does so.)

Ed: I heard your main message all right. You are seriously troubled that I don't treat you as an equal. I don't think you are right, but I want to work it out with you so you feel that I do treat you as an equal.

R.A.H.: Splendid! Ed, you have correctly discerned that you do not have to agree with Jan in order to come to clearly understand what is troubling her. But you have also come up with a very positive attitude of wanting to work with Jan so that she doesn't feel seriously troubled. An important principle can be generalized here:

Whenever one person in an intimate relationship experiences a problem, then (regardless of the differing view of the partner) *a problem does indeed exist and problem-solving is highly desirable.* It is easy for any of us in a couple relationship to decide, "I'm right, and he or she is crazy." This makes problem-solving *more* difficult!

But let's not lose sight right now of this simple exercise. Your first step is to satisfy each other *that you understand your partner's problems.* I'd like both of you to try, as your first homework assignment, to identify three problems, and by going through this first step with each of them, to make sure that you both understand the other's problem. Then at the next session, you will report back what happened. In fairness, I'd suggest that one extra problem be contributed by Ed, because Jan has already raised one.

In the time that remains for this session, let's take Jan's problem and see if we can get beyond the first step. I am going to have both of you try two brief exercises that we frequently use in REBT couples therapy. Please close your eyes. Now, Jan, will you imagine what *you* (not Ed, but *you*) could do to change any of your thoughts, perceptions, feelings, or actions to make your relationship a more equal one? In the meantime, Ed, focus on how you could alter *any* of your thoughts, perceptions, feelings, or actions to help Jan experience more equality in relating to you? Each of you is to focus on your *own* behavior (keeping your eyes closed).

(Three minutes later.) Okay, let's hear from Jan first. Both of you please keep your eyes closed until each of you has reported what you have thought and felt in the last three minutes. Now we'll move to exercise two. Be sure you still fully report to each other what you have thought and felt as you did in the previous exercise.

Jan: Yeah, well, I sort of see why Ed says these exercises are childish, but they really get to me. I focused on my behavior the way you told us to do and realized and felt that what I had really been saying by my reactions to Ed is that I feel insecure in this relationship. So the way I can help equalize things is to feel less insecure, and the way I can do that is to stop insisting that I absolutely must control how things go. Either we go for the long haul, or we don't. Either he thinks I'm an equal, or he doesn't. And, if in my non-insecure (if that's a word) judgment, he doesn't—then screw him, the haul is over, and I move on to another relationship. Ed was right in a sense to say my equality pitch was crap because I keep thinking he *has* to treat me equally and *has* to feel a certain way about me, and that the relationship *has* to work out or my world will come to an end. Now, after my three minutes of looking at my reactions, I, too, would say crap to all that. So I'm going to work on my demands and the insecurity I create with them and I'm going to try to point my behavior toward enjoying this relationship.

Ed: Wow! I take back whatever I said about these being idiotic exercises. I had a hard time not opening my eyes to make sure that was still Jan using Jan's voice. It's hard for me now to stick to my own report and not respond to what Jan said, which I think was terrific. But my focus was along the line that I've been something of a defensive asshole and I have not been willing to consider anything—including what I now consider these simple *and* valuable exercises—that did not fit within my rigid scheme. My contribution to helping Jan think and feel that I treat her as an equal will be to refuse to dismiss anything she says as crap. First, I'll listen to her and ask for confirmation: "Is this what I hear you saying?" Then I'm going to say: "Hey, please excuse me a few minutes, Jan, while I take a swig or two of exercise one." And then I will focus conscientiously on my own behavior when Jan has a problem with me, just as I have tried to do this time. Then I'll go on to exercise two and tell Jan exactly what I thought and felt that *I* could do when I did exercise one to change my feelings and behaviors that she wanted me to change.

R.A.H.: Good! You have both just indicated how you can do these two exercises as homework assignments. You have also indicated how you can have some fun with these exercises by not just seeing them as grim assignments, but as a way of communicating better, as a means to problem-solving and real enjoyment.

Let me make sure, though, that you both understand that you are free to react to what the other one reports in exercise two. But it is preferable, as both of you realized, to wait until the other's report has been made. Then there is less chance of your own focusing on self-change getting blurred by your emotional reactions to the other's report. The purpose of both exercises is to improve your communication and assist your problem-solving. Your reactions to each other's contributions are quite desirable.

Since our time is up for today, most of your reactions to what the other one has said will have to be done at home or discussed here next week. Let me caution that human endeavors—including these exercises—tend to be imperfect, so your first exercise may leave you still unsure that your partner understands your problems. The second exercise may often fail to quickly create the new behaviors that lead to the problem-solving you arrived at today.

Some problems are very hard to crack, so if you expect that success will always be quick and easy, you may give up. Finding solutions often takes long hard work, but with persistence, most problems *can* be solved. Occasionally, however, you may end up with the undesirable "resolution" of "good-bye relationship." But even that, though hardly preferable, need not be viewed as "horrible" and "awful." Because today you both seem well on your way to problem-solving. And if you are both willing to work at this, you can most likely achieve an enjoyable close relationship—and yes, even if you always have some important differences.

I tried to caution Jan and Ed against overconfidence, which can easily arise from early success and lead to giving up when real tough problems arise. Conversely, couples often get discouraged when their first efforts to handle a difficulty fall flat. Sometimes one or both parties deny the existence of a problem (you remember George in chapter two). Others pessimistically and rigidly hold that nothing can be done to improve their situation.

These attitudinal and emotional problems need to be remedied before incompatibilities can be resolved. Even with problem deniers and neurotic pessimists, persistent use of both exercises performed with Jan and Ed can bring good results.

In that case, Jan and Ed's agreeing that they could solve their problems and that each of them could alter his/her thoughts, feelings, perceptions, and actions was a tremendous help. Although it may not seem the case to some readers, it is still a radical concept—

even in psychotherapy circles—that people are able to regulate their own lives instead of letting themselves be driven by organic, unconscious, social, or cosmic forces. "You must take me as I am" and "That's just the way I am" (and, hence, unchangeable) are strongly held beliefs of many partners. The two exercises just demonstrated showed that good results can occur when neither individual holds strongly to the common belief that misery is forced on him/her by outside people or events. These same two exercises can powerfully help partners overcome their underlying IBs about themselves and each other.

Making sure that both understand each other's perceptions of problems and focusing on changing each of their own problem behaviors, and not merely their partner's problem behaviors, are helpful in solving mating difficulties. But, by doing this, couples hardly always and automatically end up with a heavenly relationship. Just as we observed that love does not necessarily conquer all in chapter three, so can we admit the same for these two REBT communication and problem-solving exercises. What else can be done to improve unheavenly relationships? Let's return to Ed and Jan in the middle of their second session.

Jan: I hate to bring this up—especially since we are solving our equal treatment problem and because we are both enthusiastic about how well the two exercises you taught us are working—but is this it? Is this all we have to do?

R.A.H.: If you hadn't brought this up yourself, I would have mentioned it soon. No, this is not a perfect ending, either for your relationship or for therapy. What we've done up to now is to get the train (that is, the relationship) on the track and work out ways to keep it on track. Your love for each other—and by that I mean your deep caring for each other and not the erotic charges you give each other—will contribute greatly to your staying on track, too. When I sort of reprimanded Jan in our last session for saying that she loved you, Ed, it was because we were trying to concentrate on a different kind of communication. Love is not only an important thing to communicate to each other, but it can also help keep you interested in and contribute solutions to your problems. There's scarcely anything better for any relationship than plenty of deep caring.

Ed: When Jan asked if this is it, I think she was reflecting that we were doing the two exercises and becoming pretty damned good at problem-solving. But we were wondering whether a long-term application of this stuff would become boring as hell.

R.A.H.: For many people it well might! Those two exercises, now that you have had a week to use them as problem-solving procedures, can be put in the cupboard until the next serious communication difficulty occurs. It would help if you practiced the techniques a little just to make sure you keep them ready for possible troubles. But even working to resolve trouble can be tempered with humor and having fun—which are very good lubricants for problem-solving.

The third exercise is broader and deeper, and is to be pursued as a kind of perpetual homework assignment—practically never to be put in the cupboard. This consists of each of you asking yourself and discussing with each other, *"How can we make life more interesting and enjoyable?"*

Jan: Sounds great but also can be overdone.—"How can we get a bigger bang out of life and to hell with other people?"

R.A.H.: That's a short-term interpretation. Only if you take the lure of an easy and quick fix—of immediate gratification. Focusing on fixing yourselves quickly often does disregard the rights and pleasure of others. But realize that for you to find ways of making life more interesting and enjoyable takes thinking, problem-solving, discussing, planning, experimenting, rethinking, rediscussing, replanning, and re-experimenting. This is longer-term, and it is hard work, not a quick fix. Working at making your lives more interesting and enjoyable is an exercise that gets built into your very philosophy of life. The process itself often gets to be interesting and enjoyable and even downright exciting. But it calls for patience and persistence in trying to understand and deal with old habits of thinking, feeling, perceiving, and acting and to convert them into more effective habits. This third exercise is endless—it is a way of life—*and*, again, it is hard work. *But* you will often find that it brings more satisfaction than any other way of life I have ever heard about.

Ed: I can tell you that Jan and I will be living exercise three and not just preaching it. I think Jan's and my working so hard for a week on the first two exercises makes it easier for us to see that focusing on how we can make life more interesting and enjoyable won't be *too* hard for us. But I still agree with Jan that it sounds rather selfish.

R.A.H.: All I can do is assure you that it usually doesn't work out that way. First of all, I have found through the years that many of us are inclined to label other people as "selfish" whenever they don't do what we want them to do. We call people "selfish" when we think they *should* be behaving differently from the way they are behaving. Second, if you decide to do things the REBT way (that is, based on long-range interest rather than immediate gratification), you realistically consider the points of view of other people. You don't let others' feelings dominate you, but you consider how they will probably react to your decisions in both the short and long run. If you use longer-term self-interest as your guide you are less likely to smoke regularly or to practice your drums at 2:00 A.M. You will probably intrude less on other people's lives than some righteous reformer who is "unselfishly" trying to keep other people from having abortions or from viewing pornography.

Ed: Does that mean you are against reform?

R.A.H.: No, certainly not! The three of us are working right now to "reform" your lives and the ways you relate to one another. But you are here by consent and not by demand and control. We are trying to help you make changes that the three of us agree are desirable. The same cooperative process can be used in the broader community. If you want to use educational methods to try to *persuade* others not to view pornography or not to have abortions, that's quite different from violently trying to *prevent* them from doing so. But back to the two of you. Why would it be preferable to help you with your emotional problems while also working on your REBT exercises?

Jan: I suspect because our doubts, fears, and skepticism should be dealt with before we can really throw ourselves wholeheartedly into living the REBT way.

Ed: Yeah, I might even add that we've not only been removing some obstacles, as Jan points out, but we have begun experiencing the increased interest and enjoyment that comes from experimenting with this approach.

R.A.H.: Fine. What, again, would be a good homework assignment for next week?

Ed: And for the next zillion weeks, if I get the aim of exercise three straight: namely, look individually and as a couple for ways of improving the interest and enjoyment of our lives.

Jan: Right. And don't forget, Ed, we can concentrate on what's interesting and enjoyable on a long-term basis—and try to have barrels of fun while we are doing all this stuff! We can use exercises one and two in case we hit any problems. But we can have lots of laughs even with problems. Right?

R.A.H.: Very right! I highly endorse your fun-seeking slant. Jan gave a particularly neat and accurate summary of where we are and where we are trying to go. I think that both of you have not only been listening, but you have also been trying to apply what you're learning. However, you don't have to be just wide-eyed Ms. Gullible and Mr. Goody-Two-Shoes. As I've said before, this is tough stuff and not all sweetness and light. You'd better work at it!

Ed: I agree. I was thinking, even before Jan spoke: "Hey, what in hell have I gotten myself into with all this REBT stuff? Life used to be a breeze." But it wasn't, really, or we wouldn't be here. As I think I said a while ago—or maybe I just thought it, I'm not sure—I'm beginning to get a bang out of this whole approach and am willing to keep working at all three exercises, especially number three.

Jan: Me, too. I may not be an easy lay, as you once said, Ed, but I seem to be a sucker for REBT.

R.A.H.: You both sound committed to giving it your best shot. Try to avoid both perfectionism and easy discouragement, but practice exercises one and two if you slack off. In the meantime, happy exercise three! See you next week.

To show you how exercises one, two, and three can be effectively used in other kinds of relationship therapy, let me (Dr. Ellis) describe the case of José and Marella, who were at continued loggerheads as to how strict they should be with their eight-year-old son, Juan. José, reared in a conventional Mexican family, thought that they should be very strict, especially when Juan neglected his chores and avoided doing his homework. Marella was much more lenient and forgiving.

During this couple's first session with me, I explained some of the principles of REBT and showed them that Marella was angry at José for being *too* strict with Juan—which he absolutely *must not* be—and that José was furious at Marella for letting Juan "get away with murder" and not be as disciplined about his chores and his homework as he *absolutely should* be. She, thought José, was turning him into a "thug"—as she definitely *must not*. They agreed with me that they were *demanding*, not merely *wishing*, that the other "correctly" raise Juan. José was also insisting that their son be "a real, disciplined male," and was often enraged at him for not achieving this "necessary" goal. They agreed that they were both *must*urbating, but I could see that they were giving only lip service to stopping it.

I started them on exercise one, listening to each other. I asked José to present his view of raising Juan to Marella. He said, "I want Juan to grow up to be a real *man*, not an undisciplined sissy like you want him to be. I'm angry that you're indulging him and turning him into a spoiled brat!"

Marella—naturally—bristled at this and immediately started to argue that José was trying to turn Juan into a male chauvinist pig—just like himself! I stopped her and insisted that she *just* repeat what she heard José say. After a few incorrect tries, she managed to say, "I hear you saying that you want Juan to grow up to be a real man and not a sissy like I want him to be. You're angry at me for spoiling him and supposedly turning Juan into a spoiled brat."

Pretty close to José's statement of his feelings, we agreed. "Now state how you feel," I told Marella, "and José, you carefully listen and repeat her view." Marella began, "José, you're much too strict with Juan. After all, he's only eight and will grow up to hate himself if you keep after him like you do. Maybe you want him to be a manly boy. But, hell, he's only a child! Call off your dogs!"

José listened carefully and repeated Marella's statement almost word for word. Then he added, "But he'd better be a little boy, not a wimp, right now!"

"None of that extra stuff!" I warned José. "Just repeat what you heard Marella say *without* saying anything extra, at least right now." He did so. I then gave Marella and José the homework assignment of each of them stating to the other partner three different problems that they had in their relationship, with the other repeating what they said until they both agreed that they really heard what their partner felt about their problems.

Then I gave José and Marella exercise two: "Close your eyes. Now will you, Marella, imagine what you (not José, but *you*) could do to curb your anger at José even though he continues to be very strict with Juan? How could *you* accept José with his present attitude, which you think is so wrong, and what could you tell yourself to reduce your anger at him? While you are doing this, will you, José, focus not on Marella's thoughts, feelings, and actions about Juan and you, but only upon what you could tell yourself to do to accept her with her present attitude, which you think is so wrong? What could *you* do to reduce your anger at her? Both of you for the next few minutes are to work at changing your *own* attitudes and feelings about the other's so-called poor behavior. Keep your eyes closed now and use the next three minutes to focus on how you could change *yourself* about this problem you both have with each other."

After I gave them three minutes Marella reported: "That was hard! It took me almost a minute to focus on me, because I kept thinking of José and how *he* should change. But I kept at it, and finally thought that, first, I could make a real effort to see that he had a genuine point of view, genuine for him, even if I strongly disagreed with it. Second, I realized—as you showed us during our first session—that when I was angry at José I had a strong *must* that was helping make me angry. Not he, but my must, was the issue. So

I found it: "José *absolutely must not* oppose me about Juan, when I'm so right and he's so wrong!" I then began to see that it was highly *preferable* that José not oppose me about Juan, but there was *no* reason that he *had* to act preferably. As soon as I told myself that, much of my anger flew out the window. I even saw that José's intentions were good, though I did not agree with them."

José listened to Marella with amazement, then reported on his own three minutes: "Like Marella, I at first had trouble focusing on *me* because I was still enraged at *her* and even thought that she was deliberately handling Juan gently in order to upset me. But I saw that my focus was still on her and remembered your instructions, so I forced it back to me. I realized that by being angry, I was hurting myself, ruining my relationship with Marella, and maybe even being unfair to Juan—who is really a great kid and I love him a lot. I saw how anger was greatly raising my blood pressure, which is much too high already. So I quickly said to myself, 'This is stupid! I'd better stop it! Even if I'm right about being strict with Juan, I don't have to be *angrily* strict.' So I made myself relax by using breathing techniques, and resolved that hereafter I would spend a hell of a lot more time *un*making rather than *making* myself angry. That resolve immediately calmed me down—and then I began to think that maybe Marella had some good points after all. But I thought of her only after, as you told us to do, I first thought of how to change *me*."

José and Marella were both delighted with each other's carrying out of exercise two, and fully agreed that, as homework, they would try to do it with three more relationship problems. They did so and had an unusually good week in working on their anger about several other household, spending, and in-law problems. They weren't exactly cured, but achieved the insight that their anger largely stemmed from themselves, not their mate's "wrongness," and therefore they could almost always reduce it by taking a few minutes to see what each of them could do, with or without the other's help, to tackle it.

By sharing what each of them did in their work on themselves in exercise two, José and Marella got additional ideas on how to curb their own anger (as well as depression) and added to their repertoire of REBT useful techniques. Then I helped them proceed to exercise three: Asking themselves and discussing with each other "How can we make life more interesting and more enjoyable?"

Although they came to therapy at first only to overcome their anger and bickering about how to deal with Juan, they found that after this largely was alleviated, they automatically enjoyed many former pursuits—such as watching television—more. But energized by me to explore greater interests and enjoyments, they did some exploration and experimenting, and added to their active participations ballroom dancing, opera-going, and joining a regular discussion group. When I last heard from them, they were considering bird-watching!

No relationship, we repeat, is perfect. Until their son, Juan, became a teenager and was on his own, Marella and José still differed about how strictly to raise him. Differed, but didn't fight about it. Each of them partly willingly accepted, without liking, the other's child-raising notions and therefore made some suitable compromises.

EXERCISES FOR CHAPTER 5

This chapter showed how REBT is often specifically designed for couples (and family) therapy. In this chapter, Jan and Ed had a communication problem—*between* them. So both *together* were shown how to do two exercises to help resolve their problem.

Oddly enough, however, the first exercise they were taught focused on how each of them could work to change *himself* and *herself* along with their working together. This is what effective couple therapy almost always seems to do. The partners, naturally, talk to each other and, with the therapist's help, work on improving their *relationship*. Isn't that what they come for? Indeed!

However, unless at least one of the two—and preferably both—see themselves as somewhat mistaken and somewhat disturbed, little progress is likely to be made. They usually have *both* individual and coupled problems—not either/or. So REBT first tends to help each of them acknowledge, understand, and work at changing his or her problems—especially disturbances—which they may well *bring to* the relationship.

As I (Dr. Ellis) tell the professionals who attend my workshops on marital and family therapy, I assume that people like Jan and Ed have their own neurotic reactions and had them long before they met each other. These reactions do not necessarily make them incompatible—but they certainly help to do so!

REBT couple counseling, therefore, usually first highlights some of each individual's personal difficulties—as Dr. Harper gently did with Ed and Jan. Before he tried to help one communicate with the other (as he did in the second REBT exercise he gave them), he instructed them to get into their own heads and communicate carefully with themselves. They did this by first acknowledging that they *could* act better with each other and second, by imagining some methods of actually doing so.

Note the inevitable interaction here between Ed and Jan's self-focus and other-focus. Their goal was to figure out how to improve their *relationship*. So, almost perversely, they first got into their *own* thoughts and feelings. But—ah!—they each thought about and felt what they could do to help *the other*. They were simultaneously working as individuals *and* as social creatures.

This is in accordance with and also emphasizes the tenets of REBT, which holds that individuals exist in their own unique right *and* as part of their social group. Both individualism and sociability seem to be innate and necessary for human survival. Both are also encouraged by social learning—though to different degrees in varying cultures. Jan and Ed came to therapy to increase their personal happiness—and to function more happily together. REBT often first gets around to their *individual* problems and solutions—so that they can communicate better *together*.

The third exercise Harper presented to Ed and Jan was for them to ask themselves and to discuss with each other: "How can we make life more interesting and enjoyable?" Harper, of course, implies interesting and enjoyable *together*. But, once again, don't they both *individually* have to do the enjoying? One would hope so!

A number of psychologists—such as Edward Sampson and Kenneth Gergen—have pointed out the dangers and limitations of our Western concepts of individualism and the advantages of some Eastern cultures' greater stresses on social sacrifice. They make a good point. But cultures that train their members to put others first and themselves second have to orient themselves toward *enjoying* this group outlook. And doesn't that include their individually enjoying it?

Ed and Jan were given REBT homework exercises. How about giving yourself some exercises to help you use the lessons included in this chapter? As noted, even making your and your partner's life more interesting and enjoyable takes thinking, problem-solving, discussing, planning, experimenting, rethinking, rediscussing, replanning, and re-experimenting. As Harper observed to Jan and Ed, "this is hard work, not a quick fix." So is mating in general!

Let us now do some exercises to help you increase your frustration tolerance and prepare you for the hard work that is required for successful mating.

Sample Exercise 5A: Making Myself Aware of My Frustration Intolerance (FI) in Aspects of Dating, Relating, and Mating and My Irrational Beliefs (IBs) That Encourage My FI

Occasions on Which I Avoided Doing What Was Beneficial or Did What Was Harmful to Me	IBs That Encouraged Me to Avoid Doing What Was Beneficial or Do What Was Harmful To Me
Spent money I could not afford to spend, knowing it would upset my partner.	I *absolutely need* the things this money will buy even though I cannot afford them. I *can't stand* being deprived and not getting what I strongly desire.
Criticized my partner severely even though I knew s/he couldn't take my criticism. Told myself to shut my big mouth but stupidly opened it and let my partner have it.	My partner is acting foolishly and I *have to* correct her/him. I *can't bear* keeping my feelings in. It's *awful* to have to shut up when I'm right about this. I *must* get my partner to change!
Refused to go out of my way to satisfy my partner's needs for more affection and sex.	I *shouldn't have to be* more affectionate and sexually involved when I don't feel like being so. It's *too* hard to push myself like this! I'm *unable* to give more than I am now giving. My partner is unfair and is no damned good for demanding more than I naturally feel like giving!
Didn't help my partner keep our apartment clean and tidy. Only helped him/her on a few occasions when I really felt like doing so and found it easy to cooperate.	My partner is too finicky and demanding—as s/he *shouldn't* be! Why should I have to work so hard and do so many unpleasant things? It's unfair! Life is too short to do the things my partner wants me to do. I never did them when I lived by myself, so I shouldn't have to do them now!

Sample Exercise 5A (cont.)

Occasions on Which I Avoided Doing What Was Beneficial or Did What Was Harmful to Me	IBs That Encouraged Me to Avoid Doing What Was Beneficial or Do What Was Harmful To Me
Kept breaking appointments with my partner and coming late when I did keep them.	I *must* do exactly what I want to do first—before I keep my appointments with my partner and before I leave early to show up on time. I have *too much* to do, and since my partner will forgive me, I'll take care of myself first and put him/her second. Time should stretch and allow me to do everything I feel like doing before I keep my appointments with my partner. I need the love and favors I get from my partner but following his or her rules about appointments is too rough, and I *can't* do it!
Kept avoiding seeing my partner's relatives and was often nasty to them even when my partner felt very upset about this.	I didn't marry my partner's damned relatives and s/he should understand this! They're stupid and obnoxious—and deserve my boycotting them and telling them off! My partner is very inconsiderate when s/he makes me visit boring relatives. S/he should be wise enough to boycott them, too!
Kept overeating in spite of my poor health and my partner's upsetness about my self-defeating food intake.	I can get away with it! I can keep eating and not ruin my health. My partner *should* leave me alone and *must* stop nagging me about my eating. S/he is after me too much and I can't tolerate that! Eating is the main pleasure I have, and I must not be deprived of good food. How *horrible* it is to be deprived!

Exercise 5A

Occasions on Which I Avoided Doing What Was Beneficial or Did What Was Harmful to Me	IBs That Encouraged Me to Avoid Doing What Was Beneficial or Do What Was Harmful To Me

Sample Exercise 5B: Disputing My Irrational Beliefs (IBs) That Encourage My Frustration Intolerance (FI)

IBs That Encourage Me to Avoid Doing What Is Beneficial or to Do What Is Harmful to Me	Disputing My IBs and Coming Up With RBs That Will Help Me Reduce My Frustration Intolerance (FI)
I *absolutely need* the things this money will buy even though I cannot afford them. I *can't stand* being deprived now and not getting what I strongly desire.	*Dispute:* Why do I *absolutely need* the things that money will buy even though I can't afford them? *Answer:* I *don't* need what I want in this respect! *Dispute:* Can I really not *stand* being deprived now and not getting what I strongly desire? *Answer:* Of course I can stand it and not die of deprivation! I can still find *much* happiness in other respects—and can arrange *later* pleasure by depriving myself *now.*
My partner is acting foolishly and I *have to* correct her/him. I *can't bear* keeping my feelings in. It's *awful* to have to shut up when I'm right about this. I *must* get my partner to change!	*Dispute:* Do I *have to* correct my partner if s/he is acting foolishly? *Answer:* Obviously not—though that would be great, *if* s/he were ready to listen. *Dispute:* Why can't I bear keeping my feelings in? *Answer:* Only because I exaggeratedly *believe* I can't bear it and because I *define* the inconvenience of doing so as *awful*—or as worse than it *should* be. *Dispute:* Does my being right about my partner's mistakes mean that I *must* get him/her to change? *Answer:* No! S/he can clearly be wrong and stay wrong—while I tactfully keep my mouth shut!

Sample Exercise 5B (cont.)

IBs That Encourage Me to Avoid Doing What Is Beneficial or to Do What Is Harmful to Me	Disputing My IBs and Coming Up With RBs That Will Help Me Reduce My Frustration Intolerance (FI)
I *shouldn't have to* be more affectionate and sexually involved when I don't feel like being so. It's *too* hard to push myself like this! I'm *unable* to give more than I am now giving. My partner is unfair and is no damned good for demanding more than I naturally feel like giving!	*Dispute:* I *preferably* shouldn't have to be more affectionately and sexually involved with my partner when I don't feel like being so. But is it true that my preference *absolutely has* to be fulfilled? *Answer:* No—only if I choose to alienate and probably lose my partner. My preferences and desires don't *have to* be realized. *Dispute:* Am I really unable to give more love and sex than I am now giving? *Answer:* Yes, if I *make* myself unable. Otherwise, I *can* give more. *Dispute:* Is my partner unfair and no damned good for demanding more affection and sex than I naturally feel like giving? *Answer:* No! Aren't *I* unfair for withholding what I can give and what will probably make our relationship better?
My partner is too finicky and demanding—as s/he *shouldn't* be! Why should I have to work so hard and do so many unpleasant things? It's unfair! Life is too short to do the things my partner wants me to do. I never did them when I lived by myself, so I shouldn't have to do them now!	*Dispute:* Why is my partner *too* finicky and demanding about my not helping keep our apartment clean? *Answer:* S/he may really be finicky but my belief about his/her being *too* finicky goes with my demand that s/he *must not* be that demanding. But s/he *must* be that finicky if he or she *is.* Too bad! But I'd better realistically accept this finickiness if I

Sample Exercise 5B (cont.)

IBs That Encourage Me to Avoid Doing What Is Beneficial or to Do What Is Harmful to Me	Disputing My IBs and Coming Up With RBs That Will Help Me Reduce My Frustration Intolerance (FI)
	choose to stay with this partner. *Dispute:* Is it really *unfair* that I have to work so hard to do so many unpleasant things to please my partner? *Answer:* No, it is painful, but not necessarily unfair. Even if it is unfair, I'd better do those things—or else calmly leave my partner. *Dispute:* Does it follow that because I never kept my apartment clean and tidy when I lived by myself, I shouldn't have to do so now? *Answer:* No, it doesn't follow at all! In this new relationship I'd better do many things that I never did before.
I *must do* exactly what I want to do first—before I keep my appointments with my partner and before I leave early to show up on time. I have *too much* to do, and since my partner will forgive me, I'll take care of myself first and put him/her second. Time should stretch and allow me to do everything I feel like doing before I keep my appointments with my partner. I need the love and favors I get from my partner but following his or her rules about appointments is too rough, and I *can't* do it!	*Dispute:* Where will it get me if I think I must do exactly what I want before I keep my appointments with my partner and before I leave early to show up on time? *Answer:* (1) Partnerless! (2) Remaining the procrastinating baby that I am! *Dispute:* Do I really have *too much* to do before I get out on time to be early for my appointments with my partner? *Answer:* No—much but not *too much* to do. Some of it I can *not* do—or sensibly can do later. *Dispute:* Should time stretch and allow me to do everything I want to do so that I can keep my ap-

Sample Exercise 5B (cont.)

IBs That Encourage Me to Avoid Doing What Is Beneficial or to Do What Is Harmful to Me	Disputing My IBs and Coming Up With RBs That Will Help Me Reduce My Frustration Intolerance (FI)
	pointments on time with my partner? *Answer:* Like hell it should! It won't. *Dispute:* Is it true that I *can't* follow my partner's rules and thereby win his/her favor that I need? *Answer:* Can't? What drivel! I foolishly *won't*. I don't *need* his/her love and favors but prefer them. So I'd better push myself.
I didn't marry my partner's damned relatives and s/he should understand this! They're stupid and obnoxious—and deserve my boycotting them and telling them off! My partner is very inconsiderate when s/he makes me visit boring relatives. S/he should be wise enough to boycott them, too!	*Dispute: Must* my partner understand that I didn't marry his/her damned relatives and therefore never try to get me to see them? *Answer:* Lots of luck! To some extent his/her relatives go with my marriage ride. Visiting them will hardly kill me! *Dispute:* Are his/her relatives really *that* stupid and obnoxious? *Answer:* Only to my prejudiced view. Even if they are, they hardly deserve my boycotting them and telling them off. That won't make them less stupid and less obnoxious! *Dispute:* Is my partner really inconsiderate of me when s/he makes me visit his/her boring relatives? *Answer:* No, s/he is merely following his/her own bent and asking me to help him/her follow it. My partner *should* stick with his/

Sample Exercise 5B (cont.)

IBs That Encourage Me to Avoid Doing What Is Beneficial or to Do What Is Harmful to Me	Disputing My IBs and Coming Up With RBs That Will Help Me Reduce My Frustration Intolerance (FI)
	her boring relatives—and even enjoy them. We can't have *everything* in common—including this one.
I can get away with it! I can keep eating and not ruin my health. My partner *should* leave me alone and *must* stop nagging me about my eating. S/he is after me too much and I can't tolerate that! Eating is the main pleasure I have, and I must not be deprived of good food. How *horrible* to be deprived!	*Dispute:* Can I really get away with eating too much and not ruin my health? *Answer:* Very unlikely! I'd be quite an unusual exception to the rule. *Dispute:* Who says that my partner *must* stop nagging me about my eating? *Answer:* I say it—and I'll thereby make myself angry and help ruin our relationship. *Dispute:* Is my partner after me *too much?* Can I not tolerate his/her nagging? *Answer:* I *see* it as too much, but it's only much. Even if s/he does it much more than other partners would, it's mainly for my good. Maybe I'd better nag myself!

Exercise 5B

IBs That Encourage Me to Avoid Doing What Is Beneficial or Do What Is Harmful to Me	Disputing My IBs and Coming Up With RBs That Will Help Me Reduce My Frustration Intolerance (FI)

Sample Exercise 5C: Tasks That I Can Make Myself Uncomfortably Do to Reduce My Frustration Intolerance (FI)

Tasks That I Can Make Myself Uncomfortably Do to Reduce My Frustration Intolerance (FI)	Rational Coping Self-Statements I Can Use to Help Myself Do These Uncomfortable Tasks
Speak up when I am afraid to be criticized by my partner or others.	If I don't force myself to speak up, I will *increase* my fear of doing so. I will train myself to speak up *less* and may sabotage our open and honest relationship.
Go for a date with a potential partner who I feel will reject me.	I have less to lose by being rejected than by not going at all. I can learn by going on the date even if it turns out badly. Rejection doesn't make *me* bad.
Take a trip to a foreign country alone.	It won't kill me to be alone. I can learn to be more self-sufficient. If I get into any difficulty it will only be inconvenient, hardly the end of the world.
Exercise regularly, though I hate to do so.	It will give me good health benefits. The pain of the exercise will be brief—the pain of not doing it may last forever!
Eat much less delicious food than I prefer to eat.	The pleasure of eating will be brief—but the pain of overeating may be long! I will enjoy the fact that I am so disciplined! I will set a good example for my partner.
Stay with a partner who is often nasty and critical when leaving this partner would be inconvenient.	I cannot enjoy my partner's nastiness but can enjoy not taking it too seriously. I can stay, without getting upset, until it is much less inconvenient to leave.

Sample Exercise 5C (cont.)

Tasks That I Can Make Myself Uncomfortably Do to Reduce My Frustration Intolerance (FI)	Rational Coping Self-Statements I Can Use to Help Myself Do These Uncomfortable Tasks
Shut my big mouth when tempted to tell my partner off.	The pleasure of telling my partner off isn't worth the pain that will almost certainly follow my doing so. I can do myself a lot of good by shutting my mouth, staying for the present, and refusing to upset myself about my partner's actions.
Force myself to help my partner when I think that s/he is demanding that I do a foolish act.	The help I give my partner won't take too long while his/her displeasure and anger if I don't give it may last forever! I can actually enjoy the pleasure of satisfying my partner even though I don't like this way of satisfying him/her.
Agree to go along with my partner's foolish expenditures when we could use the money to much better advantage.	Even though I agree to spend foolishly with my partner, I can improve our relationship. Perhaps I can show him/her *later* how foolish our expenditures were. Even when we spend money on foolish things, I can often manage to enjoy these things.

Exercise 5C

Tasks That I Can Make Myself Uncomfortably Do to Reduce My Frustration Intolerance (FI)	Rational Coping Self-Statements I Can Use to Help Myself Do These Uncomfortable Tasks
_____	_____
_____	_____
_____	_____
_____	_____
_____	_____
_____	_____
_____	_____
_____	_____
_____	_____
_____	_____
_____	_____
_____	_____
_____	_____
_____	_____

6

Better Sex for Better Couplehood

When we wrote *A Guide to a Successful Marriage*, the sixties were just beginning. Although both of us already were "established" experts on SMF (sex/marriage/family) matters, we were nevertheless rebels against the establishment and tried to communicate a much more liberal and democratic attitude toward SMF than prevailed at the time. But times have changed. In some ways, only the Far Right (now a "moral *minority*") sound the way almost everybody did in 1961. But the culture has not changed so much that people who want a liberal and democratic SMF environment can relax and feel utopia is just around the corner.

Our use of REBT from 1955 onward made us aware of several important aspects of sex therapy: (1) sexual problems are usually bound up with nonsexual problems; (2) partners can themselves check on whether each are making therapy gains; (3) each partner can help the other to learn and to use REBT principles; (4) REBT, especially through homework exercises that couples undertake, provides problem-solving methods and experience. Therapy itself becomes an effective coping experience.

While it is important for therapists to teach specialized sex techniques and skills to their clients, they should also help these clients to become adept at *human* relations. REBT, though hardly neglecting sexual coping, concentrates on teaching *general* relationship methods.

When we use REBT with couples sex therapy, the couples provide a fine source of information about their own interactions, and give us a steady workshop situation in which we (and they) test out and improve upon problem-solving skills developed in the therapy hours. Soon, if all goes well, the couple will work things out on their own, using the knowledge and skills learned in therapy.

Does this mean neglecting the methods of treating tough sex problems that we and other sex therapists—such as Masters and Johnson, Joseph LoPicollo, Helen Kaplan, Lonnie Barbach, and Bernie Zilbergeld—developed? Of course not. But we now more clearly see sex problems as part of general emotional difficulties and as being interactional as well as individual. So we treat sex issues rationally, emotively, and behaviorally, just as we treat *other* problems that commonly—and, often *more* than commonly—arise in human interactions.

To illustrate applying REBT to sexual adjustment in couples, let us return to Jan and Ed. Here are some excerpts from their sixth therapy session.

Jan: Hey, we've been doing great on all this problem-solving stuff—I mean really great! But maybe the price is too high. This guy used to be all over me, and I loved it. Now we do sex by the numbers, and we both look and act bored. What price are we paying for all this rationality?

R.A.H.: Yes, but you and Ed remember that exercise three, which we mentioned before, includes efforts to make life ever more interesting and enjoyable. Rationality helps you overcome problems, but is not an end in itself—and certainly not a substitute for sex enjoyment. In using REBT, we approach sex problems in essentially the same way as other difficulties. You two reported no sex problem before, but Jan says that you now have less sex interest and enthusiasm. Do you agree, Ed? (He did.) Okay, we don't require exercises one and two, but let's go into exercise three again, which you both have used before. (They closed their eyes, and each focused on how they could change their own behavior to make sex fun.)

Ed: This is a tough one because I think it has some paradoxes. I can think of ways to change my ways of thinking, feeling, perceiving, and acting that would probably have us panting hot, but I think I'd be a phony. And *that's* no route to long-term interest and enjoyment. But, on the other hand, I am still interested in Jan sexually as well as in several other ways.

Jan: Well, I came up with one particularly desirable behavior change on my part. After four or five really great weeks, these past few days I've been thinking, "How come you ain't hot for luscious me, man?" And I've been taking it very personally that Ed clearly wasn't. But I just realized now that I can't honestly change my *perception* of what is going on. Because Ed isn't all over me all the time may mean that he has more respect for me as a person, as an equal, which is what I was screaming for not too damned many weeks ago. Also, because I'm now more interested in Ed in a lot of other ways than as a stud, I am probably sending out fewer Cleopatra-is-ready-to-be-laid flashes and scents.

Ed: Yeah, what Jan has just said fits in with what I was going on to say. My growing interest in Jan as a person seems to interfere somewhat with my interest in her as a great lay—not easy lay, Jan, but *great* lay. And I do still think and feel that way. It was probably the things she said about seeing her more as a person than as a sex object.

R.A.H.: I think I can help here. First of all, I think you have both developed anxiety about your reduced sex interest. Being alarmed and being also very devoted to the REBT program of making life more interesting and enjoyable, you have self-consciously forced yourselves (by the numbers, as Jan said) to each show yourself and the other one how overwhelmingly passionate you were. Whenever you try too hard—because you think you *absolutely must* succeed, let's say, at table tennis—you create anxiety that is likely to mess up your game. That goes many times over for sex, which is easily inhibited by anxiety. Let me make some points that may be helpful.

First, it is usual and normal for people when they are concentrating on a number of other things—in your case, on making some difficult behavior changes—to have their libidos temporarily wane. Second, it is also common for them—especially those who have never had sexual problems—to panic if a problem suddenly arises. Third, you are now well equipped with REBT procedures to apply to this new situation, as you already have done in your experiences with exercise two. One REBT response that I'd like to remind you of is that it wouldn't be terrible, awful, and catastrophic *even* if sex for the two of you became somewhat less exciting than in the past. You do have, as you both have indicated, increasing interest and enjoyment in many other aspects of your life. So you probably *won't* have less enjoyable sex. But even if you *do*, things will not be terrible. To summarize: relax, and your sex problem may already be on the wane.

Suppose Ed and Jan had had a *real* sex problem, what could we, as REBT therapists, do to help them with it? Actually, their problem *was* quite real and, like most sex (and non-sex) problems derived from anxiety or from *must*urbating about the *necessity* of success. Their anxiety deepened as they thought they *had* to please and be totally loved by the other partner and this anxiety led to hurt and suspicion. Partly, though, because Jan brought it up quite soon in therapy and partly because both Ed and Jan were already experienced in REBT couple exercises, their sex problem was so quickly dealt with that it seemed almost "unreal." Using exercise three for the next few weeks, they focused on how they could change their own behavior so that each of them could have more sex fun. Jan focused on being more sexy in her dress, her scent, and in her verbal and gestural approaches to Ed. She also used imagery to recall how sexually exciting he was when they first met and helped herself experience quicker and more intense orgasms. Ed also actively took the challenge of focusing on Jan's whole body, instead of mainly her genitals, when they were having sex, and of giving himself and her increased sensual pleasures even when his orgasms were not intense. He made sure that he—and Jan—had more prolonged sensual enjoyment even when their sexual peaks were quick and short. He became so focused on this aspect of their sexuality that other aspects were much less boring. Jan pushed herself to focus on bodily sensitivity, too; and they both resonated to the challenge of doing so. Even on some nights when they were not sexually aroused to begin with, they ultimately became so and enjoyed their own now-enhanced sensuality.

When couples have a sex problem that is more complicated, less readily defined, more long-standing, and apparently deep-seated, REBT couple procedures are similar. Exercise one (in which they make sure they understand each other's view of the problem) may require more work in both therapy sessions and in homework assignments, instead of being quickly resolved, as happened in Jan and Ed's case. Exercise two (focusing on how each partner can change to make things better) may only be done slowly and with small advances. Exercise three (what we can both do to enjoy our relationship more) may be tougher for one or both partners but can also be a rewarding experience.

Sex compatibility in mating is not always solved, as in Ed and Jan's case, by love. Many couples—like Sid and Jo who I (Dr. Ellis) wrote about in chapter two—love each other, all right, but really *are* somewhat sexually incompatible, in which case their sex problems may erode their love.

Sex differences in couples arise for a number of reasons. For example:

1. One partner—as in Jo's case—may be relatively low-sexed and the other—as was true of Sid—relatively high-sexed. Jo really wanted sex *a maximum* of once a month and Sid wanted it a *minimum* of once a week. No great compatibility!

Possible solution: The low-sexed partner finds some sexually uninvolved, noncoital way of satisfying the high-sexed partner. Thus s/he can do so with his/her mouth, tongue, vibrator, or in some other manner, while remaining unsexy but loving and interested in the other's satisfaction. One client I saw, who enjoyed intercourse about once a month, massaged her husband's penis with her large breasts twice a week and gave him "stupendous" orgasms—which she immensely enjoyed his having.

2. One partner, for various physical reasons—such as physical impotence, pain, or severe back pain—may not be able to have some forms of "normal" penile-vaginal intercourse.

Possible solution: Again, the penile-vaginally handicapped partner may use his/her other body appendages or orifices to satisfy the other partner. One husband who had painful intercourse because of sores on his penis, and whose wife was vaginally sensitive and greatly enjoyed intromission, brought her to terrific orgasms with his fingers vigorously massaging her vagina. A wife who had dyspareunia (pain during vaginal intercourse), let her husband have anal intercourse with her, and, after a while, she began to enjoy it.

3. Some partners, for various neurotic reasons, are phobic about certain kinds of sex. One of my (Dr. Ellis') woman friends could have five or ten orgasms a night through clitoral manipulation but never overcame the trauma of her being raped by her uncle when she was fifteen, and always suffered great pain during intercourse. When I dated her I was easily able to give her powerful orgasms by manipulating her clitoral region while passionately kissing her breasts. I went with her for a full year and we never had intercourse at all but she insisted I was by far the best of the five lovers she had up to that time. Since she was fully creative and talented with her fingers, I found that she was one of the very best lovers that I had had, too!

4. Some partners take twenty or thirty minutes to come to orgasm in intercourse, while their mate may not be able to last that long or may experience pain when he or she has prolonged coitus.

Possible solution: One woman who took almost an hour to come during intercourse while her mate took only a minute or two arranged to have him copulate with her and come after a short while, then he used a vibrator to give her orgasms in ten or more minutes.

5. One partner may require fetishistic sex acts—like being tied up and beaten—which the other may not enjoy.

Possible solutions: The partner who doesn't enjoy the fetishistic acts can tolerate participating in them once in a while, providing that they have "regular" sex most of the time. Or, in return for engaging in the fetishistic act, s/he can receive some special kind of sexual or nonsexual enjoyment from the other partner. One man who didn't like vigorously pinching his wife's behind—which brought her to terrific orgasms—arranged with her to give in to his own fetish: having her masturbate him while viewing a sexy movie and risking letting the other movie-goers see what they were doing.

6. One mate may be quite monogamous while the other achieves great enjoyment from having multiple sex partners and even simultaneous ones.

Possible solution: The nonmonogamous mate may work on his/her frustration intolerance and bear up with the "horrors" of being sexually restricted to the other partner while enjoying the other aspects of their relationship. Or, as in the case of one of my clients, a man who was only interested in having sex with his wife while she wanted to have sex with her ex-husband, too, he worked out an agreement with her. Rather than lose her, he agreed to let her spend one night a month with her ex-husband as long as she agreed afterward to do anything he wanted sexually, and sometimes what he wanted nonsexually, during the rest of the month. Both of them accepted the disadvantages of this arrangement for two years, until she decided to give up her ex-husband as an additional lover.

For various reasons, mates can warmly care for each other and have little sex compatibility. Conversely, I (A.E.) have also seen a good many couples who are only compatible sexually but in practically no other way. Even after they get divorced, they sometimes get together regularly just because they enjoy sex together!

Not every sexually incompatible couple is able to work out suitable arrangements whereby both of them are satisfied in bed; and many stay together, and have quite good marriages, in spite of having little or no sex with each other for a good number of years. Defining sex only as intercourse is a serious mistake for many couples. Indeed, where one partner—either the man or the woman—insists that coitus is the only form of sex that he or she will tolerate, serious breakdown in the couple's sex participation often occurs.

Dr. Harper and I, therefore, quickly and frankly show many of our clients that sex equals sex rather than equals mere intercourse; and that there are many kinds of coital and non-coital relations they can participate in with each other when one or both of them dislike regular intercourse.

Duties, of course, can sometimes be enjoyable—such as one's duty to be helpful to one's children—and enjoyments can also be made into duties. Sex duties and sex enjoyments, therefore, are not always incompatible. Freedom and democracy in bed, however, are as good as they are out of bed. So if you and your partner will give yourself the leeway to experiment sexually, to do largely what you *want* to do and not just what you think it is your *duty* to do, and if you both will avoid turning your sex enjoyments into invariable duties, you will be following the REBT concepts of removing your needless blocks and neuroses *and* living your relationship as fully and enjoyably as you both are capable of doing.

EXERCISES FOR CHAPTER 6

As we have indicated in this chapter, sex problems almost always stem from general emotional problems rather than—as Freud wrongly thought—emotional disturbances being caused by sex difficulties. Even when sexual neuroses *seem* to start things going, they almost always have at bottom the two main issues that we have been steadily seeing throughout this book: (1) self-downing; and (2) frustration intolerance and anger.

Take, for example, Freud's famous Oedipus or Electra complex. When I (Dr. Ellis) practiced psychoanalysis, I looked for this complex and rarely found it. In a few instances, I discovered that my clients' fathers were quite jealous of their sons' attachments to their mothers, showed rage against them, and helped these sons to be afraid of having sex with women. But the vast majority of my clients who had jealous fathers were not afraid of being castrated, were quite potent with women, and often had reasonably good relationships with their partners.

Those few males I saw as clients who were afraid of being punished by other males for having sex with women were almost always putting themselves down for not being able to compete against "better" men and were telling themselves that vying for female partners was harder than it *should* be—therefore copping out of trying to win the favors of women.

I have seen relatively few males over the past fifty years who were guilty about lusting after their mothers (or sisters) and who therefore couldn't function well with female sex partners. They almost always hated themselves for doing the "wrong" thing and, as self-downers, felt undeserving and worthless. Whether or not their fathers were jealous of them was usually irrelevant.

Of all the thousands of people with sex problems that we both have seen over the years, practically all of them felt inadequate sexually because they strongly believed that they *should* be more competent than they actually were. In addition, many of them knew that they would have to make certain adjustments or changes to have satisfactory sex with a given partner—that is, do what their partner wanted sexually or nonsexually—but they found it "too hard" to do so, felt that it *shouldn't* be that hard, and therefore refused to arrange to get the satisfaction that they wanted.

So there we go again! If you or your mate are having a rough time sexually, by all means get help and find out what is blocking you. A little useful information may solve your problems. But look, also, for the possible self-downing and frustration intolerance that may well be creating your problem. If you find either or both of these, here are some exercises you can use to reduce these disturbances.

Sample Exercise 6A: Discovering My IBs That May Be Involved With My Sex Problems

My Sex Problem With My Partner Is . . .	My IBs That Lead to or Stem From This Problem May Possibly Be . . .
Low sex desire for my partner.	I *shouldn't* have to do anything to arouse myself with my partner. My partner must always want sex exactly when I want it and must go out of his/her way to satisfy me. I should always be greatly aroused by my partner and there's something very wrong with me if I am not. Maybe I don't really love my partner.
Very high sex desire for my partner when my partner has less desire.	There must be something wrong with me. If I loved my partner more, I wouldn't keep plaguing him/her for more sex. My partner should be much more desirous of me than s/he is!
I take too long to have an orgasm.	I shouldn't take so long. I must be seriously deficient! My partner will hate me for taking so long!
Having orgasms rarely or not at all.	If I don't have an orgasm that will be terrible! I'm obviously no good at sex. Arranging to have an orgasm takes too much work!
Having trouble succeeding in or enjoying intercourse.	I must have great intercourse to be good in bed! Intercourse is the *only* right way to enjoy sex with my partner. If I can't satisfy my partner in intercourse I'm not a real man or a real woman.

Sample Exercise 6A (cont.)

My Sex Problem With My Partner Is . . .	My IBs That Lead to or Stem From This Problem May Possibly Be . . .
Strongly desiring kinky sex.	I shouldn't have these kinky desires! I'm abnormal! If I engage in kinky sex I'm an evil person!
My partner doesn't have an orgasm when we have intercourse.	There's something wrong with me! I should be able to make him or her come during intercourse. I'm a failure!
I can't last in sex and come to orgasm too rapidly.	Oh, my God, this is awful! I'm just no good at sex and will never be! Normal people last longer—so I should, too!

Exercise 6A

My Sex Problem With My Partner Is . . .	My IBs That Lead to or Stem From This Problem May Possibly Be . . .

Sample Exercise 6B: Rational Coping Statements I Can Use If I Have Sex Problems With My Partner

Rational Coping Self-Statements I Can Use If I Have Sex Problems With My Partner

Even though my partner and I love each other, we differ in important ways and may not always enjoy sex at the same time together.

If my partner is more highly or more lowly sexed than I am, we can make adjustments and still usually satisfy each other.

I would *prefer* to have strong orgasms and to achieve them fairly quickly, but I don't *have to* do so.

I would prefer to be able to give my partner strong orgasms fairly quickly, but if this is not possible, we can still enjoy sex and satisfy each other.

If my partner or I have sex problems, this is not shameful. We can openly talk about them and cooperatively do our best to solve them.

If my sex life with my partner is not easily and spontaneously great, we can work at finding ways to improve it.

Kinky sex is not bad or evil as long as we mutually enjoy it and do not physically harm ourselves.

If either my partner or I comes to orgasm very rapidly, we can work at slowing down and can find various ways, and not necessarily intercourse, in which to enjoy ourselves.

Even if my partner and I never have a great sex life, we can still love each other and enjoy a fine relationship.

Exercise 6B

Rational Coping Self-Statements I Can Use If I Have Sex Problems With My Partner

_____

_____

_____

_____

_____

_____

_____

_____

_____

_____

_____

_____

_____

_____

_____

_____

_____

_____

Sample Exercise 6C: Things I Can Do to Decrease My Frustration Intolerance If My Partner and I Have Sex Problems

Things I Can Do to Decrease My Frustration Intolerance About My Sex Relations With My Partner

Be patient with my partner and explore her or his sex problems or dissatisfactions.

Show my partner what my sex preferences are but not demand that he or she fulfill them.

Discuss my and my partner's sex differences and work out some compromises when our differences remain.

If necessary for a better relationship with my partner, live with my sex frustration and work at improving our nonsexual lives.

Get some sex training so that I can satisfy my partner more in the ways he or she would like to be satisfied.

Try some new sex techniques with my partner when the usual ones are satisfying to me but not to her or him.

When I am sexually deprived with my partner, strongly convince myself that this is only inconvenient, not *awful*, and that we can still have an enjoyable relationship.

Exercise 6C

Things I Can Do to Decrease My Frustration Intolerance About
My Sex Relations With My Partner

_____

_____

_____

_____

_____

_____

_____

_____

_____

_____

_____

_____

_____

_____

_____

_____

_____

_____

_____

7

Saving Time and Money and Enjoying Life More

When we first began our research, teaching, writing, and counseling about human relations, people were greatly concerned and often disturbed about sex. But even now that people's sex problems are talked and written about more openly, difficulties among couples have hardly disappeared. However, today's social environment gives a couple (married, unmarried, homosexual, bisexual, heterosexual, ethnically the same or different) a better chance than in the past to work out ways of relating to each other.

This is not exactly true in economic affairs. The road is often limited and the hard-won freedom open to a couple in working out a satisfactory sex life is often not available in matters of money and leisure. Although social myth and personal fantasy are still rife ("You can make anything you want of yourself"), most *individuals* have restricted choice as to how to earn a living, how much money they will save from that earning process, and how much time and resources will be left for leisure-time activities.

When it comes to *couples*, things are often worse. First, even the individuals who once had a career choice have often already exercised that choice and are now highly restricted. Second, those who have not already made a career choice often have meager financial resources. Third, their communities often offer little help in working out financial problems.

How does REBT enter this rough scene to help couples? Mainly by showing them how to accept the "grim" realities of work and income, while not being too pessimistic and not cavalierly running away from them. Thus, if couples still believe in the great myths of rugged individualism and a chicken in every pot, they can be shown that today's world often mandates both partners working, sharing the responsibilities of child rearing, coping with the unleisurely tasks of shopping, cleaning, and paying bills. Also, because both partners may work and have children to care for, they may have increased expenses (such as two cars or commutes to work) and less time for being intimate and leisurely, which means they may have more practical problems to solve in their partnerships.

Let us look again at an actual couple with some of these problems. Here is how I (Dr. Harper) used REBT to work with them.

Ron: We have really been approaching this relationship quite intelligently, Bill and I both think. It's the first time I've lived with anyone, but Bill has been married before.

Bill: For a couple of years. But fortunately no kids and even more fortunately, no real fuss from my wife when I decided to stop forcing myself to pretend I was really straight. I was too scared of AIDS to do any messing around in gay places. Then I met Ron and we took HIV tests and came out clean (he'd been afraid of messing around, too, with a few exceptions, where he was just plain lucky).

Ron: So, as I was saying, we think we have worked things out pretty well. We had separately done some REBT reading and listening to tapes. So we did some more and then decided we would try living together. We have some trouble with families, friends, neighbors, and, in Bill's case, an employer. You know, "Hey, you guys can't do this dreadful thing of living together and going around together. It's degradation and degeneration, and so forth." But everybody, with the exception of Bill's employer, got used to the idea.

Bill: I ended up getting fired, but I got a better job almost immediately. Better, that is, in money, but worse in the time and energy it takes to make the better income. I could probably get even more money by suing my original employer (a conservative lawyer tells me I have a splendid case). But money isn't really our problem. And sex isn't our problem. I always heard that if it isn't money, it's sex; and if it isn't sex, it's money. But with us it's neither. Time is our problem. Time to enjoy ourselves. Time to enjoy our relationship. Time to live.

Ron: Don't wax too wildly poetic, Bill, or Doc will think all our problems come from being gay. In fact, we get that almost all the time from people who know us. They seem to say, "Hey, what have a couple of queers like you got to complain about?" This implies that only a red-blooded all-American heterosexual couple have the stern moral fiber needed to have a happy relationship. Even Bill has occasionally looked for some psychoanalytic crap about our deep-seated guilty feelings about being gay preventing our getting full satisfaction from our life together.

R.A.H.: I see Bill ready to dispute that. But please let me intervene here. Your time problem is often basic to contemporary American life. It is shared to some degree by many of us. It may get more exaggerated by special factors (such as one's sexual orientation), but it is still often the same problem. The time problem is not quite as free of money problems as I think Bill was perhaps suggesting. If you have plenty of money, you can usually buy a lot of time; and if you have little money, a lot of time often won't lead to enjoyment. And—regarding your so-called deep-seated feelings of guilt—it is more likely that because you are not enjoying yourselves, you look for and find guilt feelings about being gay (a convenient hook on which you hang your nonenjoyment). You may indeed have some other problems associated with your homosexuality, but let's view this problem of time-to-enjoy-yourselves in its own right.

Enjoying yourself involves, one, learning to function efficiently, and two, learning what is fun for you and helpful to your social group. To do so, you had better also learn to engage in *tasks* with efficiency and zest. Try not to spend money and time without providing much enjoyment in the process. REBT's answer is to have us examine what we are doing in terms of how *efficiently* and *enjoyably* we are doing it.

Ron: On the efficiency thing, we've done some work. For example, we make out a supermarket list in advance, based on the next week's planned dinners and lunches, and we fairly and efficiently divide up household chores. We have a schedule of these chores posted in the kitchen. But proceeding efficiently doesn't make for fun—we find it all a pain in the ass.

R.A.H.: You're already ahead of many couples, however, in trying to organize your tasks. Many people balk at even the thought of carefully planning the use of either their time or their money. For most of us, whether we like spending a month scaling the Himalayas or a day at the beach, we work it out better by planning it in terms of both time and money issues.

Bill: Yeah, but there you hit it, man: *work.* We work our asses off in our respective jobs. We work out ways of keeping the damned home fires burning. We work out a schedule in time and money to include dry cleaning, laundry, haircuts, and new clothes. We work at getting along with other people on our jobs and in the community. We work at our relationship and at REBT. There's plenty of work, Doc, but where is the good old fun? Right, rational Ronnie?

Ron: Right, benign basket-case Billy.

R.A.H.: Even Bill's recitation of your work woes, Ron, and your reply all indicate you have made even more progress than I first thought. You have not only made considerable headway in organizing your life together, but you show signs of beginning to accept this as a way of life and of beginning to be kind of lighthearted about it.

Ron: I think we have a way to go on the lighthearted bit, but even lightheartedness falls short of having a car load of fun, doesn't it?

R.A.H.: Yes, I'm afraid more work is indicated (both Bill and Ron groan)—work focused on how to get more fun out of work. You two are already well on your way. You have taken step one: facing the fact that modern couples had better organize themselves or they won't be able to cope and to begin to *act* on enjoying themselves. As I indicated before, many people have difficulty even facing step two: realizing that hard work is a permanent ongoing process—a way of life. As a human, you have to *get* organized, and then *stay* organized, which calls for ongoing problem-solving.

Many of us rebel at step two. We often think and feel that after step one, things must come easy—living peachy keen without any special effort on our part. We not only have this tendency built into us as humans, but we also reinforce it in each other as couples. We say to each other, "So we mowed the lawn and cleaned the bathroom. Why can't we just relax and take it easy the rest of our lives? I thought good people were supposed to live happily ever after."

You two, however, seem also to have pretty well accepted step two. As I think you might put it, "Tough shit, man! That's where life is at." It's okay to be pissed off that life is as life is, but it is foolish to let your annoyance with hassles interfere with your coping. So much for efficiency. Now we come to tough step three: enjoyment. Let's see how we can work better on that.

Ron: Sorry to interrupt, but it's all starting to sound academic and phony to me. In the real situation these three steps are all mixed in together, and we can't really tip-toe through step one and step two in order to be ready for step three, "enjoyment."

R.A.H.: You are right. No tip-toeing! In our REBT procedures we first try to demonstrate to people some of the self-defeating ways they are now behaving. At the same time, we attempt to show them how to discover *and* actually experience greater happiness and self-actualization. We also encourage them to sustain and extend their efforts when something short of a fairy godmother change is achieved. Complications can and often do develop. Some people, for example, make fine progress in learning to enjoy life and then lapse into feeling miserable about doing so—because they were presumably "put here to do greater and more noble things than to enjoy life," such as uphold family honor, serve God and/or country, or be a "wonderful" parent. Fine, if that's what they really want. But not if it's what they think they *should* and *must* want.

Bill: Back to the REBT anti-shoulds and anti-musts. Right?

R.A.H.: Yes, back to non-musturbating! So let me again stress the difficulties of getting yourself to see where you are, where you realistically want to go, and how you can rationally try to get there. By your dealing, as you might guess I would say, with your firmly entrenched hindrances to permanently incorporating the desirable changes you want. Then to go on to step three.

Ron: To even enjoy the *work* of self-fulfillment?

R.A.H.: Exactly. Working for money, for mental health, or for anything else need *not* be as unenjoyable as you make it. You can find distinct satisfaction in your careers—by yourself and with your coworkers. Yes, you *can* find ways—by using your imagination and by experimenting—to make your work more enjoyable.

Bill: And our life as a couple, too? *Really* more enjoyable?

R.A.H.: Yes—almost always, definitely yes.

Ron: In a word—how?

R.A.H.: In quite a few words, by maximizing and using your leisure. But this, not so strangely enough, means first agreeing on and carrying out your responsibilities to yourself, to each other, and even to your social group—the group in which you *choose* to live. Whether you like it or not, your couple life (like that of most people) is filled with obligations. Whether you call them "duties" or not, these obligations add to your work in leaving you little time when you are utterly "free." Damned little leisure! But, of course, this leisure time gives you more choice about when and how you will enjoy yourself.

Ron: I think I see your point. Are you saying that if we work on an *efficient* scheduling of our obligations and *determine* we are going to have fun in fulfilling this schedule that our life as a couple will become a ball?

R.A.H.: Not entirely, of course. But you and Bill do have some degree of choice about what social obligations you will fulfill, and how efficiently you will go about carrying them out. If you choose sensibly, you can do more *un*obligated tasks together and separately. But, again, you have to *strive* to do this.

Bill: Too bad, as you often say in REBT. But I don't think that will turn us off. Although we like to bitch a lot about it, we believe in working for more pleasure.

Ron: I think Bill speaks for me, too. Shall we take the homework assignment between now and our next session of analyzing our time together and devising some concrete plans for making it more efficient and enjoyable?

R.A.H.: Fine! But make enjoyment your number-one priority. The most efficient way of doing something is not always the most enjoyable way. For example, for one of you to clean the kitchen while the other does the week's shopping might be more efficient than to shop together, but you might have more fun with the latter approach.

Bill: I see what you mean.

Ron: Yes, let's try.

In this chapter, we have taken a very brief and perhaps oversimplified look at the money/leisure situation in which many contemporary couples find themselves. We intentionally didn't try to deal with a multitude of serious social problems where, for example, money is insufficient and community resources are inadequate for even minimum health and decency standards and where couples lack almost all resources to enjoy themselves. Nor did we discuss couple relationships that are seriously hampered by alcohol, drugs, illness, or other factors. What we noted, however, was that even in "good" situations, couples can find themselves in a real time and money squeeze, and we concentrated on the time factor to show how REBT can help couples maximize leisure and thereby work for greater enjoyment.

EXERCISES FOR CHAPTER 7

Saving time and money involves developing your high frustration tolerance (HFT) and your unconditional self-acceptance (USA). So do most aspects of self-discipline! You—like other people—largely overspend because you think you *need* things you can't really afford and because you *must* show others that you are as affluent as they may be. And you may unrealistically save too much money because you think that you *can't* spend normally and that you *have* to save enormously to prove that your monetary worth equals your worth as a person.

REBT does stress financial sanity and Patricia Hunter and I (Dr. Ellis) wrote a whole book dedicated to REBT and money: *Why Am I Always Broke? How to Be Sane About Money.* The following exercises bring out some of the main points in that book—namely, how to save time and money to enjoy life more.

Sample Exercise 7A: Common Problems That My Partner and I May Have in Spending Time and Money and Enjoying Life More

Common Problems That My Partner and I May Have	IBs I May Create About This Problem	RBs That I Can Use to Alleviate This Problem
Inefficiently frittering away our time.	It's too hard to efficiently keep track of our time. I *shouldn't have to* do so! We can enjoy ourselves more if we only think of the pleasures of the moment. I *can't stand* taking the trouble to be more efficient.	Yes, it may be hard to efficiently keep track of our time, but it's hard*er* not to do so! We only have *one* life to live and enjoy—so we'd better plot, scheme, and push ourselves to enjoy it! The one thing we can never regain is lost time.
Griping when money is short—and still overspending.	It's *awful* to be short of money! My partner and I *must not* be deprived of things we really want! Other people have more money than we have and it's unfair that that they do. It shouldn't be so unfair!	It's highly inconvenient to be short of money, but it's hardly totally inconvenient or *awful*. My partner and I *must* be deprived of things we really want when we're short of money. Even if other people "unfairly" have more funds than we do, that unfairness has to exist when it does. Too bad!
Dealing with household problems as a team.	I hate boring housework and I *shouldn't* have to do it! My partner finds household tasks easier to do and s/he should therefore do more	No matter how much I hate housework I darned well better do it! Even though my partner finds it easier to do than I, I can do my share and enjoy

Sample Exercise 7A (cont.)

Common Problems That My Partner and I May Have	IBs I May Create About This Problem	RBs That I Can Use to Alleviate This Problem
	than I. I'll wait to see if s/he gets going on them. Then maybe I'll pitch in, too. After all I do to please my partner sexually, s/he really should do most of the housework.	doing some of it as a team. I'll get going on it right away and serve as a model for my partner to follow. Just because I please my partner sexually and in other ways, there is no reason for me not to do my share of housework. This will thereby help us to avoid squabbles and aid our relationship.
Handling our children, especially when they are sick and difficult.	I'm no good at handling our children and therefore my partner should usually do so. I have too many other things to do, so s/he should mainly handle them. My partner *should* care for me very much and take most of the burden of handling the children off my hands.	If I'm not good as my partner at handling the children, I can learn to be better. Yes, I have many things to do, but so does my partner—let me be fair! Why should my partner care for me so much and take most of the burden of caring for the children off my hands? How about my showing him/her how much I care by doing my share of taking care of the burden of the children? Why can't I arrange

Sample Exercise 7.A (cont.)

Common Problems That My Partner and I May Have	IBs I May Create About This Problem	RBs That I Can Use to Alleviate This Problem
		for us to *enjoy* taking care of them together?
Budgeting and keeping our spending within the budget.	If there's anything I hate, it's budgeting, so I shouldn't have to do it! My partner foolishly exceeds our budget, so I might as well be lax, too. We made a mistake in arranging to pay so much rent, and now we have to skimp on everything. How awful! My partner should have stopped us from paying so much rent!	No matter how much I hate budgeting, my partner and I will get in much more financial trouble if we don't! Even though my partner foolishly exceeds our budget, I'd better help him/her stick to it and not be equally foolish! Yes, we made a mistake in arranging to pay so much rent, but it won't kill us to skimp on other things. Perhaps my partner should have stopped us from paying so much rent, but both of us *should* have kept us from making that mistake—fallible creatures that we are!
Severely criticizing my partner for his/her inefficiently wasting time, money, or perpetrating other kinds of disorganization.	My partner *should* be much more efficient! Because I am, s/he should darned well be. His/her inefficiency and wastefulness is ruining our lives! What a worth-	My partner has problems being more efficient and I'd better uncritically try to help him/her with them—or even make up for some of his/her wastefulness. It's

Sample Exercise 7A (cont.)

Common Problems That My Partner and I May Have	IBs I May Create About This Problem	RBs That I Can Use to Alleviate This Problem
	less person s/he is!	good that I'm more efficient, but that never means s/he *must* be too. Her/his inefficiency is handicapping us but it's far from ruining our whole lives. S/he is acting badly in this respect, but s/he has many other good traits and is not a *bad person.*
Making little real effort to have fun and enjoyment with my partner.	It's *too much* trouble to *make* fun and *work for* enjoyment. This should come spontaneously and naturally. My partner must love me for *myself* and not because I amuse him/her or go out of my way to create enjoyment for him/her.	I may find it trouble to make fun and work for enjoyment with my partner, but it's not *too much* trouble. I can appreciably help our relationship. It need *not* come about spontaneously but may be better if planned There's no reason why my partner must love me for *myself* if I make no efforts to amuse him/her or go out of my way to create enjoyment for him/her. If I allow us to have a dull life, s/he will find me a dull person!

Exercise 7A

Common Problems That My Partner and I May Have	IBs I May Create About This Problem	RBs That I Can Use to Alleviate This Problem
Inefficiently frittering away our time		
Griping when money is short—and still overspending		
Dealing with household problems as a team		
Handling our children, especially when they are sick or difficult		
Budgeting and keeping our spending within the budget		
Severely criticizing my partner for his/her inefficiently wasting time, money, and perpetrating other kinds of disorganization		
Making little real effort to have fun and enjoyment with my partner		

Exercise 7A (cont.)

Common Problems That My Partner and I May Have	IBs I May Create About This Problem	RBs That I Can Use to Alleviate This This Problem
Other common problems my partner and I may have (specify)		
_____	_____	_____
_____	_____	_____
_____	_____	_____
_____	_____	_____
_____	_____	_____
_____	_____	_____
_____	_____	_____
_____	_____	_____
_____	_____	_____
_____	_____	_____
_____	_____	_____

Exercise 7B: How Can My Partner and I Be Rational About Spending Money?

Question 1: What can my partner and I do if we spend foolishly and then beat ourselves mercilessly for being such awful fools?
Answer: _____
_____
_____
_____
_____
_____
_____
_____
_____
_____
_____
_____
_____
_____

Turn the page for REBT answers

REBT Answers to Question 1:

1. We can rate our behavior, our foolish spending, as bad, foolish, ridiculous, or self-defeating. But we do not have to rate our *selves*, our *beings*, our *totality* in terms of this behavior; in fact, we do not have to rate our *selves* at all, even though we engage in the behavior and are responsible for engaging in it.

2. We can always choose to accept ourselves as good or okay persons, just because we are alive. When we choose to see ourselves as bad, rotten, or inadequate persons, we really *choose* to do so, and we can always choose *not* to do this, and to say to ourselves, "I am human. I am alive. As long as I am alive and human, I can see myself as a good person. Period."

3. Yes, we are persons who are doing this foolish thing, spending too much money. But we do many other good things (such as being kind to others) and many neutral things (such a watching TV). So we are only persons *who* spend too much money, and never really *good persons* or *rotten persons!*

Question 2: Do my partner and I need people to look up to us for spending as much as they do or for being lavish spenders or great savers?

Answer: _____

_____

_____

_____

_____

_____

_____

_____

_____

_____

_____

_____

_____

_____

_____

_____

Turn the page for the REBT answers

REBT Answers to Question 2:

1. No, we don't *need* people to look up to us for *anything*—for spending as much as they do, for being lavish spenders, or for being great savers. We *want* people to like us and look up to us, but we never *need* them to do so. If they don't and even if we do the wrong thing in their and our own eyes, we can always decide that what we did is wrong and stupid but that we, the doers of this deed, are *not* wrong, rotten, or stupid *persons*.

2. Because it is preferable for people to like us, and because they give us goodies and favors when they do, we may well decide to do our spending according to their wishes. But we don't *have* to agree with them and go along with them and can be happy even if they do not like what we do.

3. If people hate *us*, instead of only disliking our *behavior*, when we overspend or underspend, they are overgeneralizing about us and have a problem themselves. Too bad, if they have such a problem, but we can live with their disapproval.

Question 3: Are my partner and I real failures for not earning more money or for failing to save more money?

Answer: _____

_____

_____

_____

_____

_____

_____

_____

_____

_____

_____

_____

_____

_____

_____

_____

Turn the page for the REBT answers

REBT Answers to Question 3:

1. No. If we don't have more money than we now have, we are failing to make and keep as much as we would like to make and keep, but we are merely failing in this respect, and are succeeding in many other aspects of our life. A "failure" would always fail—and that is not us.

2. Failing to earn and save more money than we now do is highly inconvenient, if we really want more money, but that is *all* it is. It doesn't make *us*, as *people*, bad—unless we foolishly *think* that it does.

3. Earning and having more money than we now have may be very important to us. But it is not *all*-important, not *necessary*, not *sacred*.

4. Even if my partner and I failed at everything we did in life—which is most improbable—we would not be "real failures" in the sense of being damnable and undeserving of any good things in life. We would merely be persons with real handicaps and would still deserve to live and be helped by others who fail less.

Question 4: When my partner and I spend too much money, are we doing so because we really feel very anxious, depressed, or self-hating, and, rather than face these feelings, are we trying to distract ourselves by spending, by getting immediate satisfactions by doing so, and by temporarily feeling much better than we really feel underneath?

Answer: _____

_____

_____

_____

_____

_____

_____

_____

_____

_____

_____

_____

_____

Turn the page for the REBT answers

REBT Answers to Question 4:

1. It is possible that we are spending to distract ourselves from our feelings of anxiety, depression, or self-hatred. Let us look at how we feel just before we do too much spending, and how we feel immediately afterward.

2. If we really are spending money to cover up our own negative feelings, we will thereby make ourselves *feel* better temporarily but not *get* better. In fact, by denying that we have these negative feelings, we will take away our chances of dealing with them and eliminating them.

3. When we deny our feelings of anxiety and depression, we are really telling ourselves: "It would be shameful to have such feelings! We would be no-goodniks for having them!" We therefore create symptoms *about* our symptoms—making ourselves depressed about our depression, or panicked about our anxiety. It is not *shameful*, but only *self-defeating*, to have neurotic symptoms. So we'd better acknowledge them fully—and then use REBT to reduce them instead of covering them up or temporarily distracting ourselves from them.

Exercise 7C: Do My Partner and I Spend too Much Money—
and How Can We Stop?

Question 1: Does my partner's and my overspending prove that
we are weak or stupid persons? If not, why not?
Answer: _____
_____
_____
_____
_____
_____
_____
_____
_____
_____
_____
_____
_____
_____
_____

Turn the page for the REBT answers

REBT Answers to Question 1:

---

1. No. It only proves, at worst, that we are behaving weakly and stupidly in this aspect of our lives.

2. In other respects, we may be acting quite strongly and intelligently.

3. Even if we always acted weakly and stupidly—which is most unlikely—we would be behaving foolishly but we still wouldn't be worthless, rotten persons, but people who had great handicaps. We would still deserve to live and enjoy ourselves simply because we are human and choose to live and enjoy life.

Question 2: Did our early upbringing make me or my partner an overspender? If not, why not?

Answer: _____

_____

_____

_____

_____

_____

_____

_____

_____

_____

_____

_____

_____

_____

_____

_____

_____

_____

Turn the page for the REBT answers

REBT Answers to Question 2:

No, our early upbringing probably did not make me or my partner an overspender because:

1. Even if our parents were overspenders and encouraged us to follow in their footsteps, we did not *have to* agree with and go along with them.

2. When we were children, we doubtless saw other people who were frugal and even penny-pinching. Why did we not follow *them?*

3. If our parents were thieves or murderers, would we have to imitate their kind of behavior? Of course not!

4. If our parents overspent, we could have noticed the hassles and disadvantages of their ways and could have chosen to avoid those hassles by behaving otherwise.

5. If we followed our parents' model and overspent because they did, we could have seen later how our overspending got us into trouble and therefore stopped it.

6. If we took our parents' preferences for overspending and made them into our own, we did not have to turn these preferences into absolutist musts, and we did not have to make ourselves compulsive overspenders.

7. No matter what goals and standards we adopted from our parents in our early lives, we have the ability to choose to adopt different ones today. So, as far as overspending is concerned, we'd better construct our *own* present standards and behaviors!

Question 3: What is frustration intolerance (FI)? How can I change it if I suffer from it?

Answer: _____

_____

_____

_____

_____

_____

_____

_____

_____

_____

_____

_____

_____

_____

_____

_____

_____

_____

_____

_____

_____

_____

Turn the page for the REBT answers

REBT Answers to Question 3:

Frustration intolerance means looking for immediate gratification even when it later brings me poor results (for example, smokers risk getting emphysema and lung cancer); refusing to do onerous tasks even when they would bring good results (for example, refusing to diet and exercise to lower my weight and thereby lower my blood pressure); defining a task or project as *too* hard to do and demanding that it *must* not be as hard as it is; choosing to believe that I can get good results by procrastinating on or avoiding a task when I most probably will get bad results (for example, telling myself that I need more time to get better data for a paper I am writing, when delaying writing it will most likely lead to my writing it frantically and badly at the last moment).

I can overcome frustration intolerance (FI) in several ways:

1. I can strongly convince myself that I don't *need* immediate gratification that would result in my later harm, even though I would definitely *like* to have it.

2. I can strongly convince myself that doing onerous tasks is hard but not *too* hard, that it is best to get them out of the way quickly, and that doing them (for example, exercising) won't kill me but not doing them well may!

3. I can show myself that no matter how hard certain tasks (like finishing a paper) are, it will be much *harder* if I don't do them.

4. I can write down a list of the disadvantages of procrastinating on or avoiding certain important tasks and read and think about these disadvantages several times every day to sink into my head the rational idea that I am *not* going to gain by delay and avoidance.

5. I can reinforce myself with something I find quite rewarding—such as music, reading, or socializing—every time I make myself do burdensome things that later lead to good results and every time I avoid immediate gratification that later leads to bad results.

6. I can penalize myself in some meaningful way—by doing something I really think is unpleasant—each time I indulge in harmful immediate gratification and each time I avoid doing burdensome things that will later lead to good results.

Question 4: Why is it better for my partner and I to have some long-range monetary goals and plans than to only stay with short-term objectives?

Answer: _____

_____

_____

_____

_____

_____

_____

_____

_____

_____

_____

_____

_____

_____

_____

Turn the page for the REBT answers

REBT Answers to Question 4:

1. My short-range plans will soon be fulfilled or found wanting, and I will then have to take time and effort to revise them.

2. My short-term monetary goals—for example, renting a larger apartment—may sabotage my long-range and more important goals— such as saving money to buy a home.

3. Long-range goals give me a vital interest that may enjoyably last for a long period of time and help me nicely structure a large part of my life.

4. My long-range monetary goals are more likely to be achieved because I have a longer period of time to plan for and possibly revise them.

5. My long-range monetary goals will very likely help me provide substantially for my later years, while more short-range goals may by no means do this.

Question 5: If I am phobic about financial planning and stubbornly refuse to do it, what irrational beliefs am I probably telling myself?

Answer: _____

_____

_____

_____

_____

_____

_____

_____

_____

_____

_____

_____

_____

_____

_____

Turn the page for the REBT answers

REBT Answers to Question 5:

1. "I am unable to plan. An incompetent person like me would surely screw up my planning!"

2. "Suppose my financial plans don't work out. What a hopeless fool I would be!"

3. "My relatives and friends insist that I do financial planning when I really don't want to do it. To hell with them!"

4. "It takes too much time and effort to plan. It's not worth it!"

5. "No matter how well I plan, the country's whole financial system will doubtless be screwed up and I could easily have my plans go wrong. So what's the use of planning?"

Question 6: What can I tell myself about TV, magazine, radio, and other advertising that may influence me to not overspend?
Answer: _____
_____
_____
_____
_____
_____
_____
_____
_____
_____
_____
_____
_____
_____
_____
_____
_____
_____

Turn the page for the REBT answers

REBT Answers to Question 6:

1. "The advertiser is distinctly interested in making money, not in my welfare!"

2. "No matter how good this merchandise is made to look, I don't *need* it!"

3. "I can think for myself and don't have to be so damned suggestible!"

4. "Even if the advertised product is desirable, it is hardly worth the money I will have to pay for it. Spending money on this product will deprive me of savings or of some other item that would be more useful."

Question 7: What can I say to my partner or my friends if they urge me to spend more money than is good for me to spend?
Answer: _____
_____
_____
_____
_____
_____
_____
_____
_____
_____
_____
_____
_____
_____
_____
_____
_____

Turn the page for the REBT answers

REBT Answers to Question 7:

1. "I'd be glad to go along with you, but frankly I can't afford it."

2. "I can see why you want to spend money on this thing, but it is just not the kind of thing that I want."

3. "You may think I'm cheap for not spending this amount of money, but I'd rather be thought cheap than do what I really don't want to do."

4. "I could probably afford to go along with the expenditure that you are suggesting, but it's just not what I'd like to spend my money on."

8

Getting Along Together and With Others

Up to now we have concentrated on how intimate partners can relate more effectively and enjoyably to each other. Most couples, however, do not live in isolation, and how they relate to friends, relatives, neighbors, and others can importantly affect them as individuals and as a couple. Using similar REBT principles to those we have described for improved couplehood, you can also relate better to other people.

Before we explore other-relating, let's ask ourselves whether getting along with other people is a reasonable goal. Wouldn't it be better if we all decided we wanted to learn to be wonderful people and become leaders in the community and be admired and respected for the leadership we have provided? Not exactly. While these and various other goals may be desirable for some of us, it is usually better for us first to learn how to get along with people. After you are getting along, if you have the interest, skills, time, and energy to become a community leader, splendid.

Even the goal of associating with others often cannot be approached as directly as you might want. The main reason for this is simple: as we have seen in our discussion of couples, Person A— you, let's say—cannot change anyone's behavior other than your own. No, not even the behavior of your partner, Person B. So where will you get if you tell Persons C and D, your arrogant and grouchy neighbors, to behave differently in order to enable you to enjoy them more? Nowhere! In addition, if you focus on how to alter your own behavior in order (hopefully) to change Persons C through Z, you can find this a very time-and-energy consuming enterprise—with no guarantee of success!

What can you do to enhance your relations with others? First, determine how you can *enjoy* being with others *even* when they behave badly. You can, of course, try to change other people (lots of luck!). And you can try to change yourself when you are with them so that you help them act less and less obnoxiously than they usually do. But rather than count on changed behavior from them, try to enjoy yourself more *without* such changes.

Second, agree with your partner that you will both check on each other's efforts to enjoy yourselves more with others (as well as with one another). This cross-check helps you see how "right" you are in viewing others and may increase your enjoyment of them.

The work of relating better to others mainly consists of your striving to overcome your own major irrational ideas. As a human, you may have inherited tendencies to think unhealthily or you may have had them laid heavily upon you in your early years. Also, some of your irrationality may stem from your recent thoughts about unfortunate experiences that led you to create and cling dearly to destructive thoughts, feelings, and actions. However you "got that way," only you can make yourself function more realistically and enjoyably today.

Your main laboratory for experimenting, testing, and reworking your IBs can be your relationships with others. You are also particularly fortunate, as we said above, if you have the advantage and the fun of a living-as-a-couple laboratory.

MRB stands for "more rational beliefs." We are not trying to do your thinking for you (it wouldn't be of any use to you even if we tried), but we are giving you some less irrational and more realistic thought patterns to kick around in your own head and to discuss with your partner. Maybe some of the more rational beliefs we present (reshaped to your own personality and your own couplehood) will be helpful. Maybe you and your partner will throw them all out and come up with *MRB*s that have strictly your own seals on them.

CHANGING YOUR IRRATIONAL BELIEFS
ABOUT OTHERS

Following are some important IBs about others that you can explore and work at changing.

IB: "I must be totally approved as a person regardless of how I behave."

MRB: "I will strive to do what I consider enjoyable and desirable. That usually includes accepting some of the people who show that they like or accept me as a person. But since people in their reactions tend to jump from rating my particular behavior to rating me as a total person, they are overgeneralizing and will not accurately rate me globally. Even if I could somehow get people to react to the 'real me' (which is an inaccurate abstraction), what are my chances of having them react to this 'real me' as totally lovable? Very slim! I may learn something helpful from other people's views of me, but what I learn should be balanced by what I learn from other sources."

IB: "To be worthwhile as a person I must prove to others that I am outstanding in whatever I do. To fail to do so shows that I am a failure or an inadequate person who doesn't deserve people's approval."

MRB: "It is nice if I perform well and am therefore approved by others—nice but not necessary. And my performance has nothing to do with my worth as a person."

IB: "I should judge people by who they seem to be—as *good* or *bad* individuals. If I judge them to be wrong, bad, or evil, they deserve to be damned and punished."

MRB: "Because all people are human and hence fallible, I and others will surely misbehave part of the time. None of us *is* good or bad, though we all *do* "good" and "bad" things. I can give people unconditional other-acceptance (UOA) and only rate their *deeds* and not their *selves*. I will try to help them act better but refuse to damn *them* when they don't."

IB: "Since REBT says I am not to worry about what other people think and what they tell me I ought to do, I'll always do whatever I feel like doing whenever I feel like doing it. Today I feel like staying home from work and lying on the beach smoking pot all day. So whatever else other people may be expecting, I'll avoid working. Fun's fun, man."

MRB: "Let me face it. Indulging in immediate gratification that later leads to grim results (such as getting lung cancer from smoking) is hardly *fun*. I can enjoy life more if I don't cop out but promptly and unrebelliously do difficult and unpleasant tasks for which I have responsibility. I can vigilantly try to distinguish between short-term and long-term hedonism. I won't always avoid immediate fun, but when it seriously distracts me from my commitments, I'd better be responsible to myself and to others and postpone the 'fun' till later. REBT never says I am not to be concerned *at all* about what other people think of me and my behavior, but only that I'd better not be *over*-concerned and worry *too much* about what they think."

IB: "My partner must take me the way I am. I have been molded into the kind of person that I am. The past cannot be altered, and I must go on deeply reacting in the same way that I always have."

MRB: "My past is not all-important. If I rethink my old assumptions and rework my past habits (and check from time to time with my partner on how much I am changing), I can minimize the undesirable influences from my childhood and adolescence. I can learn valuable lessons from studying my past, but I do not need to consider myself enslaved by it. Today is tomorrow's past: let's see what I can do to make it better. I hope that my partner accepts *me* with my *failings*. But to help myself and to improve our relationship, I'd better work on some of those failings!"

IB: "Since the REBT goal is to enjoy myself as much as I can, I will make as few commitments as possible and only arrange for free time, where nothing is expected of me and no responsibilities are laid on me. That's real happiness!"

MRB: "I have had my happiest times when I have been fully committed to and involved in action of some kind. I shall search and find and develop activities that challenge me and provide me with long-term expanding interest and development. I shall also try to help my partner, individually and as a couple, be committed and responsible, and thereby improve our relationship and our lives."

GETTING ALONG WITH OTHER PEOPLE AS A COUPLE

As we have noted in this chapter, getting along with other people—and especially with your partner—leads to decreased disturbance and increased happiness within and outside of your couplehood. This includes, in many cases, you and your partner getting along with other people—especially with your family members, close friends, and business associates—*together.*

You may avoid this problem, of course, by rarely having close contact with your partner's family, friends, or job associates. But is this practical—or desirable? Usually, you and s/he will want some of these contacts. Either of you may want the other to be reasonably friendly with, say, your relatives, long-standing friends, and close associates. You both may "intellectually" agree that this would be desirable, but actually find each other's intimates too boring, stupid, hostile, clinging, or otherwise obnoxious. You may then—either of you—avoid, hate, fight with, or severely criticize them. If you do, you and your partner may well have a problem!

Liane, for example, was usually friendly and warm to her husband's relatives and friends but loathed Jake's mother, Doris, whom she (and several other people) considered to be supercritical, mean, and utterly dependent upon Jake. While he acknowledged his mother's "faults," he loved her deeply, pitied her, and took good care of her, especially after his father died. Liane, using a million excuses, rarely saw Doris and when she was practically forced to do so, seethed with resentment and was often rude to her. Jake tried to help Liane to at least tolerate Doris better, but failed to do so, and was torn between his allegiance to his wife and his mother. He practically forced Liane to see me (Dr. Ellis) for therapy.

As is common in cases like Liane's, I acknowledged her rational preferences about Doris—to avoid her as much as possible and encourage Jake to be less devoted to her. But we, Liane and I, soon uncovered several IBs she strongly held to make herself angry, depressed, and self-hating: (1) "Doris *must not* be as disturbed and rotten as she is!", (2) "I *can't stand* being with her or talking to her on the phone for even a few minutes!", (3) "Jake should completely see through her and stop idiotically taking care of her!", (4) "I am angry at Jake and am destroying my relationship with him—as I absolutely must not do!", (5) "our two children must see how loathsome their grandmother, Doris, is and not love her the way they do!"

I found that helping Liane give up these IBs was quite a task, and for several weeks I thought I would never reach her. She found Doris so nauseatingly "hypocritical"—deliberately warm, loving, and forgiving to Jake and her grandchildren, and mean and nasty to Liane and just about everyone else. So she concluded that Doris was *able* to control her feelings and behaviors and act consistently polite, but she deliberately *refused* to do so. Liane was incensed at this "hypocrisy."

I got at least a foot in the door in disputing Liane's IBs when I showed her that she, too, was "hypocritically" *able* to act well to many people but presumably *not able* to change or suppress her hostility to Doris. Moreover, she, Liane, "hypocritically" let herself love and hate her own husband, Jake.

My showing Liane her own "hypocritical" inconsistencies, and her own *ability* to control her hatred when she really tried to do so, finally got to her, and she began to give up her deep resentment by changing her irrational *demands* for Doris and Jake to act well to strong *preferences*. She convinced herself, "I really *wish* Doris were less mean and overly critical of me, *but* she doesn't *have* to be. Let her remain—as she will—as sick as she is in these respects."

As she changed some of her own incensing beliefs, I showed Liane how to plan and scheme, and then how to act, *together* with Jake, when Doris visited them. Liane, for example, would work on her own incipient hostility and deliberately *seem* to agree with Doris about her being overly nice to their children; and Jake would firmly refuse some of Doris's inconsiderate demands on him, while working on his own guilt about not giving in to her. Liane and Jake *acted* so well with Doris on many planned-in-advance occasions that Liane often *felt* more forgiving and less hostile to her mother-in-law and Jake *felt* less guilty and firmer in resisting his mother's inconsiderate demands.

This case shows the general REBT procedure to help you and your partner relate better to yourself, each other, and your and his/her close associates. First, look for, find, and actively dispute your IBs that are interfering with this relating. Second, replace these IBs with RBs and preferences. Third, discuss with your partner your own and his or her dysfunctional demands that are interfering with your relationships with her/him and your close associates. Fourth, plan to act harmoniously and enjoyably when s/he is together with you and your intimates and you are together with his/her intimates.

When you actually meet together with each other's close associates, here are some questions to consider and helpful rules to know:

1. How close are your and his/her relations with other people? Casual, moderately close, really intimate?

2. How do you want your partner to feel and behave about your intimates—whether that means really feel or pretend to feel?

3. How does your partner want you to feel and behave about your intimates—again, whether that means really feel or pretend to feel?

4. Can you and your partner be comfortable with seeing your and his/her intimates always together, sometimes together, occasionally together, never together? Just because you or s/he is close to family members or other people does *not* mean that you always *have to* see them as a couple.

5. In ticklish cases—where, for example, you and your partner would prefer to see an ex-lover or someone either of you detest

alone—fully agree upon the rules of how often, how long, where and when, and other conditions of meeting this person or these people.

6. When you meet each other's intimates together, plan how you and your partner will usually act with them. Where and when? What will you usually do together? What will you particularly avoid saying and doing? Discuss this with each other before the meeting.

7. Try to figure out how you and your partner's relatives and friends can actually help or enhance your relationship. What role can they play in aiding it and helping the two of you get closer?

8. Experiment with your mutually arrived-at goals in these respects. See if they work—and change them if they don't!

9. If feelings or relationships with you and your partner's intimates seem to be becoming an obstacle to your own relationship, honestly discuss it, however difficult. See what you can do to remove these "obstacles."

10. Agree on suitable ways to handle your and your partner's relations with intimates, try them out for awhile, and from time to time review them to see if they are still working satisfactorily. If not, back to the drawing board!

Are the IBs we have just looked at, as well as your self-defeating actions, the only ways you can mess up yourself, your relationship with your partner, and both of your relationships with others? By no means! Because of your human limitations, you, like all people, may well have a boundless capacity for thinking up ways of defeating, downing, and even destroying yourself and your relationships. So watch it!

Are your more rational, healthy beliefs guaranteed to put your irrational ones permanently to rest? We hope you have not only read but *practiced* enough REBT by now to know better than that. Face it: Vigilance and hard work will keep you functioning more healthily and more enjoyably—but not perfectly.

Nor will you, by reading and heeding this chapter, get along perfectly well with your partner and with other people. We hope you will and are pretty sure that you can, but we give you no guarantees—only a fairly high degree of probability.

EXERCISES FOR CHAPTER 8

This chapter emphasized minimizing your self-defeating IBs and changing them into self-helping MRBs. And while this seems clear and obvious, it isn't as easy to do as it often seems. Many of our clients for over four decades now have promptly grasped and agreed with the "truth" of seeing their IBs and substituting RBs for them. Easily and quickly grasped. Easily and quickly agreed. But not easily achieved!

Some, of course, haven't really tried to change their IBs. "Oh, yes, you're right. My belief that I absolutely *need* other people's approval is largely false—and will get me nowhere, with them and with myself." "Right! My partner can't really love me completely at all times. No one can! I'd better give up believing that nonsense— or else I'll continually be anxious and angry. What rot!"

Good agreement—but still little change. You beautifully tell yourself sensible dating, relating, and mating philosophies. Still no real conviction about them. Only some mighty sensible beliefs—at most!

Suppose, then, that you agree with the MRBs described in this chapter. How do you *really* convince yourself of them? How do you get yourself to largely *follow* them?

In 1962, a social psychologist, Robert Abelson, pointed out that people have both *cool* and *hot* cognitions. I (Dr. Ellis) quickly saw that he was on the right track, and added that people also have warm, as well as cool and hot beliefs. Let us explain.

Cool beliefs are your descriptions of people and things, without positive or negative evaluations of them. For example, "This is a table. I see that it is round" or "Peter or Patricia asked me for a date. He or she seems to favor me."

Warm beliefs are your evaluations of your observations and descriptions, such as "I don't like this round table. I wish it were square" and "I like Peter or Patricia's asking me for a date. Good!"

Hot beliefs give you very strong evaluations of your observations and descriptions. For example, "I really hate this round table. I'm going to do my best to get rid of it and get a square one instead" or "I am completely thrilled with Peter or Patricia's asking me for a date. This is the best thing that has happened to me all year!"

Hot insistent beliefs give you very strong and demanding evaluations of your observations and descriptions, like "This round table is really disgusting! It must not remain here! I *can't stand* it. I am going to get an axe and chop it up" or "Peter or Patricia's asking me for a date is so desirable that s/he must go through with it and do whatever I want on the date! I *must not* be deprived in any way by him/her. It would be *awful* if I were. I couldn't bear it!"

Following Abelson, REBT assumes that when you are encouraged by your IBs to create unhealthy feelings and behaviors, and that when you do so consistently and have trouble changing your beliefs to preferences, thus creating healthier feelings and behaviors, you tend to hold on to your IBs very hotly—to forcefully, vigorously, and powerfully (consciously and/or unconsciously) cling to them. Therefore, if you merely dispute them mildly and moderately you may keep them *along with* the RBs or effective new philosophies that you *say* that you now believe.

When you dispute your IBs and come up with rational coping self-statements with which to replace them, you can easily "see" that these RBs are "true" or "helpful," but you may only lightly and ineffectually believe them. Thus, you can "intellectually" see that smoking is harmful, but "emotionally" believe, "It really won't harm *me*" or "I can get away with it," or "No matter how hard I try, I *can't* stop smoking!" You then may well continue to smoke!

In exercises 8A and 8B, you will figure out some rational coping self-statements, perhaps writing them out on a 3 × 5 index card to show yourself the various *reasons* why they make sense and will help you. Say them to yourself five or ten times a day and repeat them forcefully and vigorously each time until you feel that you *really* understand them and convincingly believe them. Strongly say them to yourself while you solidly *think about* why they are accurate and helpful. You will than tend to achieve "emotional" as well as "intellectual" insight into your RBs.

Sample Exercise 8A: Using Forceful and Persistent Rational Coping Self-Statements

    Rational Coping Self-Statements About Getting Along With My Partner That I Can Forcefully and Convincingly Tell Myself Until I Solidly Believe and Act on Them

I would really like to find a suitable partner, but I definitely *don't have to* find one. I won't be *as* happy by myself but I can always find *a great deal of happiness* if I remain unmated. If I am unmated, I will *try like hell* to enjoy myself and lead a full life.

I *fully realize* that it is difficult for me to find a permanent suitable partner. Very difficult—but *not impossible!* There are literally thousands—or millions!—of good partners in the world for me. And I can—if I *keep looking and experimenting*—find one. I *can*, I *can!* So I will unfrantically *keep looking, looking, looking!*

Yes, my partner *may well* be unfair to me and often. S/he *may* criticize me unduly, lie to me about something, or spend too much of our money on foolish things and unjustly deprive me. *Too bad!* My partner will *often* be far from fair! That is human nature! *Tough!* But s/he has many good points, too. *Many!* I *can* enjoy him or her *in spite of* some unfairness. It won't kill me! I can *accept* him or her with her/his faults. Because *it's worth it—really worth it!*

I *can* stand important disagreements with my partner. I may never like their position, never agree, but I can *agree to disagree!* I never have to get her/him to agree with me—though that would be great! Disagreements are interesting. I can learn from them. So can s/he. We can enjoy our disagreements. And *really* enjoy being honest about them and letting each other have them—that can be *fantastic!*

Sample Exercise 8A (cont.)

Yes, I really *dislike* doing annoying or boring things with my partner. But *I'd better* sometimes do them, without carping and
screaming. Without nastily rebelling. Some of them *go with* a
good relationship. My partner may enjoy them and I can enjoy
his/her enjoyment! Sure I can get away with balking and goof-
ing. But is it *worth* it? Rarely! So I often *will* do what I don't like
to please my partner. To enhance our relationship. *I can! I will!*

Exercise 8A: Some Rational Coping Self-Statements About Getting Along With My Partner That I Can Forcefully Convince Myself of Until I Solidly Believe and Act on Them

_____

_____

_____

_____

_____

_____

_____

_____

_____

_____

_____

_____

_____

_____

_____

_____

_____

_____

_____

_____

_____

_____

_____

_____

_____

_____

_____

_____

Sample Exercise 8B: Using Forceful and Persistent Rational Coping Self-Statements About Getting Along With My Partner's Close Associates and Intimates That I Can Tell Myself Until I Solidly Believe and Act on Them

I don't have to *like* my partner's close associates and intimates. They have a perfect *right* to be as unlikeable as they *are*. I probably can't *stop* them from being obnoxious but I *can stand it*. I am *making myself* angry at them and damning *them* for their unfortunate *behavior*. I can darned well stop my damnation and then tolerate them much better.

My partner is free to like or dislike my close associates and intimates. S/he is wrong if s/he hates *them* and not merely their *behavior*, but s/he has a right to be wrong! I would distinctly *prefer* him/her to feel and act well when s/he meets them. But s/he doesn't *have to* do so!

I am foolishly harming myself and my relationship with my partner when I ignore or act badly toward his/her close associates and intimates. But I am *not* a fool for doing so—just a *person who* acts stupidly. Let me work on myself to feel and act less angrily, and do my best to *accept* his/her friends even if I never greatly like them. *I and we* will thereby benefit!

There is no *necessity* for my partner to act well with my close friends and associates, though that would be *preferable*. Even if s/he is prejudiced against them, I can accept and care for him/her because of his/her many other good traits. I can dislike several of the things s/he does, but if I dislike *him/her* for doing them I shall help ruin our relationship.

I *can* go to the trouble of finding out how my partner feels and acts about my close associates and intimates, and I will! It's *worth* discussing this with him/her and planning how we act when we are together with our intimates. If either or both of us has IBs that are encouraging us to feel and act badly in this respect, I *can* work with him/her to find and change them.

If I or my partner am over-involved with some of our close associates and intimates, which thereby interferes with our relation-

Sample Exercise 8B (cont.)

ship, I can honestly discuss this with him/her and agree how, where, and under what conditions I and s/he will continue to have contact with these other people.

When my partner and I agree on how we will handle our relationships with close associates and intimates, so as to not seriously interfere with our closeness with each other, we shall review our feelings and actions in this respect from time to time and work to change our relationship-sabotaging behaviors.

Exercise 8B: Forceful and Persistent Rational Coping Self-Statements
About Getting Along With My Partner's Close Associates and Intimates
That I Can Tell Myself Until I Solidly Believe and Act on Them

_____

_____

_____

_____

_____

_____

_____

_____

_____

_____

_____

_____

_____

_____

_____

_____

_____

_____

_____

_____

_____

As Aesop demonstrated thousands of years ago in "The Fox and the Grapes," we are great rationalizers and excusers. We often try to fool others, but—more importantly—we try to fool ourselves, especially with our own rational coping self-statements. Even when you say them forcefully and persistently—as illustrated in exercise 8A—you can easily parrot them and, honestly and truly, have important hidden objections to and quibbles with them.

Windy Dryden, one of the most prolific and capable writers about REBT, has come up with a forceful method of overcoming this kind of insincere parroting—by showing you how to go out of your way and argue with your own rational coping self-statements until you answer your hidden objections to them and vigorously reaffirm them in a more self-convincing manner.

Sample Exercise 8C: Arguing With and Reaffirming Rational Coping Self-Statements

Rational Coping Self-Statements That I May Lightly Believe	My Arguing With My Own Rational Coping Self-Statements	My Firm Answers to My Arguing With My Rational Coping Self-Statements That I Lightly Believe
Although I'd *like* to find a suitable partner, I don't *have to* find one and can be happy by myself.	Yes, I won't *die* from not finding a suitable partner but I'd be *much less* happy and therefore depressed.	(1) Do I *have to be* much less happy? I might even be happi*er!* I can avoid and miss out on the *hassles* and *restrictions* of being mated. (2) Even if I were *less* happy without a partner, I could still be reasonably happy. Even if I were *un*happy I would never have to make myself depressed *about* my unhappiness. I could merely be *sad* and *frustrated*.
Though it may be *quite difficult* for me to find a suitable partner, it is not *im*possible! If I keep looking and looking I can still find one.	Yes, but suppose I look and look and never *do* find one? That would really be *awful!*	(1) It is most unlikely that I'll *never* find one—especially if I don't demand that I find the *best* possible partner. (2) If—which is *very* unlikely—I never find one, I can, really *can* find distinct happiness, if I *think* I can and arrange to find it!

Sample Exercise 8C (cont.)

Rational Coping Self-Statements That I May Lightly Believe	My Arguing With My Own Rational Coping Self-Statements	My Firm Answers to My Arguing With My Rational Coping Self-Statements That I Lightly Believe
Too bad if my partner is unfair! I can *still* enjoy many aspects of him/her. It's *worth* staying and continuing our relationship.	Yes, but if s/he is *really* unfair, that would make anyone, including me, angry. I *never* could stand that!	(1) His/her degree of unfairness would be very *displeasing*. But I still don't have to *demand* fairness and make *myself* angry. (2) I can always choose to *un*angrily leave my partner. (3) If I act lovingly in spite of the unfairness, I may induce him/her to be fair. (4) At the worst, I *could* stand the unfairness and still benefit from being with my partner. Although I naturally *dislike* important disagreements with my partner, I can agree to disagree. Disagreements can even be interesting.
Although I naturally *dislike* important disagreements with my partner, I can agree to disagree. Disagreements can be very interesting.	Yes, but we often disagree *so often* that that's really pretty awful! And our disagreements are so repetitive that they are damned boring. I *can't stand* them.	(1) No matter how often we disagree, it's only *awful* if I take our disagreements too seriously—which I never *have to* do! (2) Even though our disagreements are repetitive, if I really *accept*

Sample Exercise 8C (cont.)

Rational Coping Self-Statements That I May Lightly Believe	My Arguing With My Own Rational Coping Self-Statement	My Firm Answers to My Arguing With My Rational Coping Self-Statements That I Lightly Believe
		them and *not* make an issue out of them we'll deal with them quickly and unboringly. If not, I *can* still stand them.
Although I dislike doing annoying or boring things with my partner, I still do them and can enhance our relationship.	Yes, but what kind of a relationship is this if s/he keeps making me do so many annoying and boring things. I might as well mate with a porcupine.	Just about *all* relationships include many annoying and boring things. Do I really want to be *alone?* Look how annoying and boring that would be!

Exercise 8C

Rational Coping Self-Statements That I May Lightly Believe	My Arguing With My Own Rational Coping Self-Statements	My Firm Answers To My Arguing With My Rational Coping Self-Statements That I Lightly Believe

Exercise 8D: Reverse Role-Playing About My Upsetness About My Partner's Relatives

To use this REBT emotive-evocative method, you pick one of your IBs that you strongly hold and resist changing. Get a friend to hold on to this IB very firmly and rigidly, while you—playing a sensible person—persist at trying to talk him or her out of it. One of your reverse role-playing dialogues might go like this.

Your Friend (holding your IBs): I just won't allow it. I won't allow my partner, May, to continue to see Jake. Not only is he a cretin but I'd be a weak slob to allow her to see him.

You: How does allowing May to see Jake make *you* a weak slob? Even if he is cretinish, how does her seeing him affect *you?*

Your Friend: Obviously he's still after her ass—and will try to get it. What kind of man am I if I allow this?

You: What the devil does this have to do with your manhood? Let's suppose he is trying to get May into bed with him. Can't she resist? Is *she* a weakling?

Your Friend: It's too risky! I'm taking a foolish chance. I'll never forgive myself if she succumbs. And everyone will see what a stupid weakling I am!

You: Let's suppose the worst: May does go to bed with Jake. So that's bad. You trusted her too far and you made a mistake. How does that make you a wholly stupid person? Even if people *think* you are, does that *make* you one?

Your Friend: But what a mistake! I should have known! People would be right about me!

You: Maybe about your foolish *acts*. But not about *you*. You *aren't* your actions.

Your Friend: You damned well are! Certainly in this case—let's face it!

You: Now *you're* overgeneralizing. *You* do millions of acts. Most of them, in fact, pretty good. So even if *this* one is foolish, how does that make *you* a total fool?

Your Friend: Lots of people will think I am!

Exercise 8D (cont.)

You: Let them! They're wrong! You won't like what they *think*. But if you're quite determined, you'll always accept *you*, no matter what you do.

Your Friend: That's really great. If I do that I'll be able to give up my nutty jealousy. No matter what my partner does, I'll still be able to accept *me*. Her actions don't *make* me anything, no more than yours do.

You: I think you're right about that. Yes—work on that.

Whatever emotional problem you have with your mate, about upsetting yourself about his or her relations with friends or relatives, or about anything else, you can have a friend play your upset role, stick rigidly to it, and let you talk yourself (played by them) out of your disturbance. Try it and see!

9

How to Be Happy in Spite of
Your Blasted In-Laws

As we have already noted, this book is not merely an updated version of our 1961 manual, *A Guide to a Successful Marriage*. This book focuses on partnerships and relationships that go beyond conventional mating and includes new REBT ideas and practices developed since the 1960s.

However, to show you how some of the principles of REBT have consistently been useful to many individuals and couples since we started to practice them, we have taken one of the chapters from our earlier book and have included it here with a few minor revisions.

It may seem a shame to spoil a fine, forward-looking book on relationships such as this one with the unsavory topic of in-law relations, but a relationship will hardly be fine or forward-looking if this topic is neglected. Of the many couples whom we saw every year for marriage counseling, it is surprising what a high percentage were in more or less difficulty partly or mainly because of serious in-law problems.

Nor, in almost all instances, is there any good reason for this. Not that in-laws cannot be highly difficult, dunce-like, and even dangerous persons. They can be. Nor that wives and husbands cannot be childishly and exasperatingly bound to their parents. They can be. Nonetheless, according to the basic principles of REBT, much intense and prolonged unhappiness that is not specifically caused by physical pain or deprivation is illegitimate and unethical. And that goes for misery about in-laws.

Take, by the way of illustration, the case of the M's. When Mr. and Mrs. M first came to see me (Dr. Ellis), both insisted that they had just about the worst in-law problem in the world and they were seriously considering getting divorced in order to solve the problem. Mr. M alleged that his wife was completely devoted to her mother and that the mother hated him bitterly and did everything possible to break up their marriage. His mother-in-law feigned all kinds of illnesses, he said, in order to keep her daughter continually attached to her, and, far from ever trying to get along with Mr. M, the mother-in-law frankly said that his presence made her sick and that she never wanted to see him, if possible. Also, he claimed, she tried to alienate his thirteen-year-old daughter from him by telling the child what a terrible person he was.

When I heard her side of the story, Mrs. M did not claim that her husband was overly attached to his parents; in fact, she said that he really didn't seem to care for them at all. But, because he had been roundly indoctrinated by them with a sense of family obligation, he insisted on visiting his parents (who lived quite a distance away) at least once a week. In addition he never wanted to miss a single affair in which his very large family was involved. Again, complained Mrs. M, it would have been different if he really liked his family members and wanted to be with them on birthdays, anniversaries, and other occasions, but he just went, she contended, because he felt obligated. Such craven obedience to family protocol, said Mrs. M, was positively disgusting, and she didn't see why she had to suffer by being dragged along to so many of her husband's family gatherings just because he was such a moral coward.

I started work with Mr. M. During the first few weeks I saw him, his wife was busy taking care of her mother, who had just had her third so-called heart attack (entirely invented, insisted Mr. M) that year. She had no time to come to joint therapy sessions with him and me. As is usual in these cases, I began by assuming that his story about his wife and her mother was absolute gospel, and that he was not significantly exaggerating the facts involved. I was quite sure that Mrs. M, when I saw her, would tell a quite different story; but I deliberately assumed that the husband's story of his in-law difficulties was correct.

"Let us suppose," I said to Mr. M, "that you are describing the situation with your mother-in-law quite accurately, and that she actually is the kind of a woman you say she is. Why are you so upset about the situation?"

"What do you mean, why am I upset!" he fairly screamed at me. "Wouldn't you be, wouldn't anyone be upset if this sort of thing were going on in his home, and going on for the last fifteen years, mind you! Isn't that a good reason for me to be upset?"

"No," I calmly replied, looking him squarely in the eyes. "It isn't."

"It isn't! Then what is, then? What *is* a good reason to get upset?"

"Nothing," I just as calmly replied. "I never heard a good reason for anyone seriously upsetting themselves about anything."

"Oh, piddle! You don't really mean that. You're just saying that to—well, I don't know why you're saying it, but you just are."

"No, I'm deadly serious. I never heard of a good reason for anyone making themselves upset about anything. Even about physical pain. I see no reason to depress yourself. If you have a toothache, I certainly don't expect you to like it or be deliriously happy about it. But enraging yourself will hardly cure it or make it better. What's the point, then, of driving yourself into despair?"

"But how can—how can I help it, damn it? How can I help getting upset?"

"Very simply: Stop telling yourself the drivel you are telling yourself to make yourself miserable."

"Drivel? What drivel?"

"You know. Drivel such as: 'Oh, my God, how can she do this to me?' And: 'That lousy bitchy mother-in-law of mine, I hope she drops dead!' and: 'I just *can't stand* going on like this, with my wife acting in that perfectly idiotic and vicious manner!' And so on, and so forth."

"I can't see anything drivel-ish about that," sulked Mr. M. "She *is* a lousy bitch, my mother-in-law, and I hope she *does* drop dead. No, I can't see anything drivel-ish at all in that."

"Obviously, you can't, or you wouldn't keep repeating that nonsense to yourself. But when I convince you, as I intend to do, that it is utter bosh, real blather, to keep infecting yourself with this misery-creating stuff, you will probably stop doing so. And, lo and behold! Your horror will vanish."

"Quite a trick—if you can do it!"

"Yes. But it's trickier than you think. For actually, I intend to persuade *you* to do it—to get *you* to change your thinking and stop telling yourself that drivel. For I can't, of course, do it for you. I can convince you, perhaps, that what you're telling yourself is nonsense. But unless, finally, I get *you* to desist from feeding yourself this pap and get you, instead, to tell yourself good sense, all my sessions with you will go to waste."

"I still say: quite a trick—if you can do it!"

"Quite. But let's get back to the problem. You're off the wall, I insist, not because of the way your mother-in-law is—and I am taking your word, mind you, that she is that way—but because of the nonsense you're telling yourself *about* the way she is. Instead of forcefully telling yourself the truth, namely: 'That's the way the old gal is. Too bad, but there's nothing I can do to change her at her age, so I'd just better accept the way she is and stop incensing myself about it,' you're quite falsely telling yourself: 'How can she be the way she is? She *ought* not be the way she is! She *absolutely must not* be the unfair way she indubitably is!' and similar drivel."

"I still can't see why it's drivel."

"It's really very simple, if you look at it (which you're not really doing). To ask how a woman can be the way she is when, quite patently, she *is* that way is the worst nonsense under the sun. And to say that an old woman like your mother-in-law, who has been born and raised to be the way she is, *ought* not be that way is equivalent to saying that it *ought* not rain when it is raining. Also, to say that she must not be unfair when she *is* unfair is like saying the sky must not be blue because you'd *prefer* it to be some other color. It is *unfortunate* that your mother-in-law is not acting the way you'd *like* her to act. But you don't have to create a *horror* out of this *misfortune*."

"So you think that I should just accept my mother-in-law the way she is, whatever harm she inflicts on my wife, my child, and myself, and just let it go at that?"

"No, I don't think anything of the sort. I think that you should *first* accept her the way she is—by which I mean stop senselessly damning the poor woman for being as disturbed as she is. And, then, after you manage to accept her in the sense of not damning her, you can, of course, try to change her—or, more practically, perhaps change your wife's attitude toward your mother-in-law, so that it doesn't matter too much how your mother-in-law behaves.

"The way you're doing things now—making yourself terribly upset about your mother-in-law and the way she unfortunately is—you haven't any chance of changing her (except for the worse). What is perhaps more important, you are ceaselessly antagonizing your own wife, and haven't any chance of changing her attitude toward her mother, either—except, again, for the worse. Now how is all *that* kind of behavior doing you any good?"

"Doesn't look like it is doing me much good at all, does it?" Mr. M rather sheepishly admitted.

"No, it certainly doesn't. So I don't care if you ever get to love the old gal, or care for her at all. But just as long as you waste your time and energy, as you have been doing for fifteen years, hating her, you're almost bound to make matters much worse. Moreover and perhaps more important, you're also bound to keep yourself decidedly upset. And what's the percentage in that?"

"Very little, I have to say."

"Darn right, very little. So I still point out: It's not, no, it's positively not, what your mother-in-law or your wife is doing that's upsetting you; it's only your silly, childish, unrealistic *attitude* toward what they're doing that is making you miserable. And if you can take an honest and full look at your own attitude and then question and challenge it and give it a good kick in the teeth—which you definitely can, since *you* are the one who originally adopted it and have ever since been maintaining it—then practically nothing that your mother-in-law and your wife can or will do will seriously upset you. You won't *like*, naturally, many of the things they do; but you definitely will not seriously upset yourself, needlessly and gratuitously, by telling yourself—falsely, falsely, I still say—that what you don't like is *terrible, horrible,* and *awful.*"

Naturally I didn't quite convince Mr. M, in the course of this session, that all his hostility and gut-gnashing about his mother-in-law and wife were pointless, that he was mainly upsetting himself in this connection, and that he could and preferably should stop doing so. But after several more sessions of the same kind of forceful teaching of REBT, reason and I began to win out, and one day Mr. M came in and said:

"You know, these sessions seem to be doing me some good. The other day—I would hardly have believed it a few weeks ago—my mother-in-law pulled one of her very worst tantrums. She not only got my wife to run to her side again, as usual, but started her rumpus at four in the morning, when we were soundly sleeping. She said she was having another of those so-called heart attacks again. Of course, as usual, my wife fell for the whole thing, and insisted on running off to see her and getting me up, no less, to drive her there, even though she knew I had a cold myself and hardly felt like going out at that time, in the middle of the night. Ordinarily, I would have been fit to be tied, and probably would have had a battle royal with her, and ended up seething about it for days.

"But, almost to my own surprise, I said—this time, I said to myself, that is, and *not* to my wife—'Well, there it goes again. Just as I knew it would, and was predicting to myself last night. The old bat's at it, as usual, and of course my wife, poor misguided soul that she is, can't resist her yet. Well, no help for it right now. Too bad, but no help for it. Since I have to go anyway, I might as well do it with as much good grace as possible, as Dr. Ellis would say, and at least not give *myself* a hard time in the process.

"And, believe it or not, I *didn't* give myself a hard time. Though I certainly didn't *enjoy* driving Martha to see her mother, I wasn't particularly unhappy about it either. And the old bat, when she saw what kind of a calm mood I was in, even seemed to take things better for a change and wasn't so negative against me. You know, you're quite right: it *can* be done. You can think yourself out of anger just as, as you keep telling me, you think yourself into it. The other night was quite an eye-opener for me!"

And thereafter for the next few weeks of psychotherapy, Mr. M continued to work on himself and to improve significantly in his attitudes toward his wife and his mother-in-law. So significant, in fact, was the change he began to effect in himself that even his mother-in-law noticed it, and, for the first time in fifteen years, she began to look upon him differently, accept him, and stop carping about him to his wife. Coincidentally enough, her attacks of serious sickness also began to abate.

Meanwhile, as Mr. M was improving, I began to see his wife regularly. I had a fairly easy time of it with her, since she was most grateful, from the start, about what I had done to help her husband accept her and her mother. She admitted that her mother was difficult and that she herself was often put out by her tantrums. But she felt that she just had to keep catering to most of her mother's whims and she was now very happy that her husband had begun, at least partly, to see things her way and help abate the stressfulness of the situation.

As for Mr. M's allegiance to his own family, she still thought it *too* much. Again, as I usually do with my marriage counseling clients, I assumed that she was entirely right about his conventional adherence to his family's social functions, even though I already knew from talking to Mr. M, that he was not exactly that conventional, but kept up good social ties with his family because he wanted to ensure the possibility of getting a sizable inheritance from them. As I did with her husband, I showed Mrs. M that however wrong Mr. M might be in his dealings with his family, that was largely *his* problem, and there was no point in her making herself terribly disturbed about it.

"But doesn't his problem also involve me?" she objected. "Don't I have to go to these damned social affairs with him?"

"Certainly," I admitted, "his problem involves you to some extent. But not as much as you think it does. In the first place, you do *not* have to go to all the family affairs that he attends, but can frankly set, with him, a maximum number that you will attend a year, and stick to that maximum. That will make it all the more his problem if he insists on going to more than your maximum. Second, if you calm down and stop upsetting yourself *because* your husband presumably has a problem in this area, you will probably be able, two intelligent people like you, to work things out so as to minimize the effect of his problem on you. But if you continue to rant and rave, as you have been doing, instead of sitting down to a series of discussions about what to *do* about his problem, things will only get worse and worse—as they have been doing."

"That's for sure!"

"Right. So I'm not promising you any perfect solution to the problem, if you calm down and look at it *as* a problem. But at least, under those conditions there's a good chance that the two of you will come up with some kind of compromise solution. The way it is now, we get no solution, but only a continual worsening of the situation."

"But isn't it unfair that I have to be bothered by the fact that he has this problem and that I have to discuss it with him and make all kinds of compromises, when, really, he should just face the problem himself and get over it?"

"Let's suppose, for the sake of discussion, that it *is* unfair (although, actually, he could say to me that it's unfair that *you* do not see things his way and that *he* has to go to the trouble of compromising). Let's suppose that it's one hundred percent unfair to you that this kind of situation exists. Okay: so it's unfair. The world is full of all kinds of unfair things—of crooked politics, people starving to death while others live in luxury, and so on. And merely to cry and carp about its being that unfair is hardly going to help change things, is it? So if your husband is unfair in having this problem—which seems a little silly to say, doesn't it, since he hardly raised *himself* to have it—that's tough. As I said before: so it's 'unfair.'

"But the thing for *you* to do when faced with an unfair situation is: (a) try to unwhiningly change it, or (b) temporarily accept it as long as it can't for the moment be changed. And your crying and whining about how unfair the situation is are certainly not going to help you to do either (a) or (b). Are they?"

"No, I guess they aren't."

"All right," I said, "then when are you going to stop the non-sense—the nonsense, that is, that you keep feeding yourself? Granted that your husband may, as you say, have serious problems in regard to his family, but your problem is that you take his problem *too* seriously. Instead of understanding him and trying to help him *not* be so over-attached to his conventionalism, you are castigating him for his attachment—beating him over the head, as it were, for being too conformist. Will that help him be *less* conformist? Even if he is neu-rotically conformist, he probably became so because of being se-verely criticized by others and taking this criticism too much to heart. So will not your flagellating him help him become, if any-thing, *more* disturbed?"

"I see what you mean. What, specifically, then, should I do?"

"The same thing anyone can specifically do in a case like this, where an intimate associate is acting badly because of his own anxi-eties or hostilities. First, you can stop telling *yourself* how horrible his activities are. Second, you can accept him, for the time being, just because this is the way he is. Third, when you are calmly ac-cepting your husband's acts as *undesirable* but still not *horrible*, you can then ask yourself what you can do to help him feel more secure, so that he does not have to be so anxious or hostile. As we said be-fore, you can arrange various compromises, so that *you* do not have to be too badly affected even if, for the time being, he continues to act in much the same manner. In other words: the calmer you are and the more you stop giving yourself a hard time about your hus-band's behavior, the more chance you have of helping him change that behavior and of protecting yourself from the worst effects if he continues in much the same way. Does that give you a more specific idea of what you can do to try to help the present situation?"

"Yes, I think it does."

And, like her husband, Mrs. M did some tall talking to herself. She made herself less disturbed about her husband's participation in family affairs, and was able to show him understanding and help instead of carping and criticism. As a consequence, even though he still felt that it was desirable to keep seeing his family for economic reasons, he was able to compromise by seeing them less often and by frequently arranging to see them when his wife was not present. This former area of severe disagreement between Mr. and Mrs. M soon became no issue and they were able to spend much more of their time planning and engaging in more enjoyable aspects of life.

Can, in a similar manner, in-law problems be helped in other instances? To a great extent, yes. Almost always when there are serious in-law differences, the mates are disturbed because either their in-laws are not behaving in the way they think they *should* behave or their spouse is not acting toward these in-laws in the manner they think that s/he *must* act. Once the highly upset mates begin to question and challenge their own *shoulds*—rather than the behavior of their mate or in-laws—they almost immediately can begin to feel much better, less angry. And the better and less angry they feel, the greater, almost always, are their chances of doing something to improve the situation they abhor.

This is not to say that any husband or wife is not entitled to dislike the thoughts or actions of his or her spouse or in-laws. Dislike, yes—that is usually healthy. But when dislike is raised to severe hatred and continual backbiting, they foolishly add to the RB, "I wish this kind of behavior did not exist," the IB, "Because I wish this kind of behavior did not exist, it *should* not, *must* not exist!" This second belief is deadly. Tackling it—rather than tackling one's mate or in-laws—is a much better solution to this kind of problem.

In general, then, the line you can take to resolve serious disagreements that exist because of in-law difficulties may be as follows:

1. Accept your in-laws' shortcomings and/or your mate's "illogical" attitudes toward your in-laws as an undesirable but, for the time being, a largely unchangeable problem or annoyance.

2. Expect your in-laws and your spouse to act just the way they do, to be for the present just the way they are, and stop telling yourself that it is awful, terrible, and frightful that they act this way.

3. Do not personalize your in-laws' behavior toward you. Even if they are vicious, unfair, and thoroughly unreasonable, that is *their* problem and has nothing intrinsically to do with you. If they hate you, that does not make *you* a hateful person. If they are obstreperous or interfering, that does not make *you* weak. Cultivate your own garden, and take care of your own thoughts and feelings, and there is very little that they can actually do to make you disturbed.

4. By all means, if feasible, do not live too close to your in-laws. You can arrange to see them relatively infrequently, and avoid living in the same apartment house, or even neighborhood, with them if you can help it. But if you must, for some reason, see them relatively often, do not think that being with them, in, of, and by itself need be harmful. The worst they can do, normally, is act nastily toward you or call you names. Too bad! Does it make *that* much difference? What can they really *do* to you?

5. Once you understand your in-laws and their problems, by all means try to help them change for the better, if you can. But don't *expect* them to change because you *want* them to. And try to honestly see their point of view, be on their side, help them for their own sake as well as your own. Don't try to change them by criticism, carping, grim silence, or persecution. Try to *help* them change, do not blackmail or force them into changing.

6. Don't allow yourself to be exploited, physically or emotionally, by your in-laws just because you *are* related to them. You owe them: (a) normal human politeness, and (b) acknowledgment of the fact that they are the parents of your spouse, and that for his/her sake you will try to be as pleasant as possible to them. But you are not obligated to give them your complete allegiance, perform acts of extreme self-sacrifice for them, or go dramatically against your own grain. If you cannot get along well with them you can, without being downright unpleasant, calmly but firmly divorce yourself emotionally from them—and thus even, perhaps, set a good example for your spouse. But if s/he still wants to be very closely tied to your in-laws, you can calmly accept these ties, for the nonce, while intelligently and lovingly trying to deal with him/her.

7. If your in-laws, in spite of everything you can do, insist on re-

maining a thorn in your side and are truly obnoxious, and if you cannot keep them from unduly influencing your spouse, you must philosophically accept the fact that conditions in this respect are *bad*—but that, again, they are not necessarily *horrible* and *awful*. Perhaps you cannot reduce your annoyance at your in-laws' behavior but you can at least stop yourself from needlessly making yourself utterly miserable about it.

8. There is no law against your liking your in-laws and actually getting along very well with them. Particularly if you do not take them too seriously, if you realistically accept their limitations, and if you do not expect them to be perfect or act exceptionally well to you, you may find that they are quite decent, helpful, nice enough people with whom you have some things in common and can get along very pleasantly in many ways. They did, after all, bear and rear your spouse, who presumably has some really nice qualities, and it is most unlikely that they are complete ogres. The better you accept yourself, the less you personalize their views of you, and the more philosophical you are about many of life's irritations and annoyances, the more are you likely to find excellent points in your in-laws and to be able to enjoy them in important respects.

Again, as ever, we teach one main thing in this book: that almost all your severe emotional problems are your *own*. *You* have the ability to disturb or not disturb yourself, therefore—whatever problems your in-laws and their relationship with your spouse may seem to create. Your attitude toward these troubles, rather than the difficulties in themselves, will determine whether you are quite miserable or satisfied with your marriage and your life.

EXERCISES FOR CHAPTER 9

You may be fortunate enough to have a partner but not have in-laws or other close relatives of this partner. Maybe they have all died, live in Alaska, or hate social contact. Fine! Or maybe they are quite likable, a pleasure to be with. Marvelous!

If not, here are some exercises you can use to help cope with your partner's close relatives. Or, if they're no problem, perhaps you can use these exercises to bear up under the strain of dealing with your mate's annoying close friends or business associates. To some extent, these exercises probably apply to various restrictions and hassles of mating and relating. If they don't, bless your luck and skip them!

One of REBT's most useful emotive-evocative methods, which I (Dr. Ellis) developed in the 1970s, is the vigorous and forceful disputing of people's IBs. I found that a number of my resistant clients were competently disputing their IBs and coming up with sensible, rational effective new philosophies (Es) but that they only mildly or lightly believed them, and wound up with mild Es. Their quite powerful and forceful IBs, which they still held, unfortunately won out—to their great emotional loss.

So I give many of my clients the homework assignments of putting some of their IBs on a tape recorder, of very vigorously disputing these IBs, of letting their IBs and their disputing be heard by friends or group members, and of then revising their disputing, if necessary, and making it more powerful and convincing. We find this to be a useful disputing method. You can use it as follows.

Sample Exercise 9A: Vigorous and Forceful Disputing of My IBs About Dealing With My Partner's Relatives

My Irrational Beliefs That I Can Vigorously Dispute	Vigorous Disputation of My IBs	Strong Effective New Philosophies (Es)
Some of my partner's relatives are so obnoxious that I certainly shouldn't have to socialize with them.	Are they really *that* obnoxious or am *I* grossly exaggerating? Even if I'm right about them is there really *any* reason why I *absolutely shouldn't have to* socialize with them?	*Yes*, *I am* grossly exaggerating how obnoxious they are! *No matter!* However bad they are, that's the way they are! I *should* have to socialize with them if I desire to have good relationships with my mate! Being with them is bad—but being without my mate is *much, much worse! Tough turkey* if they bore me! *I can take it!*
My mate's parents really *are* rotten people! I can't find *anything* good about them. Murder is too good for them!	Are they *completely* rotten people or do they just do *some* rotten things? Isn't my raging at them *also* silly and rotten?	*No one* is completely rotten—not even them and Hitler! I'm idiotically damning *them* and not just their *behavior! Yes*, I'm ridiculously incensing myself at them and ripping up my own gut. What drivel!
Look how needy my partner is—putting up with lousy relatives like that. S/he *needs* their ass-kissing ap-	Is my partner needy—or just really appreciative of his or her relatives? Even if s/he is needy, is that utterly	How about *my* neediness?—my *demand* that my partner have the "right" relatives? It's *good* that s/he can

Sample Exercise 9A (cont.)

My Irrational Beliefs That I Can Vigorously Dispute	Vigorous Disputation of My IBs	Strong Effective New Philosophies (Es)
proval. How disgusting! I'll show him/her how revolting that is!	*disgusting? Must* I show him/her how revolting that behavior is?	find value in people that I am bigotedly condemning entirely. I am foolishly revolting *myself*. And *I'm* the one who's stupidly making myself suffer and disrupting my relationship! How revolting is *that*!

Exercise 9B: Vigorous and Forceful Disputing of My IBs About Dealing With My Partner's Relatives

My Irrational Beliefs That I Can Vigorously Dispute	My Vigorous Disputations of These Irrational Beliefs

Exercise 9C: Role-Playing About My Upsetness About My Partner's Relatives

REBT often uses J.L. Moreno's role-play exercise to help people overcome their needless upset feelings and to learn better social skills. Thus, if you are angry or overly frustrated about your partner's relatives, friends, or associates, enlist a friend to help you cope with your disturbed feelings and to train yourself to act better with your partner and his/her "terrible" associates. You play yourself during the role-play and your friend can play your mate. Your goal is to practice speaking *assertively* but not *angrily* to your partner. Thus, your role-play dialogue may go as follows:

You: I know it's your father's birthday, dear, but you know he's not exactly my cup of tea. So you can see him as long as you like, but do I really have to be there, too?

Your Mate: Oh! But he and Mom will be terribly hurt if you don't come with me. They'll know you really hate him.

You: Maybe you're right, dear. But I really don't hate him. I just hate some of the ways he acts.

Your Mate: But they'll be sure you hate him. And they'll think you also don't respect me.

You: Of course I respect and love you. And I wouldn't want to keep you from seeing your father if you really want to do so.

Your Mate: If you really loved me, you wouldn't put me in this position. You'd go, even though you don't like it.

You: I can see how you see it that way. But I *do* love you. I just hate hearing him go on and on as he usually does. None of us get a word in edgewise!

Your Mate: He's not that bad! And you'd still do it for me. You know how it would hurt me to go alone.

You: Yes, and I want to avoid that. Now couldn't we compromise? Couldn't I go for only a short while and then plead an important business appointment? We could even call them in advance and tell them I can only visit briefly.

Your Mate: Lie like that? I'd hate to make up a lie like that.

Exercise 9C (cont.)

You: Yes, so would I. But wouldn't it be, dear, the lesser of evils? And, to make things better, I could even buy him an expensive gift—like a special golf club he would like—to show him that I really like him.

Your Mate: Well—?

In a role-play like this, you work at not making yourself angry at your partner and arriving at some kind of compromise. Your role-playing friend—and other possible onlookers—critique your performance, tell you how to improve it, and get you to replay it until you do improve. If you appear to be angry, depressed, anxious, or otherwise disturbed during the role-play, stop it for a few minutes to see what you are telling yourself to make yourself upset and how you can change your self-talk to reduce your disturbance.

Thus, in the previous dialogue, if your partner said, "Lie like that? I'd hate to make up a lie like that," and you then felt anxious, the two of you—and other possible onlookers—would stop to ask, "What are you telling yourself to make yourself anxious?"

You might reply, "My partner is putting me down for suggesting that we lie. Right! I'm a lousy liar—and a no-goodnik!"

You and your partner would dispute this IB and might come up with the Effective New Philosophy that lying may indeed be bad but it never makes you a *bad person*. Then you could continue the role-play.

So again: If you really are upset about your partner's having "miserable" relatives, friends, or associates, you can use this REBT version of role-playing to retain your displeasure, but reduce your upsetness and function better with your partner and/or his or her "rotten" associates.

10

To Have or Not to Have Children—That *Is* the Question

While few people think they can, without much preparation and training, fly a jet plane, teach a course in nuclear physics or reprogram a bevy of complex computers, we keep running into hordes who not only think they themselves are naturally destined to be dandy parents, but also that others less magnificently endowed than themselves can easily and automatically undertake the glories of parenthood and turn out super-duper children. All you have to do to get an A-plus in parenting, they insist, is to be properly and legally married, for all husbands and wives—of course—are born with superlative child-raising skills and are able to bear incredibly marvelous offspring. If you sorely lack such skills, well, take a chance, anyway. What have you and your brats got to lose? As the Bible brilliantly proclaims, "Be fruitful and multiply."

Are we being sarcastic? In a word, yes. For we would like to highlight some of the common irrationalities of our society about children and parenthood. There are loads of such IBs. Even though large numbers of people hold that reproduction is to be encouraged and that child-rearing is a process for which no great knowledge or skill is needed, couples who want to *adopt* children usually have to meet fairly strict standards. These standards are often difficult to measure and/or fulfill. Couples must, for example, somehow demonstrate present and future happiness and emotional and financial stability. Couples who reveal themselves to be too old or too young, gay or lesbian, or different from arbitrarily predetermined "desirable" social or religious philosophies are often eliminated.

Our stance as a society on a couple's acquiring children seems to be: if you do it by reproduction, "feel free (but please be married)." If by adoption, "Hey, wait a minute, we are very concerned about the kind of parents and the kind of environment this child will have." We would expand considerably on prevalent attitudes about having children, but we hope we've said enough or at least cast doubt on the rationality and realism of what seems to be our society's position.

It is not the purpose of this chapter to join society in trying to persuade "a nice young married couple" that they ought or ought not to have children. All couples have the right to choose—rationally or irrationally—*not* to become parents just as they have the right to decide not to work for the government or to live in a large city or to buy an automobile. With the help of this chapter, work out the important factors in your particular situation in deciding whether or not to be parents. Let us pose some questions and hazard some "rational" or "healthy" answers—for some of our readers some of the time!

Question: Is it essential to our happiness and welfare for us to have children?

Answer: It all depends. Are you sure that you can't be happy without children or that you would be happy with children? Have all your relatives been really happy with their children? And what about their children—do they all seem top-hole? What about the background, skills, and attitudes you are both bringing into this deal? Aren't those the sort of questions your partner and you should preferably be discussing at great length?

Question: What are some important things to consider in deciding whether to have or not have children? Shall we have them just because we are happy with each other?

Answer: Probably not. Your being happy together is a good sign but hardly a *demand* for your having children. Would having them help or hinder your relationship? Hmm ... Is your marriage the kind of process that a kid will fit into and enjoy (let alone your enjoying the kid)? Or is your relationship one of those great me-thee things that leave little room for *anybody* else?

Question: How about my partner and us *liking* children and *being good* with them?

Answer: A good question. We remember a botany teacher who said he loved his children and that they loved him. But he loved it even more when he could walk away and leave the responsibility of them to his wife and to other people. We used to think he was just a funny guy whose words had no great importance. But don't they? Shouldn't you and your partner think of ways of testing whether you like kids and will get along with them well on a long-term basis? Would you be willing to provide foster home care for a while? And what does it say about having a child of your own if one or both of you isn't willing?

Question: Do we really have sufficient time together to properly raise children?

Answer: Perhaps. But don't forget that these days, with both mates often employed outside the home, a lot of couples have insufficient time together *without* children. Think carefully! What are you now doing that you would have to greatly reduce to properly raise children.

Question: Will our ideas and interests about having children change *after* we actually have them?

Answer: They well may! Jim got all fired up about being a stock broker, studied like mad, passed all the tests, had the highest sales record for several months. Then his interest fizzled. He thought, "So I make a lot of money. So I help other dopes make a lot of money. So who cares? It's a bore." Mary loved teaching third grade for three years—then hated it and became a happy paralegal. How can you and your partner really know how much, after a while, you will adore your own children? Not very easily!

Question: Now with all our doubt and confusion, do we just give up on having children?

Answer: Not necessarily. There's a long road to go before the *two* of you decide about having children. But you'd better get out of that children-are-my-destiny mood and be ready to work at deciding what you and your partner think is an intelligent decision. Yes, *work* at deciding.

These questions and answers were condensed from discussions we have had with individuals and couples through the years on the issues of having children. As therapists, we never try to persuade one way or the other. But since the weight of society has often pushed couples directly into parenthood, we encourage careful consideration of the problems of parenthood. If and when a couple determines to have a child we try to help them undertake parenthood realistically and to enjoy it fully.

Once a couple decides to have a child, we often make the following points. But these, like everything else in this book, are subject to discussion and revision by any specific couple.

1. While love is definitely not "all that matters," and certainly need not meet some special forms of expressions, partners A and B had better deeply and consistently care for each other and for their children.

2. They had better strive for both short-range and (especially) long-range enjoyment. They also had better include in their enjoyments working at improving interactions and responsibilities in their family.

3. They had better expect and accept their own and their children's mistakes and limitations. Their unperfectionistic outlooks will appreciably reduce anger, anxiety, and other strong disruptive emotions that often develop in close human relationships.

4. They had better teach their children how to minimize their mistakes and learn from them.

5. They had better acknowledge that the knowledge and skills most people bring to parenthood leave plenty of room for improvement. Just as we have noted in earlier chapters, improved family functioning usually can be achieved only by careful assessment, planned discussion, and hard work at improving family members' disturbed habits of thinking, feeling, and acting.

6. Couples had better recognize the individuality of their children. This means gradually relinquishing their control over their offspring and encouraging them to increasingly participate in decisions that affect the whole family unit.

EXERCISES FOR CHAPTER 10

The main problems concerning children that we keep encountering with our clients include:

Serious disagreements over whether or not to have them.

Disagreements over whether to have additional children.

Disagreements over how to raise the children the couple actually have.

Disagreements over whether to keep supporting the children when they have already reached adulthood.

As with other relationship disagreements you have, your problem with your partner is not so much to agree but to agree to disagree—to disagree amiably. As usual, the chief block here is, first, too much pride, which leads to self-downing.

Janis, for example, fought bitterly with Jim over whether they should have a child, even though she was highly ambivalent about bearing one at the age of thirty-nine and he was positive that having one would be a "huge mistake." But she felt that if he wouldn't even *consider* her mild wish to have a child he had no respect for her as a *person.* She viewed her giving in to him, even when she was convinced she was right, as a "terrible weakness." So she "strongly" kept fighting with Jim until she almost proved to be infertile. After she became pregnant, she still resented his previous "pigheadedness" and tended to "find" it in other respects where it really did not exist.

Exercise 10A is useful when you and your mate keep violently disagreeing about children or anything else because one or both of you cannot bear being "weak" by compromising. It is also useful when the main reason for your disagreement is your frustration intolerance. Thus, Jim kept fighting with Janis against their having a child because he knew he would enjoy one later but horrified himself about the loss of sleep and other inconveniences he and Janis would experience for the first year or two of the child's life. When he worked on his FI and decided to put up with this rough period of time, he was quite happy for the rest of his life about having a charming, bright daughter.

In the following exercise, you will be making a list of the advantages and the disadvantages of arguing with your mate to prove that you are not a weak person or to uphold your FI. Rate or evaluate each of these advantages from a low of one to a high of ten, especially in terms of enhancing and of sabotaging your relationship.

Sample Exercise 10A: Mapping Out the Cost-Benefit Ratio of Arguing With Your Mate to Prove That You Are Not a "Weak Person" or to Uphold Your FI

Advantages of Maintaining Strong Arguments With Partner	Rating of Advantages	Disadvantages of Maintaining Strong Arguments with Partner	Rating of Disadvantages
I feel like a strong person when I stubbornly hold my ground.	7	I may argue strongly but am I not really weak for *needing* to win?	10
My friends and relatives will like me for strongly holding my ground.	3	I will have more strength if I don't need my friends' and relatives' approval.	8
If I disagree about having another child, we will save a lot of money.	8	If I disagree about having a child, I will lose out on the excitement, love, and enjoyment of agreeing to have one.	8
People will look down on me for being childless so I have to keep fighting with my mate to have a child and perhaps two or three children. I must not be criticized for being childless.	5	If I agree with my mate that we don't have children and we are criticized for being childless, I can still accept myself fully in spite of people's criticism.	9

Exercise 10A

Advantages of Maintaining Strong Arguments With Partner	Rating of Advantages	Disadvantages of Maintaining Strong Arguments With Partner	Rating of Disadvantages

If you want, you can total up your ratings for the advantages and disadvantages of maintaining strong arguments with your partner—and hope that you view the disadvantages as greater and thereby give yourself incentives for making compromises and resisting continual arguments.

Sample Exercise 10B: Advantages and Disadvantages of My Partner and I Possibly Rearing Children

As in the previous exercise, you may rate each advantage and each disadvantage you expect to receive from rearing children from one to ten and see which side comes out with a higher rating. This kind of cost-benefit rating—or hedonic calculus—may be an important factor in which you or your mate decide whether or not to have children.

Advantages My Partner and I Will Probably Experience If We Rear Children	Rating of Advantages	Disadvantages My Partner and I Will Probably Experience If We Rear Children	Rating of Disadvantages
Monetary advantages, such as becoming forced to budget and save money. The self-discipline you may achieve by raising children.		The expenses you will have with your children. The time and energy you will probably spend in raising children.	
The love you will feel for your children.		The anger and FI you may feel with your children.	
The love your children will feel toward you and your partner.		The selfishness your children may exhibit toward you and your partner.	
The fine companionship you may have with your children.		The lack of companionship you may have with your children or the too-great responsibilities you may feel about being with them.	
The interesting experiences you may have with your children.		The boredom you may experience with your children.	

Exercise 10B

Advantages My Partner and I Will Probably Experience If We Rear Children	Rating of Advantages	Disadvantages My Partner and I Will Probably Experience If We Rear Children	Rating of Disadvantages

11

Happy Couplehood: Building a Deep and Lasting Relationship

Throughout this book, we have held that if you and your partner persistently apply the basic tenets of REBT, you can help yourself to long-term enjoyment of living. We have also pointed out the advantages you have, as a couple, of developing and testing out the revolutionary REBT ways of thinking, feeling, and acting. Moreover, this application can be nicely mixed with fun. Put somewhat differently, the REBT route to lasting happy relating is hard work, but the hard work itself can be a process of fun, and the fun itself can be greatly enhanced by having a partner to work and play with.

In this last chapter we want to help bring out some general points about couplehood, and we fortunately have the help of an old friend. Do you remember Charlene, the fifteen-year-old who was so distressed about her lesbian tendencies? Let us go further along with her saga by taking a look at interviews with Charlene and her partner, Nita, which took place eight years after the conversations with her reported in chapter one.

Charlene: Yes, it's been almost eight years since I saw you. I'm twenty-three now, and about to get a Ph.D in psychology from (she named a local university). You're responsible for that: you not only cured me of self-downing, but you got me fascinated with clinical psychology. I tried heterosexuality, by the way. In fact you might say I gave going straight a hell of a case, but I always got back to the proposition that this ain't me and there is no damned reason why it has to be me. I've had several brief affairs with other women, but Nita is the first person with whom I've ever felt I wanted to have a lasting relationship. She feels similarly about me. I don't want to blow this, and that's why we're here. I think that I've really lived sensibly as an individual, but I could use REBT more in an ongoing relationship.

R.A.H.: If you have been applying REBT in the rest of your life, you'll find that there is nothing amazingly different about applying it in a close personal relationship. In fact, there are various advantages, providing that both partners are willing to work in the REBT mode. What about you, Nita?

Nita: Yeah, well, I'm a little overwhelmed—first of all because Charlene is older and more experienced. I'm just nineteen and a first-semester junior and only beginning my psychology major. And she's not only a hotshot graduate student, but she's also this super-dynamo, Charlene. Then she drags me in here to see you after having talked about you for months as if you were the living Christ. I feel like a walk-on bit player who's having lunch with the two stars of the play. But let's continue.

Charlene: You have no damned business being overwhelmed. I wouldn't have brought you here if I didn't think you were great!

R.A.H.: Several important things have just emerged that I'd like to suggest that the two of you look at: (1) Nita is understandably ill at ease in this situation and picked her own way of expressing it, (2) Instead of letting Nita work out her nervousness (with help from me if necessary), you, Charlene, told her in effect that she has no damned business being "overwhelmed," and (3) It's interesting that you presumably tried to reassure Nita that I am an okay person rather than demonstrating what would seem more pertinent—that you, Charlene, accept Nita in what she finds to be a difficult situation. You both seem to know how desirable *acceptance* is but you are having difficulty displaying it. Let's try an REBT exercise. Will you both close your eyes, please? Now will each of you, keeping your eyes closed, honestly look at the negative feelings you have about each other. Don't think in terms of what you suspect the other is going to report, but get in touch with your own feelings. Focus on what you feel and not on any justification you can produce for feeling that way.

(After a minute or so.) Okay, Nita first. What did you recognize in the way of negative feelings toward Charlene? Please, both of you keep your eyes closed while Nita is talking. You'll get your chance later, Charlene.

Nita: I feel that Charlene thinks I'm inferior. Cute, but dumb. And I hate her for that. But I also feel she is conning herself into believing that she wants a long-term relationship (and that's why we are in here), when what she really wants is to sex it up with me like mad and tell herself it's beautiful love. I hate that even more, but my hate toward Charlene about that is less than it is about the cute-but-dumb theme. I also feel hostility toward myself and that sort of spills over onto Charlene because I'm such a wimp and suck up to Charlene because she's Ms. Hotshot. My hostility toward Charlene and toward myself is further reinforced by Ms. Hotshot telling me, even in here, what I'm supposed to think and feel.

R.A.H.: That's fine. Now keeping your eyes closed (both of you), see if you, Nita, can change these feelings into less disturbed and more positive ones. Please both be silent, and Nita, hold up your hand when you are ready to report. In the meantime, please be patient, Charlene. (After three minutes Nita holds up her hand.) Okay, will you both continue with closed eyes please, and Nita will you tell us what you *now* feel and, if your feelings are different, how you changed them?

Nita: It's funny, but I feel quite different. I believed up to now that REBT was largely bullshit, especially the part about how I can feel differently by thinking differently. I thought my feelings were my essence—that I feel as I feel because I am as I am. Charlene was always telling me that was a lot of crap, but I would react defensively because she *told* me to feel different. Just now, because I felt okay feeling any damned hostile way I wanted and because I was simply given an opportunity to change in case *I* wanted to do so, I did want to.

R.A.H.: How did you do it? And how do you know you are not just bullshitting yourself in some new way?

Nita: I think the main way I did it was by wanting to look realistically at what I was feeling and why. When I started looking, I started thinking, and when I started thinking I came up with the idea, which gradually became a feeling: Hey, Nita, all this defensiveness and hostility is for the birds. And I came up next with the idea that I don't have to measure up to some kind of standard that I think Charlene has set for me. I've got problems to work out, but I'm an okay person even if I don't work them out. And what's more, it won't be terrible if Charlene's and my relationship doesn't become the lasting and beautiful thing we've talked about. And how do I know I am not bullshitting myself in a new way? I guess I don't *know*, but I think the probability is that I'm thinking clearer and I'm certainly feeling better. At least it's a better-quality bullshit!

R.A.H.: Yes, it sounds as if you embraced at least two important ideas. First, you don't have to meet predetermined standards to be an acceptable person. Second, even if you don't solve your problems or work out a desirable relationship with Charlene, although I assume that is still your preference (Nita: Yes!), life won't be terrible. That's considerable progress. But let's now give Charlene her chance. Will you both please continue to keep your eyes closed, so that you keep focused. You have undoubtedly reacted to some of the things that Nita said, Charlene. So will you try as best you can to tell us what your own thinking and feeling processes have been?

Charlene: It was good to hear Nita's "yes" about wanting still to work out our relationship. I had thought I'd blown it to hell. And though I have, of course, been listening to what Nita and you have been saying, I had already looked at my thoughts and feelings and how they needed to be changed—oh, I'm sorry, not *needed*, but *had better* be changed. You see, I remember many of the lessons I learned from you in REBT years ago. And I practiced these things, and they helped me to function better and to do well in many respects and to enjoy myself along the way. *But* Nita sure as hell is right. I began to think of myself as a hotshot who could do no wrong and whose point of view was always fucking right. Anyone who disagreed with me was either a hopeless pain in the ass and therefore to be dismissed—or was a fine person, Nita being the prime example, who had to be shown the way and the light by wonderful me. I now know that I have been behaving like an asshole, but I have enough REBT left in me to know that it doesn't mean I *am* an asshole. I'm an okay person who has been *behaving* assholishly! And I am going to fucking stop behaving like that!

R.A.H.: Can you help Nita and me to understand better what got you off the REBT track? Incidentally, both of you can open your eyes now.

Charlene: Well, mostly success. I remember something back in a psychoanalytic seminar which said that the neurotic may fail because of the fear of success. But my own experience is you fail by *corrupting* success. The more I succeeded the more I came to believe I was someone who *couldn't* fail. I believed what you stressed with me years ago, that REBT works *only* if we work at it, applied only to the average stiff and not to a queen of the shitpile like me. And, you know, my experience in therapy training as well as my razzle-dazzle success in graduate school added to my belief that I could walk on water. Many clients are so grateful for any kind of help that they treat a two-bit therapist like a guru and it's easy to come to believe that you actually are one. Anyhow, it's easy to spout REBT to clients and to forget to practice it oneself. Then there are all these other kinds of therapies that distracted me from keeping the old REBT nose to the grindstone. Anyhow, even though I was going around spouting REBT principles to everybody, including Nita, I was getting more and more off the REBT practicing track. I think I'm now ripe for more personal help as well as doing my part in couple therapy.

R.A.H.: There isn't all that much difference between doing your part in couple therapy and getting some personal help. You describe

well some of the hazards of therapists getting off the personal practicing of REBT. That's why, you'll recall, I kept stressing years ago
that living the REBT way takes constant vigilance and unremitting
hard work.

Charlene: Yes, I remember, and I worked hard at it for a long
while. But I guess I began gradually to believe that it was automatic
with me, and I would just naturally do the most rational and healthy
thing. And I extended my conceit to Nita's and my relationship with
her, and assumed that I was so wonderful that any relationship she
had with me was bound to be great and beautiful. When it hasn't
worked out that way, I've blamed Nita. She, I'd think and all too
often say, was being obstinate or stupid or unappreciative or some
damned thing. So, she's right. I decided to haul her in here so you
could give her a quick fix.

R.A.H.: In any close relationship, it's common—but unproduc-
tive—to blame the partner for any difficulty that develops. Blame is
not only non-acceptance of the partner, but it arouses your mate's
defensiveness, blame, and non-acceptance. This, in turn, elicits
more of the same, on and on. When you seem to be falling into this
sort of pattern, try using the eyes-closed exercise you just experienced here. You can give yourselves instructions like these: "We
have a problem. Let's each of us focus on what each of us (*not* the
other one) can do to alleviate it." Later, you can describe to one another where each of you sees herself as being "off-track" and what
she can do to correct it.

Nita: Is it that easy? A little eye-closing exercise, and Charlene
and I will achieve beautiful bliss?

R.A.H.: No, Nita, you have just illustrated two common false assumptions about REBT. For one, you assumed that because some of
its therapy instructions are simple, REBT is easy. For example, if I
say, "If you want to develop real proficiency in understanding and
speaking Aleut, you will probably have to seek out and study with an
Aleutian," it does not mean I think it would be *easy* to do this.
Second, you assumed that using REBT for alleviating problems is
the same as saying, "All my problems will be solved. Beautiful bliss

is at hand." But we have more to do in REBT than eye-closing exercises. Charlene, you said at the outset that you had been trying to live in an REBT way as an individual, but knew little about applying it in a couple relationship. Do you want to say anything about that at this point?

Charlene: Seriously, in spite of how I just screwed up with Nita, I have really been living REBT. I've been preaching it to her while engaging in some anti-REBT rating of myself as a person. Something I've just faced today, in rating myself top-hole as a *person*, rather than rating my good behavior, I end up as far removed from the REBT way of life as I did when I rated myself as a lowly shit. So I have been ignoring REBT in my relationship with Nita. But I was talking bullshit about not knowing how to apply it to a close personal relationship. That was an excuse to myself to get Nita and me here. But we also genuinely had reason to get here because I, at least, had become confused.

Nita: (to Charlene) Your even admitting that you're confused is a new experience for me, and I like it. You seem much more available for democratic problem-solving than I have ever noticed before. (to me) I'm beginning to see what focusing can do. My sarcastic remarks earlier were, I think, partly from being *told* what to do by Charlene. I made myself over-react to that.

R.A.H.: I'm glad that you see that it was *your* over-reacting and not merely Charlene's trying to tell you what to do. Both of you can, I hope, now understand that the eyes-closed routine helps you to focus more intently on acknowledging and (sometimes) changing your thoughts and feelings. But there's no reason why enlightenment *must* invariably proceed in that fashion. If Charlene lapses into her old dictatorial habits from time to time, you can realize that she is working on reducing this tendency and you can work on being less vulnerable to it. Correct?

This first couples session with Charlene and Nita kept repeating some of the above points, but to make my points clearer, much repetition is omitted here. Remember, however, it is important to keep in mind in your own discussions with your partner—and perhaps with your therapist—that you seldom effect change without going over and over the same "simple and easy" matters almost monotonously! Comments made by Charlene, Nita, and myself in the remainder of this chapter have been excerpted from eight subsequent sessions.

Nita: At home, things go a little more smoothly than in these sessions. But what we find works best is for one or both of us to say something like, "Hey, we seem to have a problem here. Let's pause, close our eyes, and try to understand what each of us is thinking and feeling and how we might improve it." Both the pause and the self-focusing seem helpful.

Charlene: You asked our permission to use some of the things the three of us say in these sessions in a book on helping couples that you are writing. Do you really think problems of couples are the same whether they are straight, gay, addicts, or devoted members of religious sects?

R.A.H.: Partly. The particular content and seriousness of problems will vary with the characteristics and circumstances of the individuals who are paired. To have a leg amputated would obviously be a much more serious problem for a professional hockey player than for an accountant, and therefore also more serious for the hockey player's partner. Yet, *how* the two *approach* and *handle* their problems can determine the hockey player and his partner's ending up in a better long-term relationship than an accountant and his or her mate. REBT tries to offer couples (and individuals) more effective ways of dealing with *whatever* problems they encounter. So although all couples hardly have the same problems, most of them can learn to handle their difficulties and differences more wisely. I think a straight couple, for example, could just as well apply some of the things we have discussed in our sessions as could another lesbian couple.

Nita: Let me ask something at this point. I know you helped Charlene to work through the lesbian issue when she was just a kid, but she still had some doubts in recent years and I do, too. Aren't we *realistically* adding to our other life problems by insisting on a lesbian lifestyle? Women are already discriminated against in society, so when two women get together and thumb their noses at traditional values, aren't they just dipping into deep shit?

R.A.H.: No, not necessarily. As lesbians in our prejudiced culture, you just have another set of difficulties to realistically consider even though society is slowly becoming more open-minded about this issue. Even with all the usual couple problems and, with a set of unusual additional ones, you can still be happy. I have worked with people who had all kinds of disabilities and problems but who have learned through REBT to take them in stride. Many others catastrophize over a late plane or train, over their coworker's jealousy, and over innumerable other "petty" things.

Despite your doubts, you and Charlene have made the practical decision to function as lesbians. Can you reverse your decision if you are really determined to do so? Possibly, but Charlene at age fifteen was determined not to do so and neither of you show determination now. You both just have doubts now and then, which will probably get you nowhere. So *practically*, let's focus on the hard work you can do to function effectively and enjoyably together.

Charlene: How much do we have to do by rote the various exercises for couples you have taught us? How much do these procedures vary from those you use with other couples? I am interested as a budding therapist who would like to some day do couple therapy.

R.A.H.: Let me give you an imprecise answer. REBT practitioners do better when they avoid procedures that are too fixed and mechanical. They try to adapt their methods to specific personalities and situations. And they enlist aid from the couples themselves. The mates know each other and can often assist with more spontaneity and creativity than can a single client who just interacts with a therapist. REBT-oriented individual and couple therapy are different—and also similar! Both are fascinating.

Charlene: Is this, then, termination? Are you going to turn Nita and me out into the hostile fucking world?

R.A.H.: For the present, you're on your own—to use, or to not use REBT as you will. If you screw up, give yourselves unconditional self-acceptance and give each other unconditional other-acceptance and get back to working things out. If and when the going gets rough, remember the famous words of REBT: "Tough shit!" Good luck—and hard work—to both of you!

12

Summary: How You Can Use REBT to Build a Healthy Relationship

We have presented in this book many of the principles and practices of REBT, as well as suggestions on how to use them in your relationship. Let us briefly sum up our main suggestions.

First, rid yourself of the almost universal idea that your partner, by his or her "bad" behavior, upsets you. This is only partly true! Mainly, you can *take* your partner's undesirable thoughts, feelings, and actions and consciously or unconsciously upset yourself *about* them. As we say in REBT, the adversities of your life, A, may *significantly* contribute to your disturbed consequences, C, but you importantly *add* definite beliefs, B, *about* you and your partner's "wrong" actions to make yourself wind up with upset feelings and dysfunctional behaviors. A times B equals C!

This is fortunate. Because as constructivists, you and your partner have the power to construct and to reconstruct your own *reactions* to "bad" events that occur in your life. You can therefore sometimes change serious adversities themselves, and you can just about always change how you react (well or badly) to them. You can, at point B, construct both self-helping RBs and self-defeating IBs to difficulties in your relationships. RBs, as opposed to IBs, take the form of your *preferences* that adversities be reduced—for example, "I

212

don't *like* my partner's behavior and *wish* s/he would change it. But, if not, we can still have a satisfying relationship." IBs take the form of you and/or your partner's absolutistic, rigid demands—e.g., "Because I don't like my partner's behavior, s/he *absolutely must not* think, feel, or act that way! If so, it's *awful* (totally bad) and s/he is a *rotten person!*"

Using REBT helps you to clearly see your irrational *demands* on yourself, your partner, and the world, and to change them back to rational *preferences*. As this book shows, it gives you many cognitive, emotional-experiential, and behavioral techniques for doing so. It emphasizes that you and your partner often hold IBs *strongly* (emotionally) and *actively* (behaviorally) and therefore it helps both of you emotionally and behaviorally, as well as cognitively, to see and surrender your IBs and your consequent dysfunctioning.

Most partners who get themselves into trouble with themselves and with others make one, two, or three major irrational, dysfunctional demands. If you often disturb yourself and contribute to disturbing your partner, REBT shows you ways to think, feel, and act against these demands and to acquire three important constructive philosophies that can help you enormously to stop wrecking your relationship and build a lasting, loving one. These are:

Unconditional other-acceptance (UOA). Accepting, respecting, honoring, and loving your partner (and other people) even *with* his/her shortcomings and failings. Strongly seeing and feeling the Christian idea of accepting the sinner but not the sin. Despite all!

Unconditional self-acceptance (USA). Accepting your self, essence, totality, and being *whether or not* you act well and *whether or not* you are approved of by significant others. Under all conditions!

Unconditional life-acceptance (ULA) or high frustration tolerance. Accepting life with its hassles, problems, troubles, and difficulties, and creating enjoyment in it for yourself and your partner. Not always, but fairly consistently!

These are our main REBT suggestions. By all means consider and *experiment* flexibly with them. You and your partner are unique individuals. Uniquely, as a person and as a couple, experiment with these REBT methods for yourself. Once again: Good luck—and hard work—to both of you!

Suggested Reading

The following references include a number of REBT and Cognitive Behavior Therapy publications which may be useful for self-help purposes. Many of these materials can be obtained from the Albert Ellis Institute, 145 East 32nd Street, New York, NY—by phone (212-535-0822), fax (212-249-3582), or by email (orders@rebt.org). Check out the publications on the Albert Ellis website, www.Albert Ellis.org.

Alberti, R. and Emmons, R. (1995). *Your Perfect Right.* 7th ed. San Luis Obispo, Cal.: Impact Publishers. Original ed., 1970.

Barlow, D. H., and Craske, N. G. (1994). *Mastery of Your Anxiety and Panic.* Albany, New York: Graywind Publications.

Beck, A. T. (1988). *Love Is Not Enough.* New York: Harper & Row.

Broder, M. (2002). *Can your relationship be saved? How to know whether to stay or go.* Atascadero, CA: Impact.

Burns, D. D. (1999). *Feeling Good.* New York: Morrow.

Dryden, W. (1994). *Overcoming Guilt!* London: Sheldon Press.

Dryden, W., and Gordon, J. (1991). *Think Your Way to Happiness.* London: Sheldon Press.

Ellis, A. (2001). *How to Stubbornly Refuse to Make Yourself Miserable About Anything—Yes, Anything!* New York: Citadel Press.

———. (2000). *How to Control Your Anxiety Before It Controls You.* New York: Kensington Publishing.

———. (1999). *How to Make Yourself Happy and Remarkably Less Disturbable.* Atascadero, Cal.: Impact Publishers.

———. (2001). *Feeling Better, Getting Better, and Staying Better.* Atascadero, Cal.: Impact Publishers.

———. (2001). *Overcoming Destructive Beliefs, Feelings, and Behaviors.* Amherst, N.Y.: Prometheus Books.

Ellis, A., and Becker, I. (1982). *A Guide to Personal Happiness.* North Hollywood, Cal.: Melvin Powers.

Ellis, A., and Crawford, T. (2002). *Making Intimate Connections.* Atascadero, Cal.: Impact Publishers.

Ellis, A., and Harper, R. A. (1997). *A Guide to Rational Living.* North Hollywood, Cal.: Melvin Powers.

———. (1961). *A Guide to Successful Marriage.* North Hollywood, Cal.: Melvin Powers, Inc.

Ellis, A., and Knaus, W. (1977). *Overcoming Procrastination.* New York: New American Library.

Ellis, A., and Lange, A. (1994). *How to Keep People from Pushing Your Buttons.* New York: Carol Publishing Group.

Ellis, A. and Powers, M. G. (2000). *The Secret of Overcoming Verbal Abuse.* North Hollywood, Cal.: Melvin Powers.

Ellis, A., and Tafrate, R. C. (2000). *How to Control Your Anger Before It Controls You.* New York, N.Y.: Citadel Press.

Ellis A., and Velten, E. (1998). *Optimal Aging: Get Over Getting Older.* Chicago: Open Court Publishing.

———. (1992). *When AA Doesn't Work for You: Rational Steps for Quitting Alcohol.* New York: Barricade Books.

FitzMaurice, K. E. (1997). *Attitude Is All You Need.* Omaha, Neb.: Palm Tree Publishers.

Freeman, A., and DeWolf, R. (1989). *Woulda, Coulda, Shoulda.* New York: Morrow.

Glasser, W. (1999). *Choice Theory.* New York: Harper Perennial.

Hauck, P. A. (1991). *Overcoming the Rating Game: Beyond Self-Love— Beyond Self-Esteem.* Louisville, K.Y.: Westminster/John Knox.

Lazarus, A. (2001). Marital myths revisited: *A fresh look at two dozen mistaken beliefs about marriage.* Atascadero, CA: Impact.

Lazarus, A., and Lazarus, C. N. (1997). *The 60-Second Shrink.* Atascadero, Cal.: Impact Publishers.

Lazarus, A., Lazarus, C., and Fay, A. (1993). *Don't Believe It for a Minute: Forty Toxic Ideas That Are Driving You Crazy.* Atascadero, Cal.: Impact Publishers.

Low, A. A. (1952). *Mental Health Through Will Training.* Boston: Christopher.

Miller, T. (1986). *The Unfair Advantage*. Manlius, N.Y.: Horsesense, Inc.

Mills, D. (1993). *Overcoming Self-Esteem*. New York: Albert Ellis Institute.

Russell, B. (1950). *The Conquest of Happiness*. New York: New American Library.

Seligman, M. E. P. (1991). *Learned Optimism*. New York: Knopf.

Vernon, Ann (Ed.) (2002). *Cognitive and rational-emotive behavior therapy with couples: Theory and practice*. New York: Springer.

Wolfe, J. L. (1992). *What to Do When He Has a Headache*. New York: Hyperion.

Young, H. S. (1974). *A Rational Counseling Primer*. New York: Albert Ellis Institute.

Index

About the Authors

Albert Ellis, Ph.D., founded Rational Emotive Behavior Therapy (REBT), the pioneering form of the modern Cognitive Behavior therapies. In a 1982 professional survey, Dr. Ellis was ranked as the second-most-influential psychotherapist in history. His name is a staple among psychologists, students, and historians around the world. He published over seven hundred articles and more than sixty books on psychotherapy, marital and family therapy, and sex therapy. Until his death in 2007, Dr. Ellis served as president emeritus of the Albert Ellis Institute in New York, which provides professional training programs and psychotherapy to individuals, families and groups. To learn more, visit www.albertellis.org.

Robert A. Harper, Ph.D., taught psychology and sociology at Wagner College from 1943 to 1945. Harper was interested in conformity in social behavior as indicated in his 1942 dissertation, "An exploratory questionnaire study of conforming and nonconforming behavior," which he completed at Ohio State University. His work was interdisciplinary, drawing from the work of Floyd Allport, considered by some to be the founder of modern social psychology, and Walter Reckless, the sociologist who supervised Harper's dissertation.

Before coming to Wagner, Harper taught at Ohio State and Kent State universities and was an area analyst in Ohio for the War Manpower Commission (created by President Roosevelt in 1942). According to the 1945–46 Wagner College catalog, he "resigned to enter war work." For a year, he worked as a psychiatric social worker in the U.S. Army.

After leaving Wagner and the army, he became a prominent marriage and family counselor. He wrote several books with Albert Ellis, the founder of Rational Emotive Behavior Therapy including *Creative Marriage* (1961), *A Guide to Successful Marriage* (1975), and *A Guide to Rational Living* (1961, with revisions in 1975 and 1998), among others. His *Psychoanalysis and Psychotherapy: 36 Systems* (1959) was one of his most influential books. His obituary was published in *American Psychologist* in 2004 (vol. 59, no. 6, p. 562).

Ann Vernon, Ph.D., Sc.D., PPC, is president of the board of trustees of the Albert Ellis Institute, one of the first diplomates of the institute, a member of the International Training Standards and Review Committee of the AEI, a member of the Board of Consulting Advisors for the *Journal of Rational-Emotive Cognitive-Behavior Therapy*, and former director of the Midwest Center for REBT. In addition, she was selected by the American Psychological Association to do a counseling video demonstration entitled Rational Emotive Behavior Therapy Over Time: Psychotherapy in Six Sessions.

Dr. Vernon is recognized as the leading international expert in applications of RE&CBT with children and adolescents and has written numerous books, chapters, and articles about counseling this population, including *Thinking, Feeling, Behaving: An Emotional Education Curriculum, What Works When with Children and Adolescents: A Handbook of Individual Counseling Techniques, The Passport Program,* and *More What Works When with Children and Adolescents.*

Dr. Vernon is professor emerita, University of Northern Iowa, and was in private practice for many years. She currently conducts RE&CBT training programs in the United States and various other parts of the world. Ann Vernon lives in Tucson, Arizona, from October to mid May; from mid May to early October she lives in Wisconsin.

Of course she had the right child! Harry was her son—he couldn't be anyone else's.

She held out her hand, preferring to end the meeting on a note of formality. 'Thank you again for driving us home.'

'It was my pleasure.'

His hand enveloped hers and Mia felt a rush of heat invade her when she felt the strength of his fingers close around hers. She quickly withdrew her hand and hurried up the path. She heard the car start up but didn't look round. She didn't want to think about Leo Forester any more that day. She just wanted to go inside the house and get on with the evening. She and Harry had a set routine and she intended to stick to it: tea, playtime, bath, story and bed. If she stuck to it her life would feel normal—but if she deviated in any way then who knew what could happen?

Dear Reader

One of the questions I am asked most frequently is where do I get my ideas for a book? I usually reply that they come from conversations I've overheard or from something I have read in the newspapers, and this book is the perfect example of that.

I was having coffee in town when I overheard two women talking about IVF. One of their daughters was undergoing IVF treatment and this lady was worried in case something went wrong. As she said to her friend, wouldn't it be awful if the wrong embryo was implanted? It immediately piqued my interest.

I kept thinking about what would happen if a woman discovered that the child she had given birth to wasn't actually hers. Of course these things rarely happen, but what an intriguing scenario for a story...

On the surface, Mia and Leo are poles apart. Mia was brought up in care and has had to work hard to earn her living, whereas Leo comes from a wealthy family and has always enjoyed the finer things in life. What unites them is the fact that each is determined to protect their child. Discovering that Harry and Noah were born to the wrong mothers is a huge shock for them both, but they are determined not to let it affect the boys. They intend to do all they can to help the children cope with a very difficult situation and make their plans accordingly. What they don't plan on happening is that they will fall in love in the process. Dare they follow their hearts? Or could they end up upsetting the boys even more? It's another dilemma they need to resolve.

I hope you enjoy Mia and Leo's story as much as I enjoyed writing it. If you would like to learn more about my books then do visit my blog: Jennifertaylorauthor.wordpress.com. I love hearing from readers, so pop in and leave a message.

Best wishes

Jennifer

THE MOTHERHOOD MIX-UP

BY
JENNIFER TAYLOR

MILLS
BOON

First published in Great Britain 2013
by Mills & Boon, an imprint of Harlequin (UK) Limited,
Large Print edition 2014
Eton House, 18-24 Paradise Road,
Richmond, Surrey, TW9 1SR

© 2013 Jennifer Taylor

ISBN: 978 0 263 23869 3

Printed and bound in Great Britain
by CPI Antony Rowe, Chippenham, Wiltshire

Jennifer Taylor lives in the north-west of England, in a small village surrounded by some really beautiful countryside. She has written for several different Mills & Boon® series in the past, but it wasn't until she read her first Medical Romance™ that she truly found her niche. She was so captivated by these heart-warming stories that she set out to write them herself! When she's not writing, or doing research for her latest book, Jennifer's hobbies include reading, gardening, travel, and chatting to friends both on and off-line. She is always delighted to hear from readers, so do visit her website at www.jennifer-taylor.com

Recent titles by Jennifer Taylor:

THE SON THAT CHANGED HIS LIFE
THE FAMILY WHO MADE HIM WHOLE*
GINA'S LITTLE SECRET
SMALL TOWN MARRIAGE MIRACLE
THE MIDWIFE'S CHRISTMAS MIRACLE
THE DOCTOR'S BABY BOMBSHELL**
THE GP'S MEANT-TO-BE BRIDE**
MARRYING THE RUNAWAY BRIDE**
THE SURGEON'S FATHERHOOD SURPRISE†

*Bride's Bay Surgery
**Dalverston Weddings
†Brides of Penhally Bay

These books are also available in ebook format from www.millsandboon.co.uk

In memory of Jean and Bob Taylor,
the best parents anyone could have had.

CHAPTER ONE

'DR KHAPUR WILL see you now, Mrs Adams.'

'Thank you.'

Mia Adams stood up and followed the receptionist along the corridor. It had been almost six years since she'd last visited the fertility clinic. Although she had intended to come back after Harry was born, to thank everyone, somehow she had never got round to it. The journey into central London from Kent had seemed too daunting with a baby in tow, plus there'd been Chris to consider.

Although Chris had coped remarkably well with the problems of living his life as a paraplegic, there had been times when he had needed that extra bit of care and attention. Consequently, the months had slipped past before she had realised it. It was doubtful if she would ever have come back, in fact, if she hadn't received that letter.

Mia frowned, wondering once again why Dr Khapur had contacted her. Harry was five now and she couldn't understand why the consultant wanted to see her. It wasn't as if she was hoping to have another child; Chris's death two years ago had ruled out that possibility. So what did Dr Khapur want? Had something happened? Something to do with Harry?

Mia's stomach lurched at the thought. It was an effort to appear composed as the receptionist ushered her into an elegantly appointed office. Dr Khapur rose from his seat, smiling warmly as he came around the desk.

'Mrs Adams! Thank you so much for coming. Please…take a seat, my dear.'

The elderly doctor guided her towards a group of comfortable chairs near the window and Mia felt her unease intensify. Whenever she had visited the clinic in the past, she had sat at one side of that huge mahogany desk and Dr Khapur had sat at the other. Maybe it was silly but this new approach made her feel more nervous than ever so that her hands were shaking as she placed her bag on the floor.

'Did you have a good journey?' Dr Khapur

asked solicitously as he sat down. He smiled at her but Mia detected a certain strain about his expression that heightened her feeling that something wasn't right. It was an effort to reply calmly when her nerves seemed to be stretched to breaking point.

'Fine, thank you, Doctor. Chris and I moved to London a few years ago, so I didn't have as far to travel.'

'Ah, I see. Good. Good.'

He rubbed his hands together and Mia had the distinct impression that he was finding it difficult to decide how to continue. She leant forward, knowing that she had to get to the bottom of what was going on. If something was wrong, and if it had anything to do with Harry, she needed to know what it was.

'Dr Khapur, I....'

She got no further when the door suddenly opened. Mia looked round in surprise, frowning when she saw the tall, dark-haired man who had entered the room. Privacy was of the utmost importance to the clinic's clients and she couldn't understand how he had got past the receptionist. That Dr Khapur was less than pleased by the interruption was obvious from the way he jumped to his feet.

'Mr Forester, please! I really cannot allow you to come barging in like this.'

'Is this her?' The man ignored Dr Khapur as he turned to Mia and she shivered when she felt his cold grey eyes sweep over her. Colour rushed to her cheeks as she imagined what he would see. Medium height, medium build, mid-brown hair and regular features didn't add up to all that much in her opinion. Her eyes were her best feature, a pure emerald green that lit up her face when she was happy. However, as she was feeling far from happy at that moment she doubted they would do much to enhance the impression he formed of her.

She stood up, surprised that she should care one way or the other what he thought of her. She had no idea who he was even though it appeared he knew her.

'I'm sorry but what exactly is going on?' She looked away from that searching grey gaze and turned to the doctor. 'I think I deserve an explanation, Dr Khapur.'

'I…ehem…' Dr Khapur began unhappily.

'Of course you do. And if I'd had my way, you would have had that explanation months ago.' The man's voice was hard, edged with an anger that Mia didn't understand, although it still affected her.

'In that case, why don't you explain it all to me, starting with your name and why you're here?' She heard the tremor in her voice and knew that he must have heard it too but it was the least of her worries. She didn't care what he thought about her. She only cared about what he was going to say and if she was right to suspect that it had something to do with Harry.

'My name is Leo Forester.' His tone was still hard but the anger had disappeared now and been replaced by something that sounded very much like compassion. Mia shuddered. She had a feeling that Leo Forester wasn't a man given to feeling compassion very often. She was already steeling herself when he continued but there was no way she could have prepared herself for the shock of his next statement.

'The reason why I am here, Mrs Adams, is quite simple. I am your son's father.'

* * *

Leo could feel the tension that had gripped him ever since he had woken up that morning reach breaking point. Just for a second his vision blurred before he ruthlessly brought himself under control. This wasn't the time to weaken. He had to get this sorted out. It wasn't only his life that would be affected by the outcome of this meeting but Noah's as well.

The thought of his son was the boost he needed. Leo ignored the fact that Mia Adams's face had turned the colour of putty. Maybe he should have tried a gentler approach but at the end of the day it wouldn't change anything. He was her son's father even if she was going to find it very hard to accept that.

'If this is some kind of a joke,' she began, but he didn't give her a chance to finish.

'It isn't. Believe me, Mrs Adams, I wouldn't joke about a thing like this.' His tone was harsh and he saw the rest of the colour leach from her face and regretted his bluntness. For a man like him, who made a point of never regretting his actions, it came as a shock, an unpleasant one too.

He couldn't afford to make allowances for Mia Adams's feelings or Noah could suffer.

He turned to Dr Kahpur, needing to get back onto a more solid footing. 'Mrs Adams and I need to talk. Is there a room we can use?'

'I'm sorry but I have no intention of going anywhere with you until I know what's going on and why you've made that ridiculous claim.'

Leo could still hear the tremor in Mia Adams's voice but it didn't disguise the steel it held as well. He realised with a start that even though she had suffered a massive shock, she wasn't simply going to accept what he had to say. A flicker of something akin to admiration rose inside him and he nodded, trying to hide his surprise. If he rarely regretted his actions then he was even less likely to form a favourable opinion of a person with such speed.

'Of course. Perhaps Dr Khapur would care to explain the situation to you.'

Leo sat down, waiting while the others resumed their seats. Mia Adams didn't look at him as she smoothed her skirt over her knees. She appeared completely composed as she waited for the elderly doctor to begin and Leo's admiration cranked itself up another notch or two. After dealing with Amanda and her constant histrionics, it was a pleasant change to meet a woman who didn't feel it necessary to create a scene to get her own way.

'This is all very difficult, my dear,' Dr Kahpur began. 'Nothing like it has ever happened before, you understand, so it's been extremely hard to know how to handle things. All I can say is that we shall do everything possible to put matters right.'

Leo forbore to say anything, although how Dr Khapur could make this situation right was beyond him. He waited in silence for the older man to continue, wishing he would get on with it. The sooner Mia Adams was in possession of the facts, the sooner they could decide what they were going to do.

'It would be a lot easier if you'd explain why this gentleman claims he is Harry's father.' Mia Adams's tone was firm. Leaning forward, she looked Dr Khapur straight in the eyes. 'I want to know the truth, Dr Khapur.'

'I… Yes, of course you do.'

Dr Khapur looked more uncomfortable than

ever at being asked a direct question and Leo realised that they wouldn't get anywhere if he left
it to him to explain what had happened. Time
was of the essence and every wasted second was
a second too long.

'It appears there was some kind of a mix-up,'
he said shortly. He adopted his blandest expression when Mia Adams turned to look at him, the
one he used when he needed to break particularly
bad news to one of his patients. In his opinion,
the absence of emotion helped people cope with
even the worst prognosis.

The fact that he knew Mia Adams would consider this the worst thing that could have happened to her made his heart pang in sudden
sympathy but he ruthlessly blanked it out. He
wasn't interested in her feelings, he reminded
himself. It was Noah who mattered, Noah and
her child, Harry. His son.

A wave of emotion rose up inside him at the
thought. Bearing in mind that he had spent his
adult life divesting himself of any hint of emotion, it took him by surprise. It was an effort to
continue when he felt so out of control.

'It seems that the embryos were implanted in

the wrong women. My ex-wife received the embryo that had been created from your egg and your husband's sperm while you received ours. In short, Mrs Adams, Amanda gave birth to your son and you gave birth to ours.'

'No!' Mia Adams leapt to her feet. She glared at him, twin spots of colour burning in her cheeks. 'I have no idea why you're making up these ridiculous lies but I refuse to sit here and listen to anything else.'

She spun round on her heel, her back rigid as she strode to the door. Dr Khapur stood up as well but Leo didn't give him the chance to intervene as he went after her. Gripping hold of her wrist, he drew her to a halt, feeling a ripple of awareness run through him when he felt the delicacy of the bones beneath his encircling fingers. They felt as fragile as a bird's, so easily crushed that unconsciously he loosened his hold even though he didn't release her.

'I am not lying. Every word I've said is true.' He bent and looked into her eyes, feeling another frisson pass through him when he found himself suddenly enmeshed in that glittering emerald gaze. He had never seen eyes that colour before, he found himself thinking inconsequentially before he brought his mind back to more important matters.

'The child you gave birth to, Mrs Adams, is, in reality, my son. And now we need to decide what we're going to do about it.'

CHAPTER TWO

MIA SANK DOWN onto a chair, praying that she wouldn't pass out. Her head was spinning from a combination of shock and fear. It couldn't be true. Harry was *her* son; she knew he was! Maybe a mistake had been made but what proof was there that she'd been involved in the mix-up?

Oh, she could understand Leo Forester's desperation—who couldn't? To discover that the child he had believed to be his wasn't his biological child must have been a terrible shock. But there was no way that he was going to lay claim to Harry!

She looked round when the door opened, feeling her heart contract with fear when she saw Leo Forester come in. Dr Khapur had acceded to his request that they should be allowed some time on their own to talk and this time she hadn't objected. The sooner this was sorted out, the better.

'Mrs Rowlands is making us some coffee. It should be ready in a moment.'

He sat down opposite her, stretching out his long legs under the coffee table. Mia studied him in silence, wondering how it must feel to discover that everything you had believed to be true was no longer certain any more. She knew how she felt, yet there was little sign of the confusion she felt apparent on his face.

How old was he? she wondered suddenly. Late thirties? Older? His hair was very dark with only a few threads of silver shining through. It was expertly cut, too, the crisp dark waves clipped close to his well-shaped head. His features were strong and very masculine—a firm jaw and well-defined cheekbones giving him an aristocratic appearance that befitted his whole bearing. Leo Forester looked like a man who was used to being in charge, a man who rarely took account of other people's opinions. It wasn't the most comforting thought in the circumstances.

A knock on the door roused her from her reverie. Leo Forester got up to answer it, taking the tray from the receptionist and carrying it over to the table. Without bothering to ask, he poured them both coffee, pushing the sugar bowl and milk jug towards her before picking up his cup. Mia added a dash of milk to her coffee, although she didn't feel in the least like drinking it. However, it gave her something to do, a few extra minutes' grace before she had to tell Leo Forester that she was very sorry but he would have to look elsewhere for his missing child. Harry was hers, hers and Chris's, and nobody was going to take him away from her.

'Before we go any further, Mrs Adams, I want to show you something.' Leo Forester put down his cup then reached into his inside pocket and took out his wallet. Flipping it open, he passed it across the table. 'This is Noah.'

Mia reluctantly took the wallet from him and glanced at the photograph, wishing that he hadn't shown it to her. It seemed wrong to build up his hopes, wrong and unnecessarily cruel. Maybe he did believe that ridiculous claim he'd made but she knew the truth, knew that Harry was her child...

Her breath caught as her eyes alighted on the solemn face of the little boy in the photograph. He had blond hair, so blond that it appeared more silver than gold. His eyes were blue, a deep dark blue framed by thick black lashes that matched the dark slash of his eyebrows and created a startling contrast to his fairness. Just as Chris's had done.

Mia felt the ground roll beneath her feet as she stared at the picture, at the small straight nose, at the determined little chin with that hint of a dimple in it. It was pure coincidence, of course. Maybe the child did look very like her late husband but it didn't prove that he was hers and Chris's child, as Leo Forester claimed.

'I take it from your expression that there's a resemblance between Noah and your husband?'

Leo Forester's voice betrayed very little of what he was feeling and Mia was grateful for that. She seemed to be awash with so many conflicting emotions that she couldn't have coped with his as well. She gave a tiny shrug, needing to hold onto what she *knew* to be the truth. Harry was her son, not this boy.

'Chris was very fair too,' she said quietly, passing the wallet back to him.

'I wondered who Noah favoured.' Leo Forester slid the wallet into his pocket and picked up his coffee cup. His hand was rock steady as he lifted it to his lips and all of a sudden Mia found herself resenting the fact that he could behave this way. Surely any normal person would be torn in two, wondering and worrying about this situation?

'The fact that your son happens to have similar colouring to my husband is hardly proof, Mr Forester.' Scorn dripped from her voice but if she'd hoped to sting him into a reaction she was disappointed. His expression didn't alter as he looked steadily at her over the rim of the cup.

'Of course not. It will need DNA tests to confirm it. I suggest we make arrangements to have them done as soon as possible.'

'I have no intention of allowing Harry to be tested!' She glared at him, feeling a wave of anger wash away the fear that had invaded her ever since he'd made that ridiculous claim. 'I'm very sorry for you, Mr Forester. I'm sure that in your shoes I would do everything possible to get to the bottom of this matter. However, Harry isn't your son. He's mine. Mine and Chris's.'

'And if that is true then the DNA results will prove it.' He shrugged, his broad shoulders moving lightly under his perfectly tailored jacket.

That he was a wealthy man wasn't in doubt and Mia felt a fresh rush of fear hit her. Leo Forester obviously had the means to pursue this if he chose. If he decided to take it to the courts, he would be able to hire the very best lawyers to make his case. Even though she was working, she had no hope of fighting him if it came to a lengthy legal battle. She simply didn't have the money. Perhaps it would be wiser to concede this point in case the fight became more desperate in the future?

The thought of what might happen in the future made her inwardly tremble but she had learned at an early age to hide her feelings. She looked steadily back at him, wishing that she had followed her instincts and never agreed to visit the clinic. She'd had a bad feeling when that letter had arrived out of the blue, although not for a moment had she imagined that something like this would happen.

'If you're determined to go down that route then I shall agree to have Harry tested on one condition.'

'And that is?' Leo Forester raised a dark brow. His expression was as bland as ever but Mia could see a nerve tic in his jaw and realised, with a start, that he was nowhere near as composed as he was pretending to be. The thought was comforting for some reason and her tone softened.

'That Harry isn't told anything about this. He's only five and it will just confuse him if he's told that Chris might not be his daddy.'

'I have no intention of telling him or Noah anything until we get the results of the DNA tests.'

Leo Forester put his cup down with a clatter and Mia realised, with another start that he'd had to put it down because his hands were shaking. Maybe he did prefer to keep a rein on his emotions, but beneath that cool exterior there was definitely passion brewing. It made her wonder what would happen if he ever let himself go.

Mia pushed that thought aside. What Leo Forester did or didn't feel was of no consequence, except where it concerned Harry, of course. She needed to make it clear that any hopes he was harbouring about claiming her son as his own were never going to come to fruition.

'I shall arrange to have a DNA profile done on Harry. Once I receive the results, I'll contact you. Obviously I'll need an address or telephone number where you can be reached.'

'I'll give you my card.' He took out his wallet again and pulled out an ivory-coloured card. He didn't hand it over immediately, however.

'It seems pointless you having to go to all the trouble of finding someone to carry out the DNA tests, Mrs Adams. Why don't you leave me to make the arrangements?'

'Thank you but I'd prefer to do it myself,' Mia said shortly, and he frowned.

'Because you don't trust me not to pull some sort of a stunt so that the results come back in my favour?'

Mia heard the irritation in his deep voice but it didn't bother her. There was too much at stake to worry about his finer feelings, if he really had any, of course. It was disappointing to wonder if she'd been wrong about him. Maybe what you saw was what you got and in this instance it appeared that the handsome Leo Forester was a very cold fish indeed.

'Yes.' She took the card off him, annoyed that she should waste even a second thinking about him. Leo Forester had come into her life uninvited and definitely unwelcome and the sooner she got rid of him, the better. 'I have no intention of allowing you to pull the wool over my eyes, Mr Forester. Whilst I feel very sorry for the plight you find yourself in, it really isn't my concern. The only person I'm interested in is my son.'

She stood up, picking up her bag and looping the strap over her shoulder. Leo Forester stood up as well and for a moment she thought he was going to stop her again when she tried to leave. However, in the event, he merely stepped aside so she could pass.

'Thank you,' Mia murmured politely. She made her way to the door, curbing the urge to run. She wouldn't give him the satisfaction of knowing how scared she felt, how fearful of the future. *Harry was her son.* She repeated the mantra as she reached for the handle, hoping it would help her maintain her control. For some reason it seemed important that she shouldn't let Leo Forester know how terrified she was.

'Aren't you forgetting something, Mrs Adams?'

Mia had actually opened the door when he spoke and she paused reluctantly, wondering if he had done it deliberately, almost let her escape before calling her back, like a cat playing with a mouse. She glanced round, smoothing her face into a carefully neutral expression. He might enjoy playing games but she had no intention of being party to them.

'I don't think so.' She shrugged. 'What else is there to say until the results of the DNA tests come back?'

'Obviously, I need an address or, at the very least, a phone number where I can contact you.'

'Why would you want to contact me?' Mia countered. 'You and I have nothing further to discuss, Mr Forester. As I'm sure the DNA results will prove.'

Mia walked out of the door, half expecting him to call her back again, but he didn't. She made her way along the corridor, shaking her head when Dr Khapur's secretary jumped up and told her that the doctor wanted to speak to her. She didn't want to speak to him. Not right now, anyway. At some point she would need an explanation as to why she'd been involved in this ridiculous affair but not right now. Right now all she wanted to do was go home and see Harry. *Her* son, not Leo Forester's.

* * *

Leo cursed himself as he strode along the corridor. He had made a complete and utter hash of things and ended up making an already difficult situation worse. Wrenching open the door, he stepped out into the street, wondering why he had allowed Mia Adams to get to him that way. He knew what had to be done; he should do because he'd gone over it enough times. However, all the careful arguments he'd rehearsed, the calm and rational statements he had planned, had simply melted away. He had taken one look at the fear on Mia Adam's face and bottled it. Hell!

There was a taxi dropping off a fare at the corner. Leo flagged it down and gave the driver the address of the hospital. He was due in Theatre at two and it was almost that now. The taxi dropped him off outside the main doors and he hurried inside, nodding briefly to the porter.

Although he divided his time between his private practice in Harley Street and his NHS commitments, he was well known at the hospital, if not well liked. He was a hard taskmaster and he knew that the members of his team admired rather than liked him. It had never worried him before but as he made his way up in the lift, he suddenly found himself wishing that he had a better rapport with the people he worked with. If he had taken the trouble to develop his social skills, maybe he would have had better luck convincing Mia Adams to trust him.

Leo's mouth compressed as he stepped out of the lift. He wasn't given to such foolish thoughts normally and it was irritating to be beset by them today. The sooner he got himself in hand, the better. Mia Adams might be hoping this situation would go away but he knew it wasn't that simple. This was just the beginning and there was going to be a lot more upset before this matter was resolved. It wasn't only him and Mrs Adams who would suffer either. There were two little boys whose lives were going to have to change.

Mia was on duty the following morning. She took Harry to the school's breakfast club and left him happily demolishing a bowl of cereal then walked to the station. It was almost three years since she had moved to London. Chris had been offered a job with a leading firm of accountants and they had decided it was too good an opportunity to miss. The fact that Chris had been confined to a wheelchair following a climbing accident in his twenties had severely restricted his job options; however, the firm hadn't seen it as a problem.

Chris had loved the job and enjoyed every minute of his working life. Mia knew that moving to the city had been the right thing to do but she couldn't help wondering if she should move back to Kent at some point. Harry would not only benefit from all the fresh air and open spaces to play in, he'd be able to spend more time with his grandparents. The downside, of course, was that she would have to give up her job and she doubted if she would find another that would allow her to spend so much time with Harry.

As a senior sister, working as part of the bank of nurses at The Princess Rose Hospital, she could pick her own hours. She had worked mornings when Harry had been at nursery so she could be home in time to collect him at lunchtime. Now that Harry had started school, she had increased her hours and was thinking about going full time soon—heaven knew they could do with the extra money. However, as it would mean Harry having to stay at the after-school club until she got home, she had decided to leave the decision until after Christmas. Harry would have settled into school by then and she'd feel happier about leaving him for longer.

The train was late as usual and she had to run to reach the hospital in time for her shift. Penny Morrison, who organised the bank nurses, grinned when Mia came panting into the office.

'Either you're in training for the next London Marathon or the train was late. My guess is that it's the second option.'

'You'd be right too.' Mia hung her coat in her locker then took a comb out of her bag and tidied her hair. 'I wish they'd invest in some new trains. I mean, they wouldn't break down as often if they weren't so old, would they?'

'Ah, but new trains cost money and nobody has any these days, or so they claim.'

Penny picked up the spreadsheet she used to sort out where everyone was working. There were fifteen bank nurses and they covered all the departments as and when they were needed. It was a system that worked well and had reduced the high costs of hiring agency nurses to provide cover.

'Right, you're down for Cardiology this week. The ward sister has sprained her ankle and she's off sick. You might end up there a bit longer, in fact.'

'Fine by me. I've not covered Cardiology before so it will be nice to do something different,' Mia agreed. 'Anything I should know beforehand?'

'Not really. Oh, apart from the fact that one of the consultants is a bit of a tartar so watch your back.' Penny rolled her eyes. 'Jackie was there a couple of weeks ago and she's refused to go back if he's on duty.'

'Heavens! He sounds a real sweetheart, I don't think.' Mia grimaced as she took her ID out of her bag and clipped it to the pocket of her navy uniform top. One of the other nurses arrived just then so she left Penny to deal with her and made her way to the third floor where the cardiology unit was situated. Everything looked very peaceful when she arrived and she grinned at the staff nurse who'd been holding the fort until she got there.

'Either all your patients are extremely well behaved or you've sedated them. Which is it?'

'Neither.' The staff nurse grimaced. 'They're simply too scared to kick up a fuss.'

Mia laughed. 'You don't look that scary to me.'

'Oh, it's not me who's terrified them into submission.' The younger woman looked over Mia's shoulder and groaned. 'Here's your culprit now. And that's my cue to beat a hasty retreat. Good luck. You'll need it!'

Mia looked round, the smile still lingering on her lips as she looked at the man walking towards her. He was tall with dark hair lightly threaded with silver and chiselled features…

All of a sudden the room started to whirl, spinning faster and faster until she felt quite giddy. What on earth was Leo Forester doing here?

CHAPTER THREE

'THESE NOTES ARE incomplete, Sister. Make sure the file is updated before I return for my afternoon round. I shouldn't need to remind you that it's your job to ensure that all the information I require is available.'

Leo handed the file to Mia Adams. He turned to the two new F1 students who had joined his team the previous week, ignoring the wary look that passed between them. Maybe he had been rather hard on Sister Adams but he wouldn't tolerate incompetence in any shape or form.

'Mrs Davies will be having bypass surgery tomorrow. What needs to be done beforehand to ensure the operation goes smoothly?' he demanded, ignoring the voice in his head that insisted he was being unreasonable. So what if Mia Adams had taken charge of the unit only that morning? As ward sister, it was her responsibility to ensure that everything was up to date. Far too many errors occurred because staff had omitted some vital piece of information.

The thought reminded him rather too pointedly of the error that had been made over Noah. Finding out that the child he had believed to be his son had no biological connection to him and Amanda had been a terrible shock and he still hadn't got over it. He loved Noah with all his heart and there was no way that he was prepared to give him up, but he still needed to find out the truth, prove that Mia's child—Harry—was his real son. After that, well, he had no idea what would happen. It all depended on what Mia Adams decided.

The thought that so much was hanging on her decision wasn't easy to accept. Leo was used to running his life his own way and rarely made allowances for other people. It was little wonder that his tone was brusquer than ever when the students failed to answer. He didn't want to be beholden to Mia Adams, but he might not have a choice.

'I fail to see why you're finding it so difficult to come up with an answer.' He pinned the unhappy pair with an icy stare. 'This is something you should have covered in your first year as students. If you can't answer a simple question like this then you are of no use to me.'

'May I suggest we take this into the office?'

Leo looked round in surprise when Mia Adams cut in. He wasn't used to being interrupted and didn't appreciate her making suggestions. He opened his mouth to tell her that in no uncertain terms but she had already moved away. Leo frowned as he watched his team follow her to the office. They hadn't waited for his permission; they had simply done her bidding and it was a shock, an unpleasant one, to realise that they preferred to follow her lead rather than his.

'I'll come back to see you later, Mrs Davies,' he said politely, noticing for the first time that the woman was trembling. She gave him a wan smile as he moved away from the bed and Leo found himself wondering what was wrong with her. She'd appeared perfectly composed when he had arrived but obviously something had upset her.

His mouth thinned as he strode towards the office. It was Mia Adams's fault, of course. Mrs Davies had picked up on the tension and reacted accordingly. Well, he intended to take Sister Adams to task and make sure she understood who was in charge before she upset any more of his patients.

'A word, please, Sister Adams,' he began as he entered the office.

'Just a moment, Mr Forester.' She barely glanced at him as she carried on issuing instructions to one of the nurses and Leo felt his temper leap up a couple more notches. He was the consultant and although he didn't consider himself to be next to God in the pecking order, he did expect to be treated with due respect.

'After you've sorted that out, Sally, can you take Mrs Davies a cup of tea? She's a bit upset so sit with her, will you? It will help to calm her down if she has someone to talk to.'

Mia smiled at the younger nurse, giving no sign that she was worried about keeping him waiting, and Leo had to clamp down on the urge he felt to do something drastic, like shake her. Bearing in mind that he wasn't a man given to violence on any level it was a surprise to find himself reacting this way. It was little wonder that he was caught flat-footed when she turned to him.

'There's something you wish to say to me, Mr Forester?'

Her tone was cool in the extreme and he saw several members of his team glance at each other in amazement. Nobody spoke to him this way. Nobody queried his decisions or interrupted him either. Nobody had ever dared—until now. Leo's temper, which had been hovering just below boiling point, peaked and he glared at her.

'Yes. Let me make this clear, Sister Adams. When I am with a patient I don't expect to be interrupted. Do you understand?'

'Perfectly. However, I think it's only fair that I make my position clear too. The patients are my responsibility while they're on this unit. That means that if I notice that someone is in pain or upset I shall do something about it.' She paused, her emerald-green eyes meeting his across the desk, and if there was any hint of remorse in them Leo certainly couldn't see any sign of it. 'Mrs Davies was becoming increasingly distressed by the way you were speaking to your students. Naturally I took steps to resolve the matter.'

Mia held his gaze, wondering when the heavens were going to fall in on her. That Leo Forester was less than pleased by what she had said

JENNIFER TAYLOR   39

was obvious but she didn't care. Nobody should be allowed to speak to people the way he had spoken to those poor students. Maybe other folk were willing to put up with his bad temper but she wasn't, especially not after the havoc he had created in her life.

The claim he had made about Harry being his son had been on her mind constantly for the past twenty-four hours. Although she was sure it was a mistake, she couldn't quite rid herself of the thought, *what if*? What if he was right? What if Harry was his son and what if Noah was hers? What if the DNA tests proved it? Then what would happen? Her mind kept churning it all over but there were never any answers. How could there be? The situation was way beyond anything she'd had to deal with before. It made everything else that had happened in her life pale into insignificance. If Harry wasn't her son, she had no idea what she was going to do.

Thoughts flashed through her mind at the speed of light yet it felt as though a lifetime had passed when she focused on Leo Forester again. That he was furiously angry was obvious and she decided there and then that the only way to deal with him was by fighting fire with fire. Maybe it was wrong to allow their personal issues to spill over into work but she refused to bow down before him on any matter. Harry was her son. She was responsible for the patients on this unit; they were both unassailable facts.

'If you have a problem with the way I run this ward I suggest you take it up with the head of Nursing. I'm sure she will be happy to discuss any issues you care to raise.'

She picked up the file and walked around the desk, pausing when she came level with him. Even though several inches separated them she could feel the power of his anger like a living force and inwardly shuddered. Leo Forester would make a very bad enemy. It was a scary thought in view of what had happened.

'Please feel free to use my office, Mr Forester. I shall make sure you aren't interrupted.'

Mia swept out of the door, half expecting him to call her back, but surprisingly he didn't. She made her way to the nursing station and logged into the patients' records. Leo Forester was right: there was something missing from Anthea Davies's notes. The woman had had an angiogram the previous week and the results needed to be added to her file. Mia made the necessary changes and printed out a fresh sheet and placed it in the file. Contrary to what Leo Forester thought, she was always thorough, always liked to be prepared to prevent any mistakes occurring.

She sighed as she went over to the cabinet and filed the notes in their rightful place. If only the staff at the fertility clinic had been as thorough she and Leo Forester would not be having to face such a potentially life-changing situation.

Leo was tied up in Theatre for the rest of the morning. However, as soon as he'd finished he changed back into his clothes and headed for the cardiology unit. Whilst he hadn't been prepared to make matters worse by causing a scene, he had no intention of letting Mia get away with treating him that way. Maybe they did have issues, issues that none of their colleagues knew about, but he wasn't going to let her make a laughing stock of him.

She was in the men's section of the unit when he arrived, talking to one of his patients, a young man called David Rimmer who had a long history of heart problems. David had been born with several holes in his heart and had been in and out of hospital over the past twenty-two years. Recently, he had started to suffer from cardiac arrhythmia—an abnormal and rapid heartbeat— and he would be having cardioversion that afternoon. His heart would be stopped before an electric current was passed through it, hopefully shocking it back into its proper rhythm. Although Leo knew that David must be in a lot of discomfort, he grinned when he saw Leo approaching.

'Seems you've met your match at last, eh, Doc? The buzz on the ward is that Mia gave you a real rollicking this morning. I only wish I'd been there to see it!'

Leo summoned a smile, not wanting the younger man to think he was at all put out to learn that he was the subject of gossip. 'You shouldn't believe everything you hear, David. It's not always true.'

David laughed. 'You would say that! Still, it's nice to know that you're human after all. It's done wonders for your image.'

Leo frowned. How on earth could his run-in with Mia have improved his image? He glanced around the unit, feeling his surprise intensify when several patients smiled at him. Normally, he found that people were rather reserved around him, but not today. As he looked at the friendly faces turned towards him, he felt a sudden warmth envelop him. It was rather nice to be on the receiving end of smiles for once.

He cleared his throat, refusing to get carried away by such a ridiculous notion. He much preferred it that his patients should value him for his skills as a surgeon rather than as a potential friend. 'I wonder if I might have a word with you, Sister?' he said politely. Maybe he wasn't out to win friends but there didn't seem any harm in observing the niceties.

'Of course.' Mia's tone was icily polite. She turned to the younger man and Leo couldn't help feeling the tiniest bit irked when he heard the warmth in her voice as she wished David good luck. Obviously, *he* didn't rate that level of concern.

The thought was irritating, although Leo was very aware that he was behaving completely out of character. Normally, he wouldn't have cared a jot how people addressed him, as long as they weren't rude, of course. Nevertheless, Mia's distant approach stung. For a second he found himself wondering how it would feel if she addressed him with genuine affection in her voice before he dismissed the idea. It was never going to happen, not after the havoc he was about to create in her life.

He led the way into the office and closed the door. He didn't want any interruptions, nothing and nobody to throw him off course. Maybe they were facing a very difficult situation but he needed to lay down some ground rules. Mia didn't look at him as she walked around the desk and sat down. She appeared perfectly composed but Leo sensed her inner turmoil and for some reason the harsh words he'd been going to say seemed wrong. This was as stressful for her as it was for him; maybe he could afford to lighten up a little.

'Before you say anything I want to apologise. I should never have spoken to you like that this morning.'

The apology caught him on the hop. Leo hadn't expected it and found himself struggling to reply.

'No, you shouldn't,' he said more sharply than he'd intended.

She gave a little shrug, her slender shoulders rising and falling beneath her navy cotton uniform, and he felt a flash of awareness shoot through him. For the first time since they'd met, he *really* looked at her, deliberately taking stock instead of simply forming an overall impression.

Her features were neat and regular: a firm little chin; a short straight nose; softly rounded cheeks. Her skin was very pale, almost translucent in the harsh glare of the fluorescent light overhead. Her hair was a soft mid-brown, caught neatly back from her face with a plain black clip. Her eyes were her best feature, a pure emerald green that seemed to glitter with an inner fire that fascinated him. Some people might have described Mia Adams as ordinary but not him, he decided. Not when he looked into those incredible eyes.

Leo took a deep breath, used it to shore up his world, a world that seemed to be falling apart around him. First there'd been the shock of discovering that Noah wasn't his child and now this. He couldn't be attracted to Mia Adams; he wouldn't allow himself to be! However, as he

looked at that ordinary little face and those ex-
traordinary eyes staring back at him, he realised
that he might not have a choice. There was something about her that intrigued him, and it had
nothing to do with the fact that she had given
birth to his son.

Mia bit her lip, wishing that Leo Forrester would
say something. He was staring at her with the
oddest expression on his face...

He suddenly spun round on his heel and strode
out of the room, leaving her staring after him in
confusion. She hadn't expected him to let her off
so lightly. Maybe she had apologised, and meant
it too, but she'd been sure he would give her a
dressing down. He'd have been perfectly within
his rights to do so because she had overstepped
the mark that morning.

Normally, she wouldn't have dreamt of speaking to a consultant that way. But she'd not even
tried to hold back as she had told him what she
thought. Maybe this situation was unusual but
she would be extremely lucky if he didn't make
a formal complaint about her and heaven only
knew what would happen then. Staff had been

sacked for less and the thought of losing her job was worrying. She would need every penny she could earn if it came to a legal battle over Harry.

Somehow Mia got through the rest of the morning and did the hand-over. It was after two p.m. when she collected her coat from the staffroom. Penny was at her desk; she looked up and grinned when Mia went in.

'Well done, you! I hear you sent the redoubtable Leo Forester away with a flea in his ear.'

'Don't!' Mia grimaced as she shrugged on her coat. 'I suppose it's all round the hospital?'

'Of course. Suffice to say that most folk consider you to be a real heroine. Leo Forester isn't exactly top of everyone's Christmas card list,' Penny added dryly.

'I really shouldn't have said what I did,' Mia admitted. 'It was a stupid thing to do.'

'You're only human, love. Which is more than I can say for the handsome Leo. Heaven only knows how he ever became a father. Oh, he's gorgeous looking and everything, but he's so *cold*. I mean, can you imagine him letting go enough to actually make love to a woman?'

Mia felt a tide of heat sweep up her face. She

bent down to retrieve her bag from the locker, not wanting Penny to witness her reaction to the question. Maybe Penny couldn't imagine it but she could. Only too well.

Fortunately the phone rang so she was saved from having to reply. Mia mouthed 'Goodbye' and left hurriedly. If the trains were running on time, she should be home just in time to collect Harry from school. She headed out of the main doors, pulling up the hood of her coat when she discovered it was raining. Afternoon visiting was under way and there were cars coming and going from all directions. She paused to allow an expensive sports car to pass through the gates ahead of her, sighing when it stopped and the passenger window rolled down. No doubt someone was going to ask her if she knew where they could park.

'Get in.'

Mia jumped when a deep voice barked out the command. Bending, she peered into the car, feeling her heart leap when she saw Leo Forester behind the wheel. His expression was as bland as ever but she could see a spark of something in his eyes that warned her it would be a mistake to argue with him. Opening the door, she slid into the seat, buckling the seat belt as he pulled out of the gates. They drove in silence for several minutes before he spoke.

'I think it would be best if we agreed to forget what happened today. Neither of us expected to find ourselves working together, but as there's nothing we can do about it, we'll just have to get on with it.'

Mia felt a rush of relief flood through her. 'You don't intend to make a complaint about me, then?'

'Of course not.'

He sounded so surprised that she grimaced. 'I thought you might, that's all.'

'Well, you can stop worrying. I won't be making any complaints, not unless you do it again, of course. I don't think my ego could take another battering.'

The hint of laughter in his voice was so unexpected that Mia stared at him. 'I was sure you'd want to teach me a lesson.'

'I probably would have done if circumstances had been different.' His grey eyes met hers for a second before he returned his attention to

the road but it was long enough to make Mia's
heart race.

She took a deep breath, calling herself every
kind of a fool. Leo wasn't interested in her, not
the person she was. He was only interested in
Harry. She had to remember that and not allow
herself be duped into thinking that he cared about
her feelings any more than she must care about
his. It was the children who mattered, Harry and
his son Noah. And his next words confirmed that.

'I assume that you're going to collect your son
from school?' He drew up at the traffic lights and
turned to look at her. Mia steeled herself when
she saw how solemn he looked. She had a feeling
that she wasn't going to like what he had to say.

'Yes, I am. Why?'

'Because I'd like to ask a favour of you.' His
eyes held hers fast and for some reason she found
that she couldn't look away. 'May I go with you,
Mia? And meet Harry?'

CHAPTER FOUR

ONCE, JUST BEFORE he had gone off to university, Leo had made a parachute jump. All his friends had been keen to try it and he'd gone along with them. In the event, most of them had chickened out so there'd been just two of them in the plane and he'd been the first to jump. As he had stood in the doorway, watching the ground rushing past below, he had felt his stomach sink with a mixture of excitement and fear. Although he had never jumped again, he remembered the feeling quite clearly. It was exactly how he felt as he waited to meet Mia's son, scared and elated because he was about to leap into the unknown.

'There he is.'

Mia touched him on the arm and Leo flinched. He looked over to where she was pointing but he couldn't pick out one child from another. There seemed to be a sea of small excited faces staring back at him…

Leo's breath caught as his eyes alighted on a sturdy little boy with dark brown hair standing up in spikes around his head. It had to be Harry; he just knew it was! Even though he would have dismissed the idea that his genes had somehow recognised those of his son if anyone had suggested it, he knew it was true.

Anyway, the boy had his nose as well as his hair. He had his chin too *and* his cheekbones, he realised in astonishment. In fact, the resemblance was so marked that he couldn't understand why Mia hadn't noticed it. Surely she could see how alike they were, he thought as she brought the child over to meet him?

'Harry, this is Leo. He's a doctor and he works at the hospital. He very kindly gave me a lift here so I wouldn't be late.'

Leo had to hand it to her. Even though she must be finding it extremely difficult, there was no hint of uncertainty in her voice as she made the introductions. Her only concern was for her son and his admiration for her increased tenfold, especially when he found himself comparing the way she behaved to the way Amanda would have reacted.

The thought of the scene his ex-wife would have created was very hard to swallow and his mouth thinned with displeasure. Harry took one look at his grim expression and scooted behind his mother's legs. Leo took a deep breath, cursing himself for allowing thoughts of Amanda to spoil the moment. Amanda had caused enough damage without him allowing her to ruin this too.

'Hello, Harry. It's nice to meet you.' Leo fixed a smile to his mouth but Harry obviously wasn't convinced it was genuine. He shrank away when Leo held out his hand.

'He'll come round,' Mia said quietly. 'Just give him a moment.'

She led Harry to the gate, leaving Leo to follow. There were a lot of parents milling about and they soon disappeared from view. Leo experienced a moment of panic as he peered over the crowd because he still had no idea where she lived. Maybe it was selfish but he needed a few more minutes with Harry, a bit more time to get to know his son.

The words seemed to dance in neon-bright letters before his eyes. Harry was his son; he was more certain than ever it was true. But where did that leave Noah? He loved Noah with an intensity he had never believed himself capable of feeling. From the moment he had been handed the wrinkled, bloodied little bundle in the delivery room, he had known that he would lay down his life to protect him. Amanda had got over her longing for a child by then and hadn't even wanted to look at the miracle they had created, but he had been entranced, thrilled, enthralled.

When Amanda had decided after six months of motherhood that it wasn't for her, Leo hadn't argued and he certainly hadn't tried to stop her leaving. He had never actually loved her but she had been sophisticated and worldly and had suited his requirements, as he had suited hers.

Their parting had been amicable enough and he'd been relieved that he'd been left, both physically and metaphorically, holding the baby. It had meant he could bring up Noah the way he wanted, make sure Noah enjoyed a far happier childhood than he'd had. If only Amanda had stayed away none of this would have happened.

The crowd parted and he spotted Mia and Harry standing by the gates. He hurried to join them, seeing the way the child shrank back as he approached. It grieved him that he had made such a bad impression on the boy and he promised himself that he would do everything possible to rectify it. If he was to be part of Harry's life he wanted the child to feel comfortable around him.

'I'll run you home,' he said, refusing to dwell on the thought that he might not get the chance to play daddy to his son. It all depended on what Mia decided and as he had no idea what that would be, he couldn't go counting his proverbial chickens. Unlocking the car, he flipped forward the passenger seat so Harry could climb into the back. It was a tight squeeze and Leo realised not for the first time that he would have to buy something more suitable. Maybe he did love his car but with two children to consider now, it was hardly the most suitable of vehicles.

Mia made sure that Harry's belt was buckled then slid into the passenger seat. Leo closed the door and went round to the driver's side. He started the engine then glanced at her, seeing the strain that had etched tiny grooves at the sides of her mouth. His hands clenched on the steering wheel because the urge to reach out and smooth them away was almost too strong to resist. How-

ever, he had to resist it, had to resist doing anything that might alienate her.

'Where to?' he asked instead, sounding brusque
and cold when he had meant to sound warm and
approachable for Harry's benefit.

'Straight down the road and left at the junction.'

She glanced over her shoulder and smiled at
Harry and Leo saw the little boy's face immediately brighten as he checked the rear-view mirror before pulling out. That there was a deep and
loving bond between the pair was obvious and
he found himself wishing with all his heart that
Noah could have had that sort of a relationship
with Amanda. The problem was that Amanda
put herself and her needs first every time. Noah
came way down her list of priorities, somewhere
below the next designer handbag she coveted or
the next exotic holiday.

Leo could feel his mouth tightening again
and fought to control it. If he was to win Harry
round, he not only needed Mia's co-operation
but a major re-think about his own behaviour.
He sighed. He had realised from the moment he
had discovered that Noah wasn't his biological
child that his life was going to undergo a massive

upheaval, but only now did he understand how much *he* was going to have to change.

'It's the house with the red door…just there on the left. Yes, that's it.'

Mia gathered up her bag, trying to control the urge to leap out of the car. She wasn't sure why she had agreed to let Leo meet Harry but it had been a mistake. She glanced round, seeing the worry on her son's face. Although Harry was a happy and loving little boy, like most children his age he hated unexpected changes to his routine. Being ferried home by a stranger, even in such a luxurious vehicle as this, was obviously troubling him.

'Thank you again for the lift,' she said politely, turning to Leo. Although she was eager to get Harry into the house, there was no way that she was going to be rude. She summoned a smile when Leo looked at her. 'I hope we haven't taken you too far out of your way.'

'Not at all.' He shrugged. 'I live in Primrose Hill so it's only a short drive from here.'

A short drive maybe, but there was a massive difference in property prices, Mia thought wryly, glancing at the neat little terraced house they were parked in front of. She hurriedly opened the car door, not wanting to go down that route. Continually worrying if Leo intended to use his extensive resources to lay claim to Harry was counterproductive. She got out of the car then turned to unlatch the seat so Harry could get out, frowning when she found herself fumbling with the unfamiliar mechanism.

'Let me do it.'

Leo gently moved her aside and tipped the seat forward. He offered Harry his hand but the child ignored him. Jumping out of the car, he ran up the path to the house and stood there with his back towards them. Mia sighed softly.

'Harry hates it when his routine is changed. He prefers it when he knows exactly what is going to happen and when.'

'It might have helped if I'd made a better impression,' Leo observed, and Mia frowned when she heard the regret in his voice. He hadn't struck her as a man who ever regretted his actions; he came across as far too confident for that. However, it appeared she may have been wrong.

It was worrying to think that she might have misjudged him. Mia cleared her throat, not wanting him to guess how unnerved she felt. 'Children are highly susceptible to people's moods and Harry has become even more sensitive since Chris died. He was only three when it happened so he didn't really understand what was going on, but he saw how upset I was and it made a big impression on him.'

'I see.' Leo frowned. 'I didn't know that you'd lost your husband. I'm very sorry.'

'Thank you.' Mia felt a lump come to her throat when she heard the sympathy in his voice. Although she had come to terms with Chris's death, it touched her that Leo should offer his condolences and mean them too.

'Was it an accident? He couldn't have been very old, I imagine.'

'Indirectly, yes, it was.' She took a quick breath, knowing that she couldn't afford to let his response influence her. Until she was sure that she could trust him with regard to Harry, she needed to be objective.

'Chris was injured in a climbing accident while he was at university. He suffered serious spinal damage and was unable to walk afterwards.' She shrugged, aware of how hard it was going to be to remain dispassionate. Leo wasn't the sort of man one could ignore. 'As you know, being confined to a wheelchair makes people more susceptible to certain conditions and sadly that's what happened with Chris.'

'I'm sorry,' he repeated. 'It must have been a very difficult time for you.'

Mia inclined her head, deciding it was safer not to pursue the matter. Talking about Chris's death always upset her and she couldn't afford to allow her emotions to get the better of her. She quickly changed the subject to one that seemed more fitting.

'I have the address of a lab that does DNA testing. I'll collect the samples tonight and post them off first thing tomorrow morning. I should have the results back by the end of the week.'

'Will there be a problem about providing a sample of your husband's DNA?' he queried, frowning.

'No.' Mia didn't elaborate. She didn't want to explain why she had kept Chris's hairbrush. It was the last link she had to him, the only thing left of the man who had given her so much; however, there was no way she intended to explain that to Leo. She forced a smile to her lips, hating the fact that she felt so emotional. It wasn't just thinking about Chris—it was everything else, Harry and Noah and what would happen if it turned out that she and Leo really did have the wrong children.

'Anyway, I mustn't keep you. You must be anxious to get home,' she said, blanking out the thought. Of course she had the right child! Harry was her son and he couldn't be anyone else's. As the DNA results would prove. She held out her hand, preferring to end the meeting on a note of formality. 'Thank you again for driving us home.'

'It was my pleasure.'

His hand enveloped hers and Mia felt a rush of heat invade her when she felt the strength of his fingers close around hers. She quickly withdrew her hand and hurried up the path. She heard the car start up but she didn't look round. She didn't want to think about Leo Forester any more that day. She just wanted to go inside the house and get on with the evening. She and Harry had a set routine and she intended to stick to it—tea, playtime, bath, story, bed. If she stuck to it her life would feel normal but if she deviated in any way then who knew what could happen.

Mia bit her lip. There was one change to their routine she would have to make. She had promised to collect the DNA samples and she couldn't break her word even if she wanted to. What would happen if the tests proved that Harry wasn't her son? she wondered sickly. How would she cope with having her whole world torn apart?

Having a child of her own had always been her dream. She had been taken into care when her own mother had been unable to cope with looking after her. Her father had been well off the scene by then. Mia had never met him and didn't even know his name so she had spent her childhood being shunted from one foster-home to another.

She had longed for someone to love and care for her, but it hadn't happened. Her mother had refused to allow her to be put up for adoption so Mia had had to make do with temporary placements. Some had been good, others not so good, but the worst thing was that none of them had been permanent.

She had grown up longing for a home and a

family of her own, although she had been very choosy about who she had gone out with. She hadn't intended to make the same mistakes her mother had made and had turned down more dates than she had accepted. She had earned herself a reputation for being very stand-offish, in fact, and that in turn had led to the incident that still haunted her.

When the new registrar on the spinal unit where she had worked had invited her out, she had refused at first. Although Steve Parker had seemed pleasant enough, Mia hadn't been sure if it would be wise to go out with him. Steve was a bit of flirt and she had had no intention of becoming another notch on his bedpost. However, he had persisted and in the end he had worn her down.

They had gone out together several times and Mia had found herself enjoying his company. Steve had been fun and attentive and it had felt good to be on the receiving end of his compliments and feel special. Although she had never slept with a man before, she'd realised that she wanted to sleep with Steve so when he had suggested they should spend the night together, she'd agreed.

It was a complete and utter disaster. Steve was so rough and insensitive, making no allowance for the fact that it was her first time. Mia couldn't wait for it to be over and left as soon as she could. She tried to write it off to experience but it wasn't possible, not after she found out that Steve had been spreading stories about her, claiming that she was frigid and that any man foolish enough to get her into bed would regret it. However, the final humiliation came when she learned that he'd also claimed he had only slept with her to win a bet and that he was sorry he had bothered. As he'd put it, it would have been better if he'd forfeited the money!

Mia was mortified and swore she would never allow anything like it to happen again. She never went out on a date after that and might never have seen her dreams come true if Chris hadn't been admitted to the spinal unit. She nursed him back to health, sat with him while he struggled to come to terms with what had happened, and grew to love him for his humour and his courage. When he asked her to marry him, she accepted immediately, sure that it was the right decision.

And when she had Harry, she knew that she had everything she had ever wanted.

Now it appeared that nothing was certain any more. All she knew was that if she lost Harry, her life would be meaningless.

By the time Friday rolled around, Leo felt as though he was walking on a tightrope. Mia had promised that the DNA results would be back by the end of the week and they should arrive that day. His stomach was churning as he made his way to Theatre because the thought of what they would reveal was mind-blowing. If they proved that Harry was his son, what was he going to do?

He scrubbed up, nodding his thanks when the scrub nurse helped him on with his gown. His team was waiting for him, standing silently in Theatre as he preferred them to do. Some surgeons liked to listen to music while they operated but he liked silence, nothing to distract him, nothing to distract them. Heavy metal or classical—it was all the same to him. Noise.

'How's the patient?' he asked Gerry Carter, his anaesthetist. He knew that the theatre staff drew lots to decide who would work with him, the ones who lost being sent in as part of his team. It had never worried him before that he was so unpopular but for some reason he found it irritating that day. Would it hurt them to smile when he came in, to wish him good morning even? Surely he wasn't that much of an ogre that he not only scared little children but grown men and women as well?

The memory of how Harry had reacted to him had stayed with him and he found himself thinking about it again as the anaesthetist rattled out a summary of their patient's vital signs. He was going to have to do something about his attitude if he hoped to win the boy round, Leo decided for the umpteenth time. He suddenly realised that Gerry had stopped speaking and was staring at him, obviously expecting a response, although for the life of him, Leo couldn't imagine what it should be.

'Sorry. What did you say?' He gave a short laugh, faintly rusty admittedly but a laugh all the same. 'It must be my age. I'm finding it difficult to concentrate these days.'

There was a stunned silence before someone gave a little chuckle, hastily turning it into a cough when they realised what they were doing. Leo felt heat flow up his face as he wondered if he'd made a fool of himself and was grateful for the concealing folds of his mask. He concentrated on what Gerry was saying, nodding when the other man came to the end of his spiel.

'That's great. Thanks. OK, folks, let's get to work.'

Leo grimaced as he took his place at the table. Normally, he would have simply set to work without uttering a word, so why had he felt the need to say that? Surely he wasn't that desperate to improve the image his colleagues had of him? It was Harry he needed to impress, nobody else... except Mia.

Finding out that her husband had died in such tragic circumstances had affected him far more than he would have expected. He had found himself thinking about it all week, imagining how difficult the past few years must have been for her. He had also found it hard to come to terms with the fact that her husband had been wheelchair-bound. Although he knew it had nothing to do with him, he couldn't help speculating about their relationship. Had Mia undergone IVF treatment because she and her husband had been unable to make love?

He swiftly erased that thought. He needed to concentrate and he couldn't do that if he was thinking about issues that didn't concern him. The patient, Hilary Johnson, was undergoing surgery to replace her aortic valve. Leo made the first incision through the sternum then Hilary was placed on a heart-lung machine and her heart was stopped. It was an operation that was only carried out in extreme cases, when a patient was suffering life-threatening symptoms, but he had performed it many times before and worked swiftly, excising the damaged valve and replacing it with a prosthesis. He waited while the woman was removed from the machine, preferring to check for any problems before closing up. He nodded when everything appeared to be functioning normally.

'That all seems fine. Dr Halshaw, perhaps you would like to close up? It will be excellent practice for you.'

He moved aside so that his registrar could step up to the table, ignoring the startled looks that were being exchanged. He rarely invited his juniors to take part so it was a bit of a red-letter day, but maybe it was time he made some changes in work too. After all, the younger doctors were never going to progress if they didn't get any hands-on experience, were they?

'Good. You've made quite a decent job of that,' he said when the younger man had finished. He glanced around, rather enjoying the fact that everyone appeared slightly stunned to hear him praise one of their number. A sudden and wholly unfamiliar sense of mischief spurred him on. 'Thank you, everyone, in fact. You all did extremely well today.'

Leo exited Theatre, smiling to himself when he heard a babble of conversation break out as the doors swung to. Maybe it was time he tried a different approach if it stopped people becoming complacent. It would keep them on their toes if they weren't sure how he was going to react.

He showered and changed, then went to the consultants' lounge to write up his notes. Although one of the juniors would type them up later, he preferred to outline the procedure while it was fresh in his mind. He had almost finished when there was a knock on the door.

'Come,' he called, without glancing up from the screen. He saved the file before he looked up, feeling his heart give an almighty leap when he saw Mia standing in the doorway. She had an envelope in her hands and he knew—he just knew!—it contained the results of the DNA tests.

Leo rose to his feet, his head swimming as thoughts rushed through it. He wasn't ready for this! He didn't want to hear what she had to say, didn't want to know if Harry was his real son. He loved Noah and he didn't want any other child to supplant him.

'I have the results of the DNA tests.'

Her voice was so calm that it cut through all the turmoil in his head. Leo nodded abruptly. 'And?'

'I haven't opened it yet.' She showed him the envelope with its seal still intact. 'I thought it best if we read it together. That way there will be no mistake.'

Meaning that he wouldn't be able to accuse her of skewing the results, he thought wryly, although he couldn't blame her for being cautious. Whatever they discovered, it was going to have far-reaching consequences for all of them—him, her and the two boys.

'Right. Do you want me to open it?' he offered, but she shook her head.

'I'll do it.' She slid her finger under the flap and ripped it open. Taking out the single sheet of paper it contained, she read what it said before handing it to him.

Leo glanced sharply at her but he couldn't discern anything from her expression. He took a quick breath then looked at the paper, although the words seemed to dance before his eyes. He, a man who read reports far more complicated than this every day of his life, couldn't make sense of it!

'It appears you were right.'

Mia's voice was still calm, although she couldn't disguise the pain it held. Leo felt a rush of regret hit him when he looked up and saw the anguish in her beautiful eyes. All of a sudden he wished he hadn't started this, that he had just accepted that Noah was his son and carried on the way they'd been. Now it was too late to go back, far too late to take away the pain she was feeling.

'The results are conclusive. Harry isn't mine and Chris's child. We aren't his biological parents.'

CHAPTER FIVE

'DRINK THIS.'

Leo placed a cup of tea in front of her but Mia didn't make any attempt to pick it up. How could she when her hands were shaking so hard that she would only drop it? He muttered something under his breath as he picked it up and raised it to her lips.

'Come on, just a sip. It will help.'

Mia obediently took a sip of the hot liquid, feeling her stomach roil with nausea when she tasted the sweetness of the tea on her tongue. She stumbled to her feet, praying that she wouldn't disgrace herself by throwing up.

'Through here.'

He led her into the consultants' bathroom, guiding her to the basin when she began to retch. Mia bent over the sink, wishing the floor would open up and swallow her. The sheer humiliation of throwing up in front of him was just too much, coming on top of the shock of learning that Harry wasn't her son.

Tears welled in her eyes and she heard Leo sigh as he moved away. She didn't blame him for leaving. Why should he have to deal with this on top of the shock he'd had? Although it hadn't been such a shock for him, of course. He had known from the outset that Harry wasn't her child. He'd simply needed the results of those tests to prove it to her. Now they had to decide what they were going to do. About Harry. And Noah.

'Sit down.'

Mia jumped when Leo reappeared with a towel. He sat her down on the lavatory seat then rinsed the washbasin. Once it was clean, he soaked the end of the towel in cold water then wiped her hands and face.

Mia shuddered when she felt the coolness of the cloth on her skin. It felt as though the chill was invading her whole body, seeping deeper and deeper into every pore. Maybe the tests had proved that Harry wasn't her biological child but he was still her son and nothing was going to change that!

She pushed Leo's hand away, knowing that she

had to make it clear that she wasn't going to give Harry up. Even though she had no idea what she was going to do about Noah, she was sure about that. 'It doesn't make any difference what those results say. Harry is my son and I won't let you take him away from me.'

'And I won't let you take Noah away from me either.' His tone was flat yet she could hear the emotion rippling beneath the surface. If she was determined to keep Harry then Leo was equally determined to hold onto Noah.

'Then what are we going to do?' She sighed when he didn't answer. 'You must have thought about what you wanted when you started this, Leo. So what did you decide?'

'I didn't.' He ran his hand through his hair and she could see that it was trembling. Maybe he appeared to be handling the situation far better than she was, but it didn't mean he wasn't affected by it.

'You must have had some idea of what you wanted to achieve,' she insisted, more gently this time. In a way, it made her feel a little better to know that she wasn't alone in having to deal with this situation. Leo was going through the same kind of heartache that she was experiencing.

'Not really.' He gave her a tight smile. 'I acted on instinct more than anything else. Once I discovered that Noah wasn't my biological child, I set out to find out who was.'

'How did you discover that Noah wasn't yours?'

'Noah was involved in a road traffic accident several months ago and needed a blood transfusion. It turns out that he has a fairly rare blood type so I was tested to see if I could be a donor for him.' He shrugged. 'Amanda was driving and she was injured as well so they already knew that she wasn't a suitable match for him.' He laughed shortly. 'The doctor who came to tell me that I wasn't a match either didn't know what to say. I mean, it was obvious from the blood work that neither Amanda nor I were related to Noah.'

'It must have been a terrible shock!' Mia exclaimed.

'It was. I couldn't take it in at first. After all, I'd watched Noah being born and *knew* that he was the child Amanda had given birth to. How could he not be our son? I convinced myself that the hospital had made a mistake somehow.' He sighed. 'It was only when Noah was on the mend that I thought about it properly and realised that if there had been a mistake, it must have happened at the clinic. I contacted Dr Khapur and he agreed, reluctantly, to check their records.'

'So how did you discover that I was involved in the mix-up?'

'Sheer luck. Dr Khapur was very disinclined to discuss the matter from the outset. Every time I phoned to speak to him, he was unavailable.' He shrugged. 'In the end, I took matters into my own hands and went to see him. His secretary tried to fob me off, but I told her that I intended to sit there until Dr Khapur would see me. He must have realised that he had no choice in the matter and invited me into his office. Your file was on his desk along with Amanda's and I asked him, point blank, if you were involved.'

'And he confirmed that I was? So much for patient confidentiality!'

'No. To give him his due, he tried to deny it, but I could tell he was lying and insisted that he told me the truth otherwise I'd go straight to the Human Fertilisation and Embryology Authority and make an official complaint.' He sighed. 'I'm not proud of the fact that I resorted to threats but I needed answers. Anyway, it did the trick because he admitted that it was possible you were the other party and that he had asked you to come and see him. I don't think he meant to let it slip when you were due to visit the clinic but he was very flustered by then. I decided that I needed to speak to you myself and made sure I was there.'

'I see.' Mia frowned. 'That explains how you happened to be there the other day but it doesn't explain how the mix-up occurred. Do you have any idea what happened?'

'Not really. All I can gather is that you and Amanda had embryos transferred on the same day. I can only assume that something went wrong during the process.'

'It's incredible.' Mia shook her head. 'I mean, there are strict guidelines laid down to avoid something like this happening. Chris and I chose that particular clinic because of its excellent reputation, in fact.'

'No doubt we shall find out what went on eventually, but at the moment we have more pressing matters to worry about.'

'Namely two little boys,' Mia agreed sombrely.

'Exactly.'

Leo looked round when he heard voices coming from the other room. It was lunchtime and his colleagues were starting their breaks. He couldn't bear it if people found out about what had happened and started gossiping. Noah went to school with several of the other consultants' children and Leo didn't want him overhearing something he shouldn't, even though he would have to be told at some point.

The thought of how confused Noah was going to be when he found out that Leo wasn't his *real* father was too painful. Noah had been through enough in the past six months and Leo was determined that he was going to protect him from any more unhappiness. He came to a swift decision, hoping that Mia would agree.

'I don't know about you, Mia, but I really don't want people finding out about this. To my mind it's a private matter and we need to deal with it ourselves.'

'I agree, although I shall have to tell Chris's parents, of course.' She shook her head. 'Heaven knows how they'll react. They adore Harry, all the more so because he's their last link to Chris.

They'll be devastated when they find out he isn't Chris's son.'

'Obviously, you can't keep it a secret from them,' Leo agreed, although he had no such compunction when it came to his own parents. Sir Iain and Lady Davina Forester weren't exactly doting grandparents, but then they'd never been doting parents either.

He dismissed the thought with an ease that should have worried him, but he'd had years to come to terms with his parents' lack of interest. So long as he had performed well at school and behaved impeccably out of it, they had been perfectly content. However, they had never loved him the way he loved Noah.

No one had ever loved him like that, he thought suddenly. Amanda certainly hadn't, not that he'd wanted her to. That kind of love came with far too many strings attached and he preferred his life to be free of such complications. That's what had attracted him to Amanda in the first place— she hadn't been the clingy type and had been perfectly happy doing her own thing while he did his. It had never worried him that she hadn't loved him so it was a surprise to find himself wondering how it would feel to be loved totally and with an all-consuming passion.

'It's other folk I'm concerned about,' he explained, getting back to what really mattered. 'Noah goes to school with several of the other consultants' children and I don't want him to become the subject of gossip, especially when it will only upset and confuse him.'

'I feel the same about Harry. There's quite a few children at his school whose parents work at the hospital.' Mia shook her head. 'The less everyone knows about this, the better.'

'In that case I think we need to be circumspect.' Leo glanced round when he heard someone rattle the doorhandle. It struck him how odd it would appear if he and Mia were seen leaving the bathroom together. People were so quick to add two and two and come up with the wrong answer.

The thought of the answer they might come up with sent a rush of heat through him and he cleared his throat. He made a point of never being seen alone with any female members of staff. His private life was his concern and not the basis for gossip.

After his divorce had become common knowledge there had been a lot of speculation but he had soon nipped it in the bud. The few relationships he'd had since splitting had been conducted well away from the hospital. They had been brief affairs, based on sexual need rather than anything else, and he had made sure that the women involved had understood that. Thankfully, there were a lot of women in his circle who felt the way he did. They didn't believe in love either and were happy to satisfy their needs on a no-strings basis.

He couldn't imagine Mia agreeing to that kind of a relationship. She would expect more than that. Far more than he could give.

The thought caught him flat-footed so it was a relief when Mia took charge. Standing up, she pointed to the second door that opened into the bathroom. 'Where does that lead?'

'To the consultants' rest room.' Leo gathered his wits, which seemed to be racing in several different directions. He and Mia weren't ever going to have a relationship that was based on anything except their boys. 'There shouldn't be anyone using it right now but let me check to make sure.'

Mia stepped back to let him pass as Leo went to the door. The bathroom was a little too small for two people and he flinched when his hand brushed against her arm. He could feel the silky-soft down on her skin tickling the back of his hand and shuddered. He hadn't touched a woman in any way that wasn't connected to his work since Noah's accident and the speed with which he found himself responding shocked him. He could feel feather-light tingles spreading over his skin, as though each tiny hair had triggered an individual response.

His mouth thinned as he opened the door and checked the room was empty. He wasn't attracted to Mia for the simple reason that he refused to allow himself to be attracted to her. It was Noah who mattered, Noah and Harry, not him and what he did or didn't feel. Mia may have given birth to his son but it had been purely an accident. It didn't mean there was a bond between them.

Opening the door to the corridor, Leo checked there was nobody about then ushered her out. He watched her make her way to the lift, wondering all of a sudden if he was right to write her off. Mia had not only given birth to his son but she had loved and nurtured Harry for the past five years. She had played a major role in Harry's life and nothing could change that. That she was destined to play a role in *his* life from now on was a given too.

Leo took a deep breath as he watched her step into the lift. He couldn't ignore Mia even if he wanted to.

It was raining when Mia woke up on Saturday morning. It had been a miserably wet summer and now it appeared that autumn was repeating the trend. She grimaced as she headed downstairs. She had promised Harry they could go to the park that morning and only hoped the rain would stop. Harry would be so disappointed if the promised trip had to be cancelled.

She gave Harry his breakfast then sent him into the sitting room to play while she tidied up. She had just finished washing the breakfast dishes when the phone rang and she hurried to answer it, hoping it wouldn't be her parents-in-law. She and Harry were going to their house for lunch the following day and she really needed to work out how to break the news to them that Harry wasn't their grandson if she wasn't to give them the most terrible shock. She sighed as she picked up the receiver because no matter how she phrased it, Joyce and Edward were going to be dreadfully upset.

'Mia? It's Leo Forester.'

Mia started when she recognised the deeply assured tones flowing down the line. 'How did you get my number?' she demanded, then pulled a face. It wasn't exactly the friendliest thing to have said, bearing in mind that she and Leo were going to have to work together in the coming weeks...

Or, rather, years, a small voice inside her head amended.

'Directory enquiries,' he replied succinctly, his tone not altering.

Mia rolled her eyes. It would take more than the odd snappy remark she came out with to dent his composure! 'I see.' She took a deep breath to calm herself. She needed to behave as coolly and as rationally as Leo did if they were to sort out this mess. 'Has something happened?'

'If you mean have I heard from the clinic then no. They are maintaining a strategic silence, probably because their lawyers have instructed them to do so.'

'Lawyers!' Mia exclaimed. 'You really think they've taken legal advice?'

'Of course. Apart from the fact that we'd be well within our rights to take them to court and sue for compensation, they have committed a massive error, one that could mean their licence is revoked.'

'But we're not going to sue them, are we?' Mia asked, her heart sinking at the thought of the ensuing publicity if the story came to light.

'I'm not planning to do so and I assume you aren't either. However, the mistake will have to be reported to the HFEA.'

Mia sat down abruptly on the stairs. 'I can't bear the thought of this getting out. We both agreed that we don't want people talking for the boys' sake, but we may not be able to stop it.'

'It won't come to that. This is a private matter, Mia, and I shall make that perfectly clear to all involved. It won't be only the clinic that could find itself facing a lawsuit if details of what has happened gets into the newspapers.'

'Thank you. I can't tell you how relieved I am

to hear that. I couldn't bear it if Harry's life was blighted by this.' She took a wobbly breath. 'Obviously, I'll pay half the costs if we do have to go to court, although it may take me some time to raise the money, I'm afraid.'

'Don't worry about that. I shall bear any costs involved.'

'Oh, but I couldn't let you do that! It wouldn't be fair.'

'I suggest we sort it out if and when we need to.' He changed the subject, making it clear that he didn't intend to discuss the matter any further. 'Are you doing anything special today?'

'Not really,' Mia told him, realising that it was pointless arguing. She had a feeling that once Leo made up his mind, it was difficult to get him to change it, although she had no intention of allowing him to foot the bill if they did end up in court. She would start saving towards it and that way she wouldn't be beholden to him.

The thought of being in debt to Leo made her feel more than a little uneasy, although she wasn't sure why. It was an effort to concentrate when he continued.

'Good. I've promised Noah that I'll take him

to the park this morning and I was hoping that you'd agree to bring Harry along too. The sooner the boys meet the better, plus I'm sure you must be anxious to see Noah.'

Mia bit her lip, unsure what to answer, unsure how she felt even. Meeting Noah was the next logical step yet the thought scared her. Harry was her son and she didn't want their relationship to change in any way. However, once she met Noah, it would be impossible to maintain the status quo.

'I know how scary it is, Mia. I felt exactly the same the other day when I met Harry, as though I was leaping into the unknown. But you need to meet Noah, not just for your sake but for his.'

Leo's tone was persuasive. It held a concern that she hadn't heard in it before and she shivered. It was hard to deny him anything when he spoke in this winning way.

'You're right, it is scary. I… Well, I don't want to do anything that might upset my relationship with Harry,' she told him honestly, and he sighed.

'I understand. I'm terrified that having Harry around will somehow alter how I feel about Noah. Crazy, isn't it? I mean, there's no basis for thinking such a thing, is there?'

Mia smiled when she heard disgust in his voice this time. 'I don't think we should be too hard on ourselves, Leo. I mean, how many people have to go through something like this? There aren't any rules so we have to rely on our instincts and that's what's so scary.'

'Don't tell me you're a control freak too?' he demanded wryly, and she laughed.

''Fraid so. I like things to be just so and preferably the way I want them to be.'

'Then pity help those two boys, that's all I can say. Having one parent who's a control freak would be bad enough, but to have two? Well!'

Mia chuckled. 'I'm sure they'll survive. Anyway, what about your wife? Surely she isn't as set on having everything done her way as we are?'

'Believe me, my *ex*-wife makes us look like beginners when it comes to being demanding. What Amanda wants takes precedence every time.'

His tone was so cold that Mia shivered. The thought of the other woman having anything to do with her beloved Harry was very hard to accept. 'I see. I'm not sure if I'd be happy at the thought of Harry spending time with her after hearing that,' she told him truthfully.

'There's no need to worry. Amanda isn't the least bit interested in Harry.'

'She knows about the mix-up, though?' Mia queried, wondering if he was telling her the truth. She couldn't imagine any woman not wanting to meet her own child but, there again, why would Leo lie about it?

'Oh, yes. I told her what had happened. Suffice to say that Amanda was more concerned with how it could impact on her rather than on Noah or Harry.'

He didn't say anything else. Although it appeared that his ex-wife wasn't involved, Mia couldn't help feeling uneasy. She simply couldn't accept that any woman, no matter how self-centred, could ignore what had happened. She realised that she needed to find out exactly what she was dealing with and the only way to do that was by asking Leo straight out. She was just about to do so when Harry appeared.

'Can we go to the park now, Mummy?' he demanded plaintively.

'Soon, sweetheart.' She placed the receiver to her ear again as Harry reluctantly went back to the sitting room.

'I take it that you and Harry were planning to go to the park too,' Leo observed. 'Excellent. It'll appear far more natural if we happen to meet up. We don't want to make a big deal of this, do we? The boys will only get suspicious and start worrying that something is going on.'

'Which it is.' Mia sighed. 'I wonder how they'll get on with each other. That's something else we need to think about.'

'Let's take it a step at a time, shall we?'

They made arrangements to meet in the playground before Mia hung up. She went to tell Harry that they would be leaving shortly and sent him off to find his trainers. He whooped with delight as he tore up the stairs. He was obviously looking forward to the outing and she only hoped it would work out for all of them, Harry, Noah, Leo and herself.

Her heart gave a little jolt when it struck her that she was about to meet her real son. Although she had seen that photo of Noah, she knew nothing about him—what he enjoyed, if he was athletic or musical or neither. As Leo had said, it was like leaping into the unknown so no wonder she found the idea daunting. Still, at least Leo would be there, she consoled herself, and for some reason the thought made her heart leap once more.

CHAPTER SIX

IT HAD STOPPED raining by the time they arrived at the playground. Leo looked around but he couldn't see any sign of Mia. Noah ran off to play on the slide, ignoring the other children as he climbed the slippery steps.

Leo sighed as he watched him. Noah had always been a quiet child and he had become even more withdrawn since the accident. He wasn't sure if it was the prolonged stay in hospital that had affected him or Amanda's disappearance. Amanda hadn't made any attempt to see Noah in the last six months. She hadn't phoned or even emailed to ask how he was either. Discovering that Noah wasn't her biological child had given her the excuse she'd needed to cut him out of her life.

Although she had never been around very much, Leo knew that Noah must miss even the sparse contact he'd had with the woman he believed to be his mother. It made him realise how careful he needed to be when he introduced Noah to Mia. The little boy could resent Mia's sudden intrusion into his life.

It was something else to worry about, one more thing to add to the ever-expanding list. Not for the first time, Leo wished that he had let sleeping dogs lie. What had he hoped to achieve? All right, so he and Mia would get to know their real children but was that enough to justify disrupting Harry's and Noah's lives? Children needed stability but what hope did they have of giving the boys that when they were about to rock the very foundations of their existence?

'Hello! This is a surprise. I didn't expect to see you here.'

Leo looked round when he heard Mia's voice. Fixing a smile to his lips, he went to meet her, trying to ignore the way that Harry shrank away when he approached. It was obvious that the child's initial opinion of him hadn't improved.

'I've brought my son, Noah, here to play,' he explained, refusing to feel hurt. It was his own fault that he'd made such a bad impression on Harry and it was up to him to do something about it. His smile deliberately widened. 'That's him, over there on the slide.'

Leo pointed to Noah, who was surrounded by several other children, a couple of whom also had blond hair. He felt Mia stiffen and instinctively reached for her hand. 'He's the one wearing the red jacket. He's at the top of the slide now.'

'Yes, I can see him.'

Leo heard the tremor in her voice and realised that she was deeply affected by her first actual sighting of Noah. His fingers tightened around hers as a wave of tenderness washed over him. He knew how she felt because he had felt the same when he'd first seen Harry—shocked and amazed by the resemblance the boy bore to him. When Harry ran off to play on the swings, Leo led her over to a bench.

'It knocks you for six, doesn't it?' he said as they sat down. 'I mean, you try to prepare yourself but it's still a shock when you see them for the first time.'

'It is.' She could barely speak and he heard her take a quick little breath. 'He's so like Chris—his hair, his build, the way he tilts his head—everything!'

'I was just as stunned when I saw Harry,' he admitted. 'He has my nose and my chin, the same colour hair.' He gave a self-mocking laugh, trying to lighten the mood in the hope that it would help her. 'His hair even sticks out like mine does if I don't get it cut every couple of weeks!'

Mia turned and stared at him. 'You think Harry looks like you?'

'Of course. Surely you can see the resemblance?'

Leo frowned as she turned and stared at the little boy. He couldn't believe that she hadn't noticed how alike they were. His eyes rested on her as she studied Harry and he saw to the very second when what had been so clear to him from the moment he had laid eyes on the child became clear to her too. Her face was very pale when she turned to him, so pale that he thought she was going to faint and he gripped her hand harder, ruing the fact that he'd felt it necessary to point out the resemblance. The last thing he'd intended was to upset her.

'I can see the resemblance now.' She bit her lip. 'I don't know why I didn't spot it before.'

'Probably because this has been such a shock

for you,' Leo said soothingly, surprised that he should feel it necessary to offer comfort. Although it went against the grain to be rude, he wasn't known for being compassionate. In fact, if he was honest, he rarely took account of other people's feelings, mainly because he didn't expect them to take account of his. However, for some reason, he felt a need to soothe her, to comfort her, to make this meeting as easy for her as it could possibly be.

'Do you think so?' Her eyes held his fast and he could see the plea they held. 'Maybe I was deliberately trying not to see how like you Harry is because it would mean those test results are right.'

'They are right, though.' Even though he hated to upset her, Leo knew that he had to make this most important fact absolutely clear. 'You read the letter, Mia. The results prove conclusively that Harry isn't your son.'

'But they don't prove he's yours!' She shot to her feet, her eyes spitting fire at him. 'There was nothing in that report to say that you are his father, Leo. Absolutely nothing!'

'I know.' Leo rose as well, realising they were attracting attention. He lowered his voice, hating the thought of people overhearing their conversation. 'Which is why we need to send off more DNA samples, but from you and me this time as well as from the boys. I'll get it organised and then we'll know for sure what we're dealing with.'

'It's that simple, is it?' She sat down abruptly and Leo saw the anger drain out of her. 'We send off more samples of hair and saliva and they'll send us back another report to say that Child A belongs to this or that parent.'

'No, it isn't simple,' he said sharply. 'Nothing about this situation is simple, Mia. It's a mess, and there's no point pretending that it isn't going to cause a massive upheaval for us as well as for Harry and Noah. However, the only way we'll get through it is by working together. If we start fighting then we'll achieve nothing apart from destroying the lives of two innocent little boys. Is that what you really want?'

'Of course not.'

Mia took a deep breath and tried to get a grip on herself. It wasn't easy but, as Leo had pointed out, nothing about this situation was easy. She looked across the playground, feeling her heart ache when she saw Harry at the top of the slide. He must have sensed she was watching him because he turned and waved, his face breaking into a mischievous grin as he propelled himself at top speed down the slide. He came running over to her, bubbling with excitement.

'Did you see how fast I went, Mummy?'

'I did,' she replied, giving him a hug. 'You're a proper little demon on the slide!'

He laughed happily as he ran off to have another turn. Mia turned to Leo, knowing that she owed him an apology. It wasn't like her to create a scene but there again she'd never had anything like this happen to her before. 'I'm sorry. I'm afraid it all got the better of me but it won't happen again.'

'It's been a shock for both of us,' he said quietly, and she shrugged.

'Yes, but that isn't an excuse.' She paused, not wanting to cause another upset, but she needed to be absolutely sure of the facts. 'I think we should have those tests done as soon as possible. We need to be certain that we know exactly what we're dealing with.'

'I agree. We can't afford to make another mistake, not when it could impact on the boys.' He shrugged. 'Maybe there is a resemblance between Noah and your late husband, and maybe I do think that Harry looks a lot like me, but it isn't proof. It will be safer if we see it written down in black and white before we make any plans.'

'What sort of plans?' Mia said swiftly. 'I made it clear that I won't allow you to take Harry away from me.'

'And I made it equally clear that I am not prepared to give up Noah,' he said curtly, interrupting her.

'Then what exactly are you talking about?'

'I'm not sure.' He frowned. 'The boys are far too young to tell them what has happened—it'll only confuse them. But obviously we each need to maintain contact with our real child or it could cause problems in the future. I don't want Harry to grow up thinking that I wasn't interested in him and I'm sure you don't want Noah thinking that either.'

'Of course not. So what do you suggest?' Mia said slowly. 'That we meet up on a regular basis so we can get to know the boys and they can get to know us?'

Leo looked across the playground. Mia followed his gaze, her heart contracting when she realised that Harry and Noah were on adjoining swings. They had no idea what had happened and it was up to her and Leo to make this is as easy as possible for them.

'Won't they think it strange, though?' she said, turning to him. 'I mean, we can't keep on *bumping* into each other, can we?'

'No. They're bright kids and they'll soon realise something is going on. We have to find another way to go about this and the only thing I can come up with is if we let them think we're going out together.' He shrugged, ignoring her gasp. 'There are lots of kids at Noah's school whose parents have split up and are in new relationships and I imagine it's the same at Harry's school. If we tell them that we're seeing one another, they'll think it's quite normal. What do you think?'

What did she think? Mia was lost for words, quite frankly. It was mind-boggling to imagine herself dating Leo...

Wasn't it?

Heat roared through her veins as she looked

at his handsome face and realised that the idea wasn't so outrageous after all. 'I...um...'

She got not further when Harry appeared. 'I'm thirsty, Mummy. Can I have a drink, please?'

'Of course you can, darling.' Mia shot to her feet so fast that she almost dropped her bag. She slung the strap over her shoulder, pinning a smile to her lips as she turned to Leo. She needed to think about what he'd suggested, see if she could come up with a better idea. The last thing she needed was to become even more involved with him than she already was.

'It was nice to see you again, Leo. Enjoy the rest of your day.'

'You too,' he replied politely, rising. Noah came running over and he put a protective hand on his shoulder. 'This is Mia, Noah. Say hello to her and Harry, her son.'

'Hello,' Noah muttered, scuffing the toe of his trainer on the ground.

'Hello, Noah. It's good to meet you.'

Mia felt a rush of emotions overwhelm her as she studied the child's downbent head. Close to, the resemblance to Chris was even more marked. Not only did Noah have Chris's ash-blond hair and black brows but his nose was the same shape too. All of a sudden she knew that no matter what it took, she had to get to know him. He was her child, hers and Chris's, and even though she had no idea if she would ever be able to tell him that she was his mother, she couldn't bear the thought of not being involved in his life.

Her head lifted and she looked Leo straight in the eyes. 'I think your suggestion might work. Let's talk about it next time we meet, shall we?'

'Of course.'

Leo didn't say anything else as she led Harry away but he didn't need to when his expression said everything for him. Mia shivered as she and Harry made their way to the café. Maybe Leo had made the suggestion purely to help the boys but they both knew it could have repercussions for them too.

She bit her lip, trying to contain the rush of excitement that filled her as she recalled the way he had looked at her just now. That he was aware of her as a woman wasn't in doubt. However, her feelings for him were far more complicated. Since Chris had died she hadn't dated, hadn't been interested in going out with other men. She never really had been, if she was honest. What had happened with Steve Parker had put her off the idea of dating and if she hadn't met Chris then she doubted it she would have found the courage to try it again.

However, Leo was different. Very different. Pretending that they were seeing one another for the sake of the boys wouldn't be easy. What would be easy was making the pretence real.

Leo was glad to go into work on Monday morning. At least while he was working he would have less time to worry about what had happened on Saturday. He sighed as he made his way to Theatre. He had spent the remainder of the weekend thinking about his meeting with Mia and what had transpired.

Suggesting that they should pretend to be involved for the sake of the boys had been an off-the-cuff idea. However, as soon as he'd broached it, it had become increasingly attractive. It had been ages since he'd been out with a woman and he would appreciate some female company; however, he knew that it wasn't the reason why he found the idea so appealing. Getting to know Mia seemed as important as getting to know Harry, strangely enough.

Leo cursed softly as he thrust open the door to the scrub room. What in heaven's name was wrong with him? He could have his pick of women, women who were far more beautiful than Mia. This situation was skewing his thinking, making him come up with the craziest ideas. His only interest in Mia was as the mother of his son!

'Oh, please, *please,* don't make me do this! I'll do anything—scrub toilets, wash out sick bowls—anything at all if you'll spare me this. It's Monday and I really can't face the thought of two hours locked up in Theatre with our beloved leader!'

Leo came to a halt when he found Declan Murphy on his knees in front of Janice Lang, the theatre sister. The F2 student was staring beseechingly up at her, his face bearing an expression guaranteed to appeal to even the hardest heart. Janice and the rest of the team were laughing so hard that they didn't notice he had come in. It was only when he approached them that they spotted him. Declan obviously realised something was wrong when everyone hurriedly moved away. He looked round, his freckled face paling when he saw Leo.

'A moving performance, Dr Murphy.' Leo smiled thinly as his errant F2 scrambled to his feet. 'Your talents are obviously wasted working in this particular type of theatre. You should apply to RADA and see if they can offer you a place.'

'I...erm... Thank you,' Declan faltered, then gulped when he realised what he had said.

Leo headed into the shower room, managing to contain his mirth until he had turned on the water. Declan's face had been an absolute picture, he thought as he stepped under the jets. It would be a long time before he pulled a stunt like that again! It made him realise all of a sudden that it wasn't always necessary to play the heavy-handed boss. Sometimes a dash of humour could be far more effective.

Leo frowned as he pulled on fresh scrubs. He was very aware that the idea would never have occurred to him in the past. Was it this situation with Noah and Harry that was making him behave so differently? he wondered. Finding out that Noah wasn't his son had knocked the feet from under him; nothing seemed certain any more, including his own actions. Where once he would have known he was right, now he found himself questioning his decisions.

It was what had happened that weekend. He'd kept thinking about that suggestion he'd made to Mia, wondering if it had been the right thing to do. Normally, he wouldn't have given it a second thought but it had been on his mind, day and night: should they pretend to be dating for the sake of the boys or was it tempting fate?

His mouth thinned as he slid his feet into a pair of rubber clogs. There was no chance of him becoming romantically involved with Mia or any other woman! He had learned his lesson after what had gone on with Amanda and he had no intention of placing himself in the same position again. So maybe his heart hadn't been broken when Amanda had left him but his pride had been dented and that had been enough to put him off forming another long-term relationship. Even if he and Mia did decide to carry through with the idea, their relationship would only ever be make-believe.

He pushed open the door to Theatre, wondering why he still felt so ambivalent. As long as they both understood what they were doing, there wouldn't be a problem.

Would there?

CHAPTER SEVEN

MIA ARRIVED EARLY for work on Monday morning. Amazingly the train had been on time and she'd been spared the usual last-minute dash from the station. At least something was going right, she thought as she made her way to the staffroom.

She sighed as she hung her coat in her locker. Lunch with her in-laws the previous day had been even worse than she had feared. Joyce and Edward had been devastated when she had told them about Harry. They had refused to believe her at first and it was only after she had shown them the results of the DNA tests that they had accepted it was true.

She and Harry had left soon after lunch. Although they usually spent the afternoon with Chris's parents, Mia had realised that the couple had needed time on their own to come to terms with what had happened. Their goodbyes had been stilted, all the more so because Joyce had hurried away in the middle of waving them off. Although Mia sympathised with her mother-in-law, she hoped that Joyce wouldn't allow this development to affect her relationship with Harry. Harry needed his grandparents' love and support more than ever now.

Penny was on holiday that week but she had left the roster pinned to the notice-board. Mia grimaced when she discovered that she was covering Cardiology again. Along with the stress of breaking the news to Chris's parents, she had found herself constantly thinking about Leo's suggestion. Whilst she was still determined to get to know Noah, she was no longer sure if it would be wise to let the boys think she and Leo were involved. Harry, in particular, could find it upsetting to think there was another man in her life, especially when he seemed to have taken such a dislike to Leo.

Mia made her way to the unit and did the hand-over then went to check on the patients. She was surprised to find David Rimmer in the end bay. He had been discharged following his successful cardioversion and she hadn't expected to see him again.

'I'll have to add your name to the coffee list if you're going to be a regular,' she said, smiling at him. She picked up his chart, sighing when she discovered that he had been admitted suffering from the same symptoms as before: a rapid and irregular heartbeat.

'Milk and two sugars, please,' he said chirpily, although Mia could tell the effort it cost him.

'I'll make a note of that.' She gently replaced the oxygen mask over his face and shook an admonishing finger at him. 'Now leave that on or it will be water not coffee for you, my lad.'

'Yes, Mum,' David retorted cheekily. He looked past her and grimaced. 'Is she always this bossy, Doc?'

Mia looked round, feeling her own heart race when she saw Leo standing behind her. He was dressed in theatre scrubs, the soft green fabric outlining the powerful muscles in his chest. He looked so big and overwhelmingly male that she found herself responding in a way that shocked her.

Sex had never been a major issue in her life.

She'd only slept with Steve before she had married Chris and it had been a complete disaster. That was why she'd had no qualms about marrying Chris. The fact that they'd been unable to make love because of his injuries hadn't worried her, although Chris had fretted about it.

There had been no reason to revise her opinion either, yet she couldn't pretend that she wasn't affected by Leo's nearness. All of a sudden the doubts that had plagued her all weekend came rushing back. What would happen if she found herself falling for Leo and wanting to turn fiction into fact?

Leo had no idea what Mia was thinking but he could tell there was something troubling her. He had to make a determined effort to concentrate as he replied to David's question. 'I really couldn't say. However, I suggest we focus on you rather than on Sister Adams.'

His tone was chilly and he cursed himself when he saw the younger man's face fall. There really hadn't been any need to speak to David that way but he'd reacted instinctively. The suggestion that he knew Mia well enough to comment on her behaviour had hit a nerve, coming on top of his earlier thoughts.

He deliberately cleared his mind of any more foolishness as he explained to David that he was going to try another round of cardioversion. He wasn't attracted to Mia and he didn't intend to be attracted to her either. He had enough to contend with without complicating matters any more.

'But what's going to happen if it does it again?' David said, anxiously. 'You can't keep on stopping and starting my heart, can you?'

'No,' Leo agreed. 'We've already tried various combinations of drugs and they've been less than successful so it could be that an ICD is the answer.'

'What's that?' David asked him, frowning.

'An implantable cardioverter defibrillator,' Leo explained dryly, and smiled. 'You can see why it's called an ICD for short.'

'Too right!' David rolled his eyes and Mia laughed.

Leo cleared his throat, determined to ignore the effect the sweetly husky sound was having on him. So what if his blood pressure *had* risen a couple of notches and his breathing *did* seem a little more laboured than usual? He was a normal healthy male, with normal healthy appetites—he would have responded the same way to any woman.

'Basically, an ICD is used to treat anyone who has a dangerously abnormal heart rhythm.' Leo made himself focus on what he was saying. It wasn't like him to become distracted when dealing with a patient and he didn't intend to let it to happen again. 'Size-wise, it's slightly bigger than a matchbox and consists of a pulse generator plus one or more electrode leads, which are placed in the heart via a vein.'

'How does it work?' David wanted to know.

'The device constantly monitors your heart rhythm. If it detects a dangerous rhythm it can deliver three different treatments to restore the heart to a normal rhythm. Pacing, which is a series of rapid, low-voltage electrical impulses, cardioversion, which is one or more small electric shocks, or defibrillation which consists of one or more larger electric shocks.'

'I see. How is it fitted, though?' David grimaced. 'You said that the electrode leads are placed in the heart so does that mean I'd need an operation?'

'Yes.' Leo could tell that David wasn't happy at the thought of undergoing more surgery. David had been in and out of Theatre many times and most of the operations he'd had had entailed a lengthy stay in hospital afterwards. He hastened to reassure him.

'However, the device will be inserted under a local anaesthetic, although you will need to be sedated as well. It usually takes about an hour or so and then we will keep you in overnight so we can check it's working properly.' He shrugged. 'After that, you'll need to have it checked occasionally but that's all.'

'Really!' David exclaimed. He turned to Mia and grinned. 'Reckon the doc is telling me the truth or has he missed out the gory bits in case he scares me?'

'I'm sure Mr Forester wouldn't mislead you.' Mia glanced at him and Leo felt his blood pressure perform another of its new tricks, shooting skywards before he could stop it. It was all he could do to maintain a neutral expression as she continued in the same husky tone that was having such a devastating effect on him.

'He strikes me as someone who always tells the truth, no matter how unpalatable it is. I think you can trust him, David. I do.'

Mia wasn't sure why she had said that. Maybe she had wanted to reassure David but she knew it wasn't the only reason. She waited in silence while Leo explained to David that he would be taking him down to Theatre that afternoon. She did trust Leo and it was a surprise to discover she felt this way.

Growing up in care had made her wary of trusting anyone. Every time she'd formed an attachment to one of the care workers, they had either left or she had been sent to yet another foster-home. The experience had made her develop a protective shell and she had never allowed anyone inside it. It wasn't until she had met Chris that she had felt able to lower her defences. She had trusted Chris and now it appeared she trusted Leo too. It was unsettling to admit it.

Mia roused herself when she realised that Leo had finished. Leaning over, she once again fitted the oxygen mask over David's nose and mouth.

'Keep that on and I'll fetch you a cup of coffee. Deal?'

'Deal!' David high-fived her and settled back against the pillows. He looked exhausted as they moved away from the bed.

'I hope the ICD works,' she said quietly as they made their way to the office. 'He looks worn out.'

'No wonder, after what he's been through,' Leo replied in a tone that made her glance at him.

Colour swept up her face when she saw the awareness in his eyes because she knew what lay behind it. It was that comment about trusting him that was causing him to look at her this way. Why in heaven's name had she said it? It had been a stupid thing to say...a stupid thing to *think* in the circumstances. She couldn't afford to trust him until she was sure what his intentions were towards Harry.

Panic shot through her as she went into the office. Had she allowed herself to be lulled into a false sense of security? What if Leo hadn't been telling her the truth and intended to try and claim Harry? They said that blood was thicker than water and if Harry was his son he could be planning to gain custody. The thought was more than she could bear and she swung round.

'What I said just now was purely for David's benefit.' She carried on when Leo said nothing. 'Whilst I trust you to do whatever is best for your patients, I have reservations when it comes to Harry.'

'You still believe that I might try to gain custody of him?' He sounded so cold that Mia shivered.

'I think it's possible—yes.'

'Then all I can do is repeat what I've already told you. I have no intention of trying to take Harry away from you, neither do I intend to allow you to take Noah away from me.' He pinned her with a cold-eyed stare. 'The old cliché about trust being a two-way street is very true, especially in this instance. I have to trust you, Mia, just as you have to trust me, whether we like the idea or not.'

He didn't say anything else as he turned and walked out of the door. Mia bit her lip, wondering why she felt like crying. There'd been something beneath the ice in Leo's voice, a kind of raw hurt that had touched her. She knew that she had upset him, hurt him, wounded *him*, the person he was, not the man he portrayed to the world. Beneath that coldly aloof exterior was a warm and loving man, a man who was as afraid to open his heart as she had been before she'd met Chris.

Her breath caught. She and Leo had more in common than just the boys, it seemed.

Leo spent the afternoon seeing patients at the private practice in Harley Street he shared with several other top-notch consultants. They covered a wide range of specialities from cardiology to oncology and were kept incredibly busy even in these straitened times.

People were prepared to spend money on their health and his view was that it was their decision, although, unlike some of his colleagues at the practice, he didn't subscribe to the theory that the service he provided to his private patients should be any better than what he offered to his NHS patients. He put one hundred per cent effort into helping *all* his patients.

His last appointment had phoned to cancel so he had an early finish for once. He drove home, wondering if he should make the most of the time and take Noah out. There was a new animated film showing at the cinema and he was sure that Noah would enjoy it...or at least he *thought* he would.

He sighed as he parked in the driveway. Noah had become so withdrawn since the accident that it was impossible to predict what he liked any more. Whenever he suggested they should do something, Noah always agreed but he never showed any real enthusiasm. He seemed happier at home, playing in his bedroom, in fact. Leo had tried to draw him out but he had failed to get to the root of the problem. Noah just shook his head whenever Leo asked him if he was worried about anything.

He knew that he needed to find out what was wrong but he didn't know how to set about it. Maybe Mia could suggest something?

He frowned as he let himself into the house. It was worrying to realise that he was starting to think of Mia in those terms. She might be Noah's biological mother but she knew absolutely nothing about him. She hadn't walked the floor, night after night, when Noah was a baby, trying to get him off to sleep. She hadn't been there when Noah had chickenpox and cried continuously. She hadn't even been there when Noah was rushed into hospital following the crash, so ill that the doctors had given him only a thirty per cent chance of surviving.

He had gone through all that on his own, walked the floor with him, soothed and comforted him, cried at the thought that he might lose him. So why on earth did he imagine that Mia could offer any advice? Was he looking for a way to create a stronger bond between them, to draw her deeper into his life? And if so, why? Was it really for the sake of the children or for himself?

Leo had no idea what the answers were to any of those questions and it troubled him to feel so unsure. He liked his life to be free of uncertainties but in this instance it wasn't possible. He drove the questions from his mind with a ruthless determination that made him feel a little better. So long as he could master his own thoughts he would be fine.

Noah was in the kitchen, eating his tea. Mrs Davies, their housekeeper, collected him from school each day and stayed with him until Leo got home. She smiled when she saw him coming in.

'You're nice and early for a change, Doctor. Noah's not finished his tea yet.'

'My final appointment cancelled,' Leo explained, trying not to feel hurt when Noah didn't look up. Before the accident, Noah would have come running to greet him but these days he barely acknowledged him. It was as though the child blamed him for what had happened even though Amanda had been driving. Maybe he *would* mention it to Mia, he decided. If she could shed any light on Noah's behaviour it would be worth the risk.

Leo wasn't sure exactly what risk he was taking and refused to speculate. Drawing out a chair, he sat down beside his son and ruffled his hair. 'Did you have a good day at school?'

Noah nodded as he spooned spaghetti hoops into his mouth and Leo bit back a sigh. It was obviously not one of Noah's better days if he was refusing to talk to him. He persevered, determined to break down the barriers the child had erected between them. He loved Noah with all his heart and he couldn't bear to think there was something wrong with him and not be able to do anything about it.

'I thought we could go and watch that new film that's on the cinema seeing as I managed to get home early. What do you think? It's another one about that panda and you loved the first one, didn't you?'

Noah looked up, his expression betraying the tiniest hint of enthusiasm. 'Do we have to go in the car?'

'Nope.' Leo grinned, determined to make light of Noah's aversion to going anywhere by car. This was something he did understand, only too well. It was an effort to clamp down on the rush of anger at the thought of what Amanda had done but he'd be damned if he would upset Noah when he had finally made a breakthrough. Anyway, presenting a pleasant face to the world was a skill he needed to develop if he wasn't to completely alienate Harry.

Thinking about Harry reminded him of all the upset that was going to happen when Noah found out the truth about who his parents actually were. Not for the first time, Leo wished that he had left well alone and never started this. He and Noah could have carried on the way they'd been, and Mia and Harry could have done the same. They'd have remained oblivious of the true facts and that would have been far better for all of them.

Wouldn't it?

'We'll go on the bus. It stops right outside the cinema so there's no point taking the car and getting stuck in traffic.' Leo adopted a deliberately upbeat tone, not wanting Noah to suspect anything was wrong. So maybe he wasn't sure if it would have been better for him if Mia had never found out about the mix-up but that was his problem. If he and Mia had never met then he would never have felt he was missing out, would he?

He hurried on, refusing to dwell on that thought. 'Tell you what—we'll have an ice cream before the film starts, if you fancy it.'

'Yes!' Noah's face lit up. Pushing his plate away, he shot to his feet and went haring out of the kitchen to get ready.

'He's not finished his tea,' Mrs Davies said, shaking her head.

'Sorry.' Leo grimaced. 'My fault, I'm afraid.'

'Not to worry.' She cleared away the plate. 'It's nice to see him looking more like himself, isn't it?'

'It is.'

Leo felt a lump come to his throat and stood up. The fact that Mrs Davies had noticed the change in Noah only made it worse. As he went to get changed, he promised himself that he would do whatever it took to help Noah get over the accident. And if that meant involving Mia then that's what he would do, no matter what the cost to him personally.

CHAPTER EIGHT

NORMALLY, MIA WOULDN'T have taken Harry out on a school night but she decided to make an exception that night. He'd seemed unusually subdued when she had collected him from school and a little gentle probing had eventually elicited the answer. Harry was upset because he thought that Grandma was cross with him and he didn't know what he'd done wrong.

Mia's heart was heavy as she assured him that he had done nothing wrong and that Grandma had been feeling poorly and that was why she hadn't stayed to wave them off. This was the very thing she had wanted to avoid and she had no idea what she was going to do if Joyce reacted the same way again when they next went to visit her.

Perhaps it would be safer if she left it a couple of weeks and gave Joyce and Edward time to come to terms with what had happened, yet that would probably upset Harry too. He loved his grandparents and he would miss not seeing them, especially when they had always made such a fuss of him in the past. Talk about being stuck between a rock and a hard place!

In an effort to take Harry's mind off it, she suggested they go out for tea at a fast-food restaurant. It worked as Harry could hardly contain his excitement at the thought of the forthcoming treat. They caught the bus, which was another thing Harry loved doing. Catching a train or taking the bus was far more exciting than travelling by car!

The restaurant was busy and they had to queue up to place their order, Harry, predictably, opting for the meal that came with a free toy.

Mia ordered a chicken wrap, nodding when the young man behind the counter told her he would bring it over. Picking up their tray, she looked for somewhere to sit but every table was taken. It was only when she realised that someone was waving to her that she spotted Leo sitting near the window and her stomach sank. The one thing she had never expected was that he'd be here.

She made her way to his table, forcing a smile

when he stood up. 'Thanks for letting us share your table. It's packed in here tonight, isn't it?'

'It is indeed.' He took the tray from her while she slid into the booth, and quickly decanted its contents onto the table. He looked up and frowned. 'Aren't you having anything?'

'A chicken wrap. They said they'd bring it over when it was ready.'

Mia slipped out of her coat, wishing that she'd worn something a bit smarter than the ancient jumper she had changed into after work. The elbows were wearing thin and the front was decidedly bobbly so it could hardly be called flattering. She sighed as she helped Harry unpack his food so he could get at the free toy. What did matter what she wore? Leo wasn't interested in her; he was only interested in her son.

'I see Harry's opted for the same deal as Noah.'

Leo's voice held a hint of amusement and Mia felt a little shiver run through her. She looked up, feeling her heart jolt when she saw a matching amusement in his eyes. He looked so much more approachable when he let down his defences, she decided, then wondered why the thought worried her so much. She cleared her throat.

'I think it's the free toy that's the big attraction rather than the food.'

'I'm sure you're right. They certainly know how to push all the right buttons when it comes to attracting the kids.'

He laughed and she felt the hair on the back of her neck lift. He really did have the sexiest laugh, deep and soft and as rich as melting chocolate.

'They do. No wonder they make so much money.' Mia's own laughter sounded strained but thankfully Leo didn't appear to notice.

'Pity I don't have shares in the company. I'm sure they're doing a lot better than the ones I do have.'

Mia smiled politely, although she was hard pressed not to let her anxiety show at the reminder that Leo had a lot more resources at his disposal than she had. He had promised that he wouldn't try to gain custody of Harry and she had to believe him. She helped Harry unpack his chicken nuggets, sighing when she realised that she had forgotten to get any tomato sauce to dip them in. She was about to go and fetch some when Leo pushed a small container across the table.

'Is this what you're after? I got way too much. Noah won't eat it all so Harry may as well have it.'

'Oh, right. Thanks.' She passed it to Harry. 'Say thank you to Leo, darling.'

'Thank you,' Harry muttered with a sad lack of grace.

Leo shook his head when Mia went to remonstrate with him. He waited until the child was busily occupied with his meal. 'Leave it. If you tell him off, it will only make matters worse. I'm afraid Harry isn't all that keen on me.'

'That's no excuse for being rude,' Mia countered.

'Normally, I'd agree with you but this situation is difficult for all of us.' His expression was sombre all of a sudden. 'It can only get even more difficult too. Heaven knows how these two will react when we tell them what's happened.'

'Don't.' Mia shivered. 'I can't bear to think about it. Yesterday was bad enough.'

'Yesterday. Why, what happened?'

'We went to visit Chris's parents.' She lowered her voice, although Harry and Noah were playing some sort of complicated game that involved their toys crashing into each other and couldn't possibly hear her. 'My mother-in-law was terribly upset—they both were, although Chris's dad handled it better. It ended up with her disappearing when she was supposed to be waving us off. Poor Harry thought he'd done something wrong and upset her. That's why I brought him out for tea, to take his mind off it.'

'Hell! That's the last thing you need, Mia.' He reached across the table and touched her hand. 'I'm so sorry. It's all my fault. I should never have started this, should I?'

'I don't think you had any choice once you realised there'd been a mix-up at the clinic.'

Mia withdrew her hand simply because it would have been far too easy to leave it where it was. The warm strength of Leo's fingers made her feel safe, secure, protected even, and she knew it was dangerous to feel that way. Leo's only interest in her was as the mother of his son and she mustn't forget that, must never open herself up to that kind of heartache. People could and did let you down; she knew that only too well. Maybe Chris had never failed her but that didn't mean Leo wouldn't.

'No. You're right. I couldn't have ignored it. It wouldn't have been right for any number of reasons. But it's still hard to accept that my actions are going to cause an awful lot of upset for you, Harry and Noah.'

'And for you too,' she pointed out, determined to stick to the subject under discussion. Allowing herself to be sidetracked by how she felt was stupid. 'This is bound to have an effect on you, too, Leo.' She glanced at Noah and bit her lip. 'If you love Noah the way I love Harry then I can imagine what you're going through.'

'I'm terrified that it will be the final straw when he finds out I'm not his real dad.'

Mia frowned. 'What do you mean, the final straw?'

'Just that Noah hasn't been himself since the accident. He's become very withdrawn.' He spread his hands wide open in a gesture that hinted at the frustration he was feeling. 'When I suggested coming out tonight, it was the first time I've seen him show any enthusiasm for ages.'

'He's been through a lot,' Mia observed, feeling a little knot of anxiety gather in her chest as she looked at Noah. Maybe she didn't have any real role in his life, but she did care about him. 'Being injured so badly must have shaken him. He's bound to behave differently for a while.'

'So you think that's what it is? He's still shocked because of the accident?'

Leo's tone was urgent and her frown deepened. 'I think so but what do you think? You know him better than I do.'

'I'm not sure—that's the truthful answer.' He shook his head. 'I've tried everything I can think of to get to the bottom of what's wrong with him. I've tried talking to him about the accident but he just clams up whenever I mention it. I even suggested he should draw me a picture of what happened but he wouldn't do it. Basically, he's shut me out and I don't know how to get through to him.'

'Have you tried counselling?' Mia suggested, feeling more concerned than ever.

'Oh, yes. He simply refused to say anything when I took him so that was that.'

'What about his mother? Will he speak to her?'

'I doubt it even if I knew where she was.' His tone was grim. 'The last I heard, Amanda was holidaying on some yacht in the Caribbean or, rather, *recuperating*, as she put it. She hasn't been in touch for months and I doubt if she'll bother now.'

'Because Noah isn't hers?' Mia said, appalled.

'Yes. Amanda had gone off the idea of motherhood even before Noah was born. In fact, if I hadn't threatened to tell everyone what she was planning, she would have aborted him.'

'No! But why go through all the discomfort of IVF if she wasn't committed to having a child? Did she do it for you?'

'Amanda never does anything for other people,' he said dryly. 'No, all her friends were having babies and she decided that she wanted one as well. I tried to talk her out of it but she was adamant.' He shrugged. 'She became even more determined when she failed to get pregnant. It turned out that her ovaries were blocked and the only way she could have a child was through IVF, so that's what we did.'

'But she changed her mind once she was pregnant?' Mia said, frowning.

'Yes. She hated being pregnant, hated feeling sick, hated being fat, hated everything about it. If I hadn't laid down the law, she would have got rid of Noah without a second thought.' His expression was grim. 'It was no better after Noah was born. Amanda wasn't interested in him and left when he was six months old.'

'How awful! It must have been very difficult for you.'

'Not really. To be frank, it was a relief not to have to put up with her constant complaints. I applied for sole custody of Noah and it was granted, although I did agree to allow her access. However, her visits were infrequent to say the least. She hadn't seen Noah for almost a year when she turned up one day and asked if she could take him out. I wasn't keen but there seemed no reason to refuse so I agreed. And that's when the accident happened.'

His tone was harsh. 'So as far as I'm concerned Amanda isn't involved in this. It's you and me who need to decide what to do, so if you want out now that you know Noah has problems, you'd better say so, Mia. The last thing I want is him getting hurt any more.'

Leo could feel anger welling up inside him. He wasn't sure what had triggered it, apart from the fact that thinking about Amanda always left him feeling out of sorts. Mia drew back and he could tell that she was offended but so what? He needed to make it clear that once they involved the children there was no going back.

'And the last thing I want is Harry getting hurt either. It seems we agree on something.'

Her tone was sharp. Leo felt his temper leap another notch up the scale. He wasn't used to people speaking to him that way and didn't appreciate it. He glared at her. 'Then we need to formulate some sort of a plan, don't we?'

'Hopefully, something better than the last one you came up with,' she shot back.

'About us pretending to be seeing one another?' His brows rose. 'And what was wrong with that, may I ask?'

'Oh, nothing, except that I'm as likely to agree to go out with you as with Jack the Ripper!'

She turned to Harry, ignoring Leo as she told the child that it was time they left. Leo forced down his anger as he told Noah that it was time they left too if they weren't to miss the start of the film. Noah gathered up his plastic toy and put it carefully in his pocket.

'Can Harry come with us?' he asked, looking beseechingly at Leo.

'I'm not sure if Harry's mummy wants him to stay out late,' Leo hedged, because it was the last thing he wanted. Oh, not that he didn't want Harry to accompany them, but if Harry came then Mia would have to come too. The thought of being subjected to any more of her pronouncements didn't exactly fill him with joy. Comparing him to Jack the Ripper indeed!

'Can Harry come with us, Mia? Please?' Noah begged, and Leo immediately forgot his injured feelings. Having Harry go with them was obviously important to Noah and that was all that mattered.

He looked at Mia and shrugged. 'It's up to you, but Harry is very welcome if he'd like to come. You too obviously.'

Mia took a deep breath. She wasn't sure why she had gone off at the deep end. Maybe it was because Leo believed that she was no more trustworthy than his ex-wife had been but it had been wrong of her to react that way. They would never deal with this situation if they started quarrelling with each other.

'If Harry wants to go then I can't see that it's a problem.' She dredged up a smile when Harry whooped in delight. 'I think that's a yes.'

Leo laughed and she was relieved to see no trace of annoyance on his face. 'Seems like it. OK, guys, let's go. We'd better get a wriggle on if you want to buy some popcorn before the film starts.'

'Yes!'

The two boys went racing to the door and Mia hurriedly followed them. 'Wait!' she ordered before they had time to go charging outside. She took hold of their hands, bending so she could look from one excited face to the other. 'There are a lot of cars out there so you're to hold my hands and not go running off. Understand?'

They both nodded, holding obediently onto her hands as she led them outside. The cinema was at the far side of the complex and they skipped along beside her, chattering excitedly about the film they were about to see. Mia paused outside the cinema so Leo could catch them up, surprised by the pensive expression on his face as he ushered them inside. She waited until the boys had gone to select their popcorn before she asked him what was wrong.

'Nothing. In fact, everything's better than it's been for a long time.' He looked at the children. 'I was starting to think that I'd never get through to Noah, but tonight he seems so much more like his old self and it's all thanks to you and Harry.'

He turned and Mia's breath caught when she saw the way he was looking at her. Maybe it was gratitude that had prompted it but it felt good to see warmth in his eyes after the chill that had been there earlier. She realised that she wanted him to look at her this way all the time and it was scary to know how vulnerable she was. She mustn't make the mistake of thinking that Leo cared about her for her own sake.

'I'm glad we could help.'

She gave him a quick smile then went to pay for the popcorn. Leo had the tickets when they went back and he shepherded them into the auditorium. The theatre was packed but they had numbered seats right in the middle. The film started almost immediately and the boys were soon engrossed. Mia stared at the screen, although she took in very little of what was happening. Leo was sitting at one end and she was at the other, with Harry and Noah in between, and she told herself that she was glad. At least it meant she didn't have to sit beside him.

Her breath caught as she found herself imagining how it might have been if they had sat next to each other. She would have felt the warmth of his body, heard him breathing, smelled the scent of his skin, that clean fresh aroma that was such an intrinsic part of him. Feelings she had never experienced before suddenly swamped her and she bit her lip. She could feel her body growing hot and languid, hear own breathing becoming laboured, feel her nose tingling as though the scent that filled her nostrils was real.

Was this how passion felt? she wondered. This awakening of the senses, this heightening of awareness? Although she had loved Chris, they had been unable to make love—his injuries had made it impossible. They had shared kisses and caresses, though, and she had enjoyed them, but she had never been aroused to passion. If she was honest, she had believed that she was incapable of feeling passion but if that were true why did she feel this way?

Mia sat there in the darkness and tried to work it out but it was impossible. Impossible to take these feelings and categorise them, explain them or will them away. All she knew was that she was twenty-nine years old. She had been married. She had borne a child. Yet she had been an innocent, untried, untested, unaroused.

Until now.

Leo stared at the screen. The colours were so vivid that they made his eyes ache but he was afraid to close them. There were thoughts lurking in his head, ones he didn't want to encourage. He needed to concentrate on the film and shut them out, turn his mind away from those tantalising images of him and Mia sitting close together, holding hands, sharing a kiss, sharing more.

He cursed softly, turned it into a cough when Noah glanced at him. He turned and grinned at his son because Noah was his son no matter who his biological parents were. Mia might be Noah's mother but he was Noah's dad and he intended to be his dad for evermore. Nothing was going to get in the way of that, nothing was going to part him from this child he adored, neither Mia nor this crazy attraction he felt for her.

'OK?' he whispered, struggling to get a grip. One thing could lead to another and before he knew it, he'd be in so deep he'd never get out. He had been attracted to other women in the past and had parted company from them when the time had come, but he couldn't do that with Mia, could he? She was part of this whole package, her and Harry, and Noah and him. They were all bound up together so that if you wanted one you had to have the other as well. Mia and Harry came as a pair. Just like him and Noah.

'It's great!'

Noah grinned at him then turned back to the screen and Leo felt his heart overflow. He couldn't describe how wonderful it felt to see the child looking so happy. It had been a long haul to reach this point and there could still be problems ahead, but Noah would get there eventually. He was sure of that, just as he was sure that meeting Mia had been the trigger. Noah had formed a bond with her and Harry and that was what had made the difference. He would always be grateful to her for that.

He glanced along the row, felt his breath catch when he caught sight of her. She was staring at the screen but he knew that she wasn't thinking about the film. There was just something about her expression, a certain set to her features that told him it was the last thing on her mind.

Leo turned away, staring sightlessly ahead. He could no longer see the eye-aching colours flashing across the screen or hear the raucous music. He was being drawn into a world of his own, a world that he really, *really* didn't want to inhabit.

He groaned quietly, unable to fight off temptation any longer. Pictures immediately flooded his mind, pictures of him and Mia touching, kissing, caressing, making love. He knew it was wrong to indulge himself this way. If he followed through on such thoughts it could be a disaster, and not just for him but for Noah and Harry. He had dated enough women both before and after his marriage ended to know that physical attraction didn't last. Oh, it might take a month or two but it always faded, and that would complicate matters even more.

He could deal with the thought of Mia being Noah's real mother, accept that she had given birth to his son. What he couldn't handle was the idea of her once having been his lover. That would be a step too far!

CHAPTER NINE

IT WAS GONE seven by the time the film ended. Mia took hold of Harry's hand and briskly led him outside, wanting to bring the evening to a speedy conclusion. Turning, she smiled politely at Leo, who was in the process of zipping up Noah's coat.

'Thank you for inviting us. We really enjoyed it, didn't we, Harry?'

'It was brilliant!'

Harry grinned at them and she saw Leo's expression soften. It touched her that it so obviously meant a lot to him to have earned Harry's approval, but she hardened her heart. She couldn't afford to let her emotions run away with her again.

Heat rushed up her face as she recalled in vivid detail how she'd felt in the cinema and she turned away, making a great production of fastening Harry's jacket. Maybe she was attracted to Leo but nothing was going to come of it; she would make sure of that. It would be foolish in the extreme to get involved with him when the situation they faced was already so fraught.

'I'm glad you enjoyed it, Harry. Noah enjoyed having you along. Maybe you'd like to come round to our house one day and play with him, if your mummy doesn't mind, of course.'

Mia looked up when she heard the hesitancy in Leo's voice. It wasn't like him to exhibit anything other than supreme confidence, so it came as a surprise. 'Of course I don't mind,' she said quietly, wondering what could have dented his legendary self-assurance.

'Good.' He gave her a quick smile and she realised that she must have imagined it. There was certainly no sign of indecision as he turned to Harry. 'How about if you come round on Saturday? Would you like that? Noah and I can pick you up around ten if you fancy it.'

'Yes!' Harry exclaimed, obviously delighted at the thought of seeing his new friend again.

Mia didn't share his joy, however. Leo had made no mention of her going along and she wasn't sure if she was happy to let Harry go off on his own with Leo just yet. Maybe he was Harry's real father but she knew very little about him apart from the fact that he was a first-rate surgeon.

'Noah's daddy and I need to talk about it first,' she cautioned. She shook her head when Harry's lower lip jutted ominously. 'I'm not saying that you can't go, darling, but Leo and I need to sort out the details.' She gave a forced little laugh, hating the fact that she'd been made to take on the role of the bad guy for spoiling the promised treat. 'Why, I don't even know where Noah lives!'

'You're right,' Leo said with a grimace. 'Sorry, Harry. I should have asked your mummy first before I suggested it.'

'Never mind.' Mia tried to shrug it off as an oversight, although she wasn't happy about his high-handed behaviour. If he thought he could walk all over her, he could think again! She took hold of Harry's hand. 'I'll give you a call and see what we can work out. OK?'

'Fine. You should have my phone number but I'll give it to you again just in case.' He dug in his pocket and came up with a scrap of paper, scribbling down his telephone number before handing it to her. 'We live in Primrose Hill—I should have written the address down as well.' He took the paper from her and wrote down his address then gave it back to her. 'If you do agree to let Harry come I promise I'll take very good care of him, Mia.'

'I'm sure you will,' Mia agreed, wondering if he was deliberately making it appear as though she was fussing. Her smile was strained as she slipped the paper into her pocket. If Leo was planning to play these sorts of games, she had no intention of letting him get away with it. 'Right, it's time we went home. Say goodnight, Harry.'

She led Harry to the bus stop after he'd said goodbye. Fortunately their bus arrived almost immediately so they got on board and climbed the stairs as Harry loved sitting on the top deck. Mia caught a glimpse of Leo and Noah standing at the bus stop before their bus pulled away and had to clamp down on the anger bubbling inside her.

Was Leo trying to gain the upper hand by offering Harry treats? She hoped not. The situation was difficult enough without that sort of added pressure. Harry was her son no matter what the

DNA tests said and she wasn't going to allow anyone to lure him away. How would Leo feel if she tried to do the same to Noah? she wondered, and shivered. She could imagine only too easily how Leo would react.

Leo made his way home, very much aware that he had upset Mia. He got Noah ready for bed then went downstairs, wondering what to do. Normally, he wouldn't have cared two hoots. Although he was never deliberately rude, he did tend to be a little too forthright so there'd been a number of occasions when he had unwittingly hurt someone's feelings. Normally his solution was to ignore it because in his experience folk got over it in the end. However, he couldn't seem to take that approach with Mia. He had upset her and he regretted it. Very much.

He went into his study and picked up the phone then hesitated. Would a phone call be enough or would it be better if he spoke to her face to face? He would hate to think that she didn't believe he was genuinely sorry, especially when it could have a detrimental impact on their future dealings. He needed Mia on his side, although he

JENNIFER TAYLOR   149

wasn't prepared to delve too deeply into all the reasons why it was so important to him.

He phoned his housekeeper instead and asked her if she would mind sitting with Noah as he had to go out. As soon as she arrived, he left. He glanced at the dashboard clock as he started the car: half past eight. Not too late to go calling by most people's standards so, hopefully, it wouldn't be too late for Mia. He certainly didn't want to upset her any more than he already had!

Mia had just made herself a cup of tea when there was a knock on the front door. Putting the cup on the table, she went to answer it, wondering who it could be. She rarely had visitors and it was too late for any salespeople to call. Opening the door, she gasped when she found Leo standing outside.

'What are you doing here?'

'I was going to phone but then I decided it would be better if I spoke to you face to face,' he said quietly.

'Really?' Mia replied, hoping he couldn't tell how on edge she felt. Having him turn up like this was a shock and not a pleasant one either after what had happened earlier. She squared her shoulders, determined to stick to her decision not to allow him to ride roughshod over her. If he had come to harass her about allowing Harry to visit his home this weekend, he could think again.

'So, what do you want? Or do I need to ask?' Her smile was tight. 'If you've come to *browbeat* me into agreeing to let Harry come and play with Noah then forget it, Leo. I make the decisions where Harry is concerned, not you.'

'I know. And I'm truly sorry if you thought I was trying to force your hand.' He grimaced, his handsome face filled with contrition. 'I'm so used to getting my own way that it's hard to accept that I need to consult you when it comes to Harry.'

'Oh. I see.' Mia was nonplussed by the apology and had no idea what to say. She bit her lip and heard him sigh.

'I never meant to upset you, Mia. The last thing I want is you and me falling out.'

'Me too. We've enough to contend with without us being at odds.'

'Too right we do.' His tone was wry. It matched the smile he gave her as he stepped away from the door. 'Anyway, I won't keep you. I just wanted to make my apologies and smooth things over.'

'I appreciate that.' Mia took a quick breath, wondering why she felt so loath to let him leave. She didn't bother trying to work it out as she opened the door wider. 'Would you like a cup of tea, seeing as you're here? I've just made a pot and you're very welcome to share it with me.'

'Thank you. I'd like that.' He smiled at her as he stepped into the tiny vestibule. 'A cup of tea sounds like just the thing to seal a friendship.'

Mia smiled politely as she led the way into the living room, although she couldn't help wondering if they would ever be friends. Necessity had brought them together rather than choice and there was no way of knowing if they would get on in the long term, just as there was no way of knowing if friendship would be enough. She bit her lip. Having Leo as her friend might be good, but having him as her lover would be even better.

'I'll get your tea. Milk and sugar?'

Mia forced the thought aside, terrified that he would pick up on it. She didn't want Leo to be her lover; the idea was ridiculous. It would only complicate matters even more, especially if they fell out as lovers so often did. Imagine how difficult it would be to see and speak to Leo, to have any dealings whatsoever with him if they'd been intimately involved. No, she must forget how she'd felt in the cinema and focus on what really mattered, Harry and Noah. She may not have given birth to Noah but he was still her son and she cared about him.

'Just milk, please.' Leo looked around the room, smiling when he spotted a photo of Harry on the mantelpiece. He picked it up, shaking his head in amazement. 'There's a photo of me at about the same age and we could be two peas in a pod.'

'Really? You must let me see it one day.' Mia went over to the shelves in the alcove next to the chimney breast and picked up the photograph album. 'There's a lot more photos in here if you'd like to have a look at them.'

'I would. Thank you.'

Leo took the album from her and she sucked in her breath when their hands touched. He took it over to the sofa and sat down, opening it at the first page. He seemed engrossed when she left the room and it was a relief. At least Leo hadn't experienced that flash of awareness that had shot through her when their hands had touched. It would be so much harder if he had, so much more difficult to fight her feelings if she knew that he felt the same.

She took a deep breath, forcing down the rush of sensations that had filled her. They were the parents of their two beautiful boys. It was enough of a bond between them and they didn't need anything more.

Leo inhaled sharply as Mia left the room but his heart was racing. He couldn't remember the last time he had felt this way—probably never. Whatever relationships he'd had in the past, he had always been in control. Even when he had asked Amanda to marry him it had been a conscious decision, weighed up and evaluated beforehand. Love hadn't entered into it, desire had been merely a bonus. He had enjoyed sleeping with Amanda enough to overlook her more irritating traits, although even that hadn't lasted much beyond their honeymoon. Desire rarely did last in his experience. So why had he reacted so strongly when his and Mia's hands had touched? Why did he want it to happen again?

And, most worrying of all, why did it feel as though his brain was engaged this time and not just his body?

'Here you are.'

Leo jumped when Mia reappeared with a cup of tea for him. He took it from her, taking care not to touch her this time. Once was enough if his current parlous state of mind was anything to go by. 'Thanks.'

He took a sip of the hot liquid then looked for somewhere to put the cup down. Mia hurriedly moved a small table closer to him.

'Use this.'

'Thank you.'

He placed the cup on the table and sat back in his seat, determined to project the right image. Maybe he did feel at sixes and sevens but it would pass and he'd soon be back to his usual self. He frowned, wondering why the idea seemed less appealing than it should have done. He liked his life free of emotional ties, apart from the ties he had to Noah obviously. So why did he find himself wondering if he was missing out?

'Harry really enjoyed the film. He talked about it all the way home.'

'Did he? That's good.'

Leo dredged up a smile. His life was fine and there was nothing he lacked. He had enough money to buy whatever he wanted and go wherever he chose. He enjoyed his work and wouldn't wish to do anything else. If he needed to satisfy his more basic needs then it was easy enough to find an attractive woman to satisfy them with. He had everything he could possibly want.

Except Mia.

The blood rushed to his head so that he missed what else she said. There were reasons why he and Mia could never get involved, important reasons like the effect it could have on the boys, but it didn't make a scrap of difference. Leo realised with a sinking heart that it was what he wanted. Badly. He, Leo Forester, erstwhile master of his own destiny, had no control whatsoever in this instance.

Mia's voice faltered. Leo was staring at her, although she doubted if he'd heard a word she had said. She had no idea what was going through his mind but if his expression was anything to go by, it wasn't pleasant. She cleared her throat and saw him jump. 'Penny for them. You were miles away.'

'Was I? Sorry.'

He turned to the next page in the album, studying a photo of Chris holding Harry on his lap. Harry had been just a few weeks old when it was taken and he was staring at the camera with that intensity that very young babies often displayed. Mia drummed up a laugh. She really didn't want to know what Leo had been thinking. Something warned her it would be too disturbing.

'Harry was about six weeks old when that was taken,' she explained, clamping down on the rush of heat that scorched her veins. To imagine that Leo was experiencing the same kind of uncertainty as she was would be asking for trouble. 'He'd just had a bath and Chris was giving him a cuddle before I put him to bed.'

'He looks very contented.'

'He was. He was such a good baby, ate and slept exactly like the textbooks said he should do.' She smiled reminiscently. 'Chris and I used to say that we'd won the jackpot when we got Harry.'

'Noah was the exact opposite,' Leo said wryly,

and she was relieved to hear him sounding more like he normally did.

'Was he?' she said quickly, wanting to keep the conversation on track. It was easier when they focused on the children, less stressful.

'Mmm. He never slept and as for feeding…! We were lucky if we could get a couple of ounces of milk down him.'

'It must have been very difficult for your ex-wife,' she observed, wondering if that explained why Noah's mother had abandoned him. A lot of women suffered from postnatal depression and it could be that Noah's mother had been one of them.

'Amanda had very little to do with looking after him. She hired a nanny to care for him when she left hospital,' Leo said shortly.

'I see,' Mia replied, because there wasn't much else she could say. She had loved looking after Harry and had relished every moment, but maybe she was being uncharitable. After all, she hadn't suffered all those sleepless nights, had she?

Leo didn't say anything else as he turned to the next photo, which happened to be one of her sitting on a rug in the garden, holding Harry. He studied it intently, rather too intently, in fact. Mia gave a nervous little laugh.

'The bags under my eyes were the result of rushing around all over the place. Harry wasn't responsible for them.'

'I never noticed them.' He looked up and his grey eyes seemed to shimmer with silver fire as they rested on her. 'I was just thinking how happy you look, Mia. Happy and fulfilled.'

'I was.' Mia felt a lump come to her throat. It was silly to feel so touched by the observation but she couldn't help it. 'I loved being a mum and to cap it all, Chris was so well at the time too. It was one of those perfect times in your life when everything comes together.'

'You must miss him, your husband, I mean.'

'I do. He was so brave. It doesn't seem fair that after everything he'd been through, he should have died like that.'

'What happened exactly?'

'He developed a DVT. Chris had no idea, of course. He wasn't aware of any pain but I realised something was wrong when I saw how swollen his leg was.' She sighed. 'He was rushed into hospital and given drugs to dissolve the clot but part of it must have broken off. He had a massive heart attack and there was nothing anyone could do.'

'It must have been horrendous for you.'

The sympathy in his voice brought tears to her eyes and she blinked them away. 'It was. Harry had just turned three and all I could think about was that now he would grow up without a father. I know how it feels not to have a family and it broke my heart to think that Harry would miss out on so much.'

'Did your father die when you were young?' Leo asked, and she shook her head.

'No. Or, rather, I don't think he did.' She saw him frown and realised that she would have to explain. Her tone was brisk because she didn't want him to think that she was looking for sympathy. 'I never knew my father. He was well off the scene by the time I was born. I don't know that much about my mother either as I was taken into care when I was eighteen months old and had very little contact with her after that.'

'Good heavens!' Leo exclaimed. 'I had no idea that you'd had it so tough.'

'There's no reason why you should have

known,' she countered. 'Anyway, it's all in the past. It doesn't affect me now.'

'Oh, I think it does.' He looked at her and Mia shuddered when she felt the intensity of his gaze envelop her like a physical force. 'The way you were brought up has made you the person you are today, Mia. It's one of the reasons why you're such a good mother, in fact.'

He paused and she steeled herself for what he would say next. 'I only wish that you'd been around when Noah was born. It would have made the world of difference to him, I'm sure.'

CHAPTER TEN

'SO, IS THERE anything you'd like to ask me, David?'

Leo waited while the younger man gave it some thought. It was Friday morning and a slot had un-expectedly become vacant in Theatre. As soon as he had found out, he had contacted David Rimmer and offered him the chance to have the ICD fitted. The sooner it was done the better, in his opinion.

'I don't think so.' David frowned as he turned to Mia. 'Is there anything else I need to know, do you think?'

'No. I think Mr Forester has covered every-thing, David.' She squeezed the young man's hand. 'My advice to you is to let him do what he does best—mend wonky hearts!'

David laughed, obviously relieved to be given such straightforward advice. Leo smiled too, although his own feelings were far more complicated. Ever since Mia had revealed what a difficult time she'd had growing up, his emotions had swung from one extreme to the other.

Whilst he admired her fortitude, he wished with every scrap of his being that she hadn't had to experience so much unhappiness in her life. It made his own upbringing seem like a walk in the park by comparison and he found himself wondering if he was guilty of self-indulgence. Maybe his parents hadn't smothered him in love but they had always been there for him.

It was unsettling to find himself re-evaluating yet another aspect of his life. He pushed the thought aside while he concentrated on David. 'As I explained the other day, you'll be having a local anaesthetic, not a general one. You'll be sedated as well but you will be conscious throughout the procedure.'

'So basically I'll know what's going on but won't be able to kick up a fuss if I don't like it?' David observed wryly.

Leo laughed, very much aware that he wouldn't have laughed a few weeks ago. He would have maintained a strictly professional front rather than encourage a patient to speak to him this way, but that had been before he'd met Mia. Meeting her had changed him. It was another disquieting thought.

'That's right. Once I have you on the table, there's no backing out. Still, look on the bright side. The ICD will mean that you'll see a lot less of me in the future.'

'Bonus!' David declared. 'Although I have to admit that I'll miss Mia. She makes a wicked cup of coffee.'

'Flatterer,' Mia retorted, laughing.

She straightened the sheet then followed Leo to the door. He paused so she could catch him up, thinking how pretty she looked. The navy-blue colour of her uniform suited her, he decided, highlighting the chestnut lights in her hair and bringing out the glorious emerald-green shade of her eyes. His gaze ran over her as he took appreciative stock. She was neither too fat nor too thin but just perfect. It was only when he realised that she was looking expectantly at him that he rallied.

'I'm not anticipating any problems. David should be back on the ward later this morning. Are his parents coming in?'

'Yes. He told them to wait until after the op so it will be nearer to lunchtime before they get here.'

'Good. Right, it looks like we're good to go.' Leo turned to leave, not wanting to linger in case it became a habit. Work was work and they'd agreed to keep it separate from their private lives. A frisson shot through him and he had to remind himself that the only private life he and Mia had revolved around the children.

'Before you go, Leo, I just want to make sure what the arrangements are for tomorrow,' she said, putting her hand on his arm.

Leo sucked in his breath when he felt the hairs all over his body stand to attention. It was just a touch, he told himself sternly, but it was hard to think of it as *just* anything. 'Tomorrow?'

'When Harry comes to play with Noah.' She frowned. 'You are still expecting him? He's talked about nothing else all week and he'll be really disappointed if he can't come.'

'Of course he can come!' Leo exclaimed. 'I didn't think you were keen on the idea, that's all.'

She sighed. 'I wasn't when you first suggested it but now I've accepted that you aren't trying to lure Harry away, I'm fine with it.'

'I would *never* try to lure him away from you, Mia.' He covered her hand with his, feeling his heart leap when he realised how small and delicate it felt compared to his. An unfamiliar rush of tenderness filled him and his tone deepened. 'I give you my word on that.'

'Thank you. I appreciate it more than you can imagine.'

Her voice had softened, the husky tones making all those pesky hairs start saluting again. Leo felt the fledgling tender feelings change to something deeper and drew in his breath. Even though he knew it was inappropriate to behave this way at work, he couldn't help himself. It was only when he heard footsteps coming along the corridor that he managed to get a grip.

He stepped back so that Mia's hand slid from his arm. 'I'll pick Harry up around ten if that's all right with you?'

'Fine. I'll make sure he's ready.'

She smiled but he could see the awareness in her eyes and knew that she felt the same as he did. He turned away, barely acknowledging the greeting as he passed one of the nurses. His head was spinning as thoughts whirled around inside it. He was attracted to Mia and she was attracted to him too but they couldn't act upon their feelings. They had to concentrate on Noah and Harry, on making sure that what had happened at the clinic didn't ruin their young lives.

Leo took a deep breath as he stepped into the lift. He might want Mia but he could never have her. The sooner he accepted that, the easier it would be.

'My, my, you two looked very cosy. Do I detect a hint of romance in the air?'

Mia started when Penny Morrison stopped beside her. Taking a deep breath, she turned to her. 'Don't be silly. Mr Forester and I were discussing a patient.'

'Really? So that's why you were staring into each other's eyes.' Penny grinned. 'Pull the other one, Mia. That's got umpteen bells on it!'

Mia sighed. She knew it was pointless trying to convince Penny that she was telling the truth. After all, she and Leo had been staring at each other. She ditched that thought because she couldn't deal with it right then. Maybe later she would be able to make sense of what had happened but not now.

'You're adding two and two and coming up with five hundred. Leo and I were sorting out what time he can collect Harry tomorrow.'

'Harry? And why should *Leo* be making arrangements to collect him?' Penny demanded, emphasising Mia's use of Leo's first name.

'Because Harry and Noah are friends and they want to spend the morning together,' Mia explained, deciding it was easier to ignore the unspoken question. She would only dig herself an even deeper hole if she tried to explain how she happened to be on first-name terms with one of the consultants.

'Friends? How come?' Penny followed her into the office, making it clear that she wasn't about to give up. 'I mean, how did they meet? I know for a fact that Mr Forester's son goes to a private school so it can't have been there.'

'Of course not. Harry and I happened to bump into him and Noah at a fast-food place on Monday.' Mia shrugged. 'We ended up going to the cinema together to see a film. Harry and Noah just seemed to hit it off, so Leo invited Harry round to play with him tomorrow.'

'Fancy that. Maybe the Ice Man is human after all.'

Penny shrugged and Mia was relieved to see that her friend had accepted her explanation. When Penny turned her attention to the reason for her visit—a timetable glitch—she breathed easier. Although she hated misleading Penny, it was vital that nobody found out what was going on. The last thing she wanted was the boys overhearing something they shouldn't.

Mia sat down to update David Rimmer's notes after Penny left, wondering if it was possible to stop people finding out. At some point, she and Leo would have to tell the boys what had happened and there was no knowing how they would react. It could be that they would have to inform their schools too and the thought of more people knowing that Harry was actually Leo's son and Noah was hers filled her with dread. The more people who knew, the harder it would be to keep it a secret.

It was early when Leo got up on Saturday morning. Mrs Davies didn't come in at the weekend unless he was seeing patients at his rooms in Harley Street. Since Noah's accident, he had tried to keep Saturdays free. Although he was aware that several of his colleagues weren't happy with the arrangement, helping Noah overcome whatever was troubling him took precedence.

Once breakfast was over, he sent Noah upstairs for his coat. Although they were far too early to collect Harry, he couldn't see any point in them waiting around. He sighed, aware that he was as eager to see Mia as Noah was to see his new friend. He was acting like a teenager in the throes of his first crush…except he hadn't acted this way when he *had* been a teenager! It was worrying to realise that Mia had this effect on him, especially when he knew it couldn't lead anywhere.

It was just after nine when he drew up outside her house. He helped Noah out of the car and ushered him up the path. Mia must have heard them because she opened the door before he could knock.

'I take it that Noah couldn't wait either,' she said, smiling at him. 'Harry was dressed and all ready to go by seven!'

'Was he?' Leo smiled back, trying to ignore the leap his pulse had given when she'd opened the door. Maybe he was having some sort of mid-life crisis, he mused, and that explained why he was acting so out of character. He tested out the theory as he followed her inside but he wasn't convinced. He sighed. Maybe he should stop trying to analyse what was happening and just get on with it. 'Good. I don't feel as guilty now for landing on your doorstep at this hour of the morning.'

'Oh, there's no need to feel guilty. We've been up for ages. Still, at least it meant you didn't catch me in my pyjamas.'

'Er…no.' Leo managed to hold his smile but all of a sudden his mind was awash with pictures of Mia in her nightclothes or, more accurately, out of them. He cleared his throat. 'I'll give Harry his lunch if that's all right with you and bring him back around four?'

'That's fine.' She looked round when Harry and Noah came racing into the room. 'Did you hear that, darling? Leo says you can have lunch with Noah.'

Her tone was bright and breezy, so why did Leo have the feeling that she knew exactly what he'd been thinking? He turned to the boys, eager to hide his confusion. He preferred to keep his feelings under wraps. He had always been highly successful at doing so too and it worried him to know that Mia could slip past his defences so easily.

'Right, guys, let's get going. Say goodbye to your mummy, Harry.'

He waited while Harry gave Mia a hug, somewhat surprised when Noah hugged her as well. Noah had been so withdrawn lately, shying away whenever Leo had tried to hug him, but obviously he felt comfortable about hugging Mia.

It was something he knew he would take on board. As he led the boys out to the car, he couldn't help wondering if this was the turning point he'd been hoping for. Having Mia around could be exactly what Noah needed, even though the child had no idea who she really was. He sighed as he started the engine. It made it more imperative than ever that he keep a rein on his feelings. He couldn't afford to do anything that might harm Noah's relationship with Mia.

Mia set to after Leo left and got all the jobs that needed doing finished in record time. She looked around the pristine kitchen and sighed. Maybe it was easier to get the housework done without Harry constantly interrupting her but she did miss him. She glanced at the clock and grimaced: it was only eleven a.m. Leo had promised to have Harry home by four. which meant she had five hours to kill. How on earth was she going to fill in the time?

She made herself a cup of coffee and sat down at the table to drink it. When she had been in the children's home, she had longed for time on her own, she remembered wryly. Once she had left care, she had found a flat—a bedsit really—and revelled in the fact that she had her own space at last. She had lived on her own until she had married, in fact, and had enjoyed it, but not any longer. She couldn't bear to imagine how lonely her life would be if she didn't have Harry.

She stood up, refusing to sit there and think depressing thoughts. Leo had promised that he wouldn't try to take Harry away from her and she believed him. She went upstairs to her bedroom and opened the wardrobe. She had been meaning to sort through Chris's clothes and give them to a local charity shop and now was the perfect time to do it.

Mia set to work, not even stopping for lunch.

She hadn't realised just how much there was of Chris's belongings but by the time she heard a car drawing up outside, she had everything sorted. She ran downstairs, smiling as she opened the front door. 'Hello, sweetheart. Have you had a lovely time?'

'It was brilliant!' Harry declared. 'Noah has this *huge* garage and a hundred million cars. We played with them for ages!'

'How wonderful.' Mia turned to Noah. Leo hadn't made it up the path yet as he was on his phone. It was obviously an important call because he looked very grave. She smiled at the little boy, her heart turning over when once again she was struck by his resemblance to Chris. Maybe it was the fact that she had spent the afternoon sorting through Chris's belongings but she felt very emotional all of a sudden. 'Did you enjoy it too, Noah?'

'Yes.' He smiled shyly up at her. 'Harry's my best friend and he said he wants to come and play with me again if you'll let him.'

'Of course he can,' Mia assured him, giving him a hug. 'And you can come and play with him too, if you want to.'

She straightened up as Noah nodded, feeling her pulse leap when she found herself staring into Leo's eyes. 'Noah was just telling me what a lovely time he and Harry have had,' she explained, trying not to read too much into the way he was looking at her, but it was impossible. To know that Leo wanted her this much was both scary and exciting.

She hurried on, terrified that she would do something stupid. She and Leo could never be more than friends. She had to remember that and not be tempted to put her own needs ahead of the boys'. 'Thank you for inviting Harry. He enjoyed every minute.'

'It was my pleasure, Mia.'

His voice sounded so deep as he said her name that she shivered. She turned away, her heart racing. She knew so little about desire yet that was what she was feeling. She wanted Leo, wanted him to say her name again as he kissed her, caressed her, made love to her, and the strength of her feelings shocked her. She had never wanted any man like this, had never felt this need growing inside her, consuming her. So why did she feel this way about Leo? Why did the sound of his voice saying her name fill her with such longing? She had no idea. What she did know was that she and Leo could never be lovers.

CHAPTER ELEVEN

LEO'S CHEST FELT tight as he followed Mia inside. He took a deep breath but no amount of oxygen could ease the restriction. His hands clenched as he struggled to contain the feelings that were running riot inside him. Maybe she did want him every bit as much as he wanted her but nothing was going to come of it.

He followed her into the sitting room and looked around. He had no idea what she had been doing but she'd obviously been busy because there was a smudge of dirt on her cheek. His hand half lifted to wipe it away before he thought better of it. He didn't dare touch her, couldn't take that risk. One touch wouldn't be enough—he'd want more and more, he'd want it all.

His vision blurred as pictures danced before his eyes, pictures of him stroking and caressing every inch of her satin-smooth skin, and a groan broke from his lips. How the hell was he going to cope when the mere thought of making love to her could push him to the edge?

'Leo? Are you all right?'

The question broke into his thoughts and he rallied. 'Sorry. I was just trying to work out what to do.'

'Why? What's happened? Can I help in any way?'

Definitely, Leo thought wryly, although he managed not to say so. 'Not really. One of my patients has been rushed into hospital. He was due to have bypass surgery but he's been putting it off for months now. There's no way we can delay any longer, though. It needs sorting out a.s.a.p.'

'Surely Dr Wilson can deal with him?' Mia suggested, frowning.

Leo's hands clenched once again as he fought to control the urge to smooth away the tiny lines puckering her brow. He had never wanted to touch a woman as much as he yearned to touch her and it was hard to accept that he was no longer in full control of himself. 'He could, only the patient has requested that I perform the surgery. He's one of my private patients,' he added by way of explanation.

'Oh, I see.' Mia grimaced. 'That makes a difference, doesn't it?'

'It does.' He sighed as he glanced at Noah. Maybe it was a shock to find himself responding this way but he would deal with it. He didn't have a choice. 'I've no idea what I'm going to do about Noah. Normally, I'd ask my housekeeper to mind him but she's away for the weekend. The only thing I can think of is to contact an agency and hire a nanny for the night.'

'There's no need to do that!' Mia exclaimed. 'Noah can stay here. In fact, he can have a sleepover with Harry.'

'Are you sure?' Leo said in surprise.

'Of course I'm sure.' She laughed. 'Although I should warn you that it's doubtful if there'll be very much sleeping done!'

Leo laughed too. 'If today is anything to go by then you could be right. The two of them have never stopped chattering all day long.'

'It's great that they get on so well, isn't it?' Mia glanced at the boys, who were busily engaged in building a tower out of some plastic blocks. She sighed. 'Hopefully, it will make it that much easier when we tell them what's happened.'

'Let's hope so,' Leo agreed quietly. That Mia was as worried as he was by the thought of how the boys were going to react when they found out the truth was obvious. Reaching out, he squeezed her hand, wanting to offer whatever reassurance he could. 'They'll both be in the same boat and that's bound to help.'

He removed his hand before he was tempted to let it linger. Turning to Noah, he quickly explained that he had to go to the hospital to see someone who was very sick but that Mia had invited him to stay with Harry for a sleepover. Both boys let out a huge cheer at the news, making it clear that they loved the idea. They went thundering up the stairs, leaving him and Mia alone. Leo summoned a smile.

'That seemed to meet with everyone's approval. You're sure you don't mind, though? It seems a bit rich to put on you like this.'

'You're not putting on me. I'm only too happy to help, especially when it means I'll have the chance to get to know Noah a bit better. Is there anything I need to know—food he's allergic to or hates, things like that?'

'No, nothing. He's not keen on cheese but apart

from that he eats most things.' He glanced at his watch and grimaced. 'I'll have to go. If you need me then phone. OK?'

'Of course, but there's no need to worry. Noah will be perfectly fine.'

'I know he will.' He headed out to the hall then paused. Mia had followed him and all of a sudden he couldn't contain his feelings any longer. Bending, he brushed her cheek with his lips, feeling a rush of sensations flow through his body. It was all he could do to draw back but he had a patient waiting and he couldn't waste any time. 'I trust you to look after Noah not because he's your son, Mia, but because you're you. You'd never let anything bad happen to him.'

'Thank you.'

Leo heard the catch in her voice and knew that his words had touched her. He opened the door, knowing that if he didn't leave now, he might not leave at all. He drove straight to the hospital, forcing himself to concentrate on what lay ahead. It was easier that way, less stressful to think about the complexities of the surgery he was about to perform than his own feelings. Maybe a time would come when he would have to face up to how he felt but not right now. Right now he was going to save a man's life. That took precedence over everything else.

By ten o'clock the house was quiet at last. Mia made herself a cup of tea and took it into the sitting room. Sinking down onto a chair, she sighed wearily. Harry and Noah had had the most wonderful time. She'd made a makeshift tent for them out of an old clothes airer covered with a sheet and they had played in it all evening. They'd even had their tea in there, wolfing down fish fingers and chips followed by ice cream. It had taken all her ingenuity to persuade them to vacate it for their bath but they had finally given in and spent the next hour splashing about. Now they were tucked up in bed and, hopefully, asleep.

A light knock on the front door roused her. Mia went to answer it, surprised to find Leo outside. 'I didn't realise you were coming back!' she exclaimed as she let him in.

'I wasn't planning to but I felt like some company. I hope you don't mind?'

'Of course not.' She led him into the sitting room. 'Sit down. You look worn out.'

'I feel it.' He rested his head against the cushions and sighed. 'It's not been the best of evenings. The patient I was operating on died in Theatre.'

'Oh, I'm so sorry. What happened?'

'We'd not even started when he had a massive infarct. James and I did everything we could but it was no use.' He ran his hands through his hair. 'I keep going over it, wondering if there was something we missed.'

'I doubt it. If you and Dr Wilson did all you could then there was nothing anyone could have done.' She shook her head when he went to speak. 'I mean it, Leo. You did your best and it didn't work. You can't go blaming yourself when it wasn't your fault.'

'I suppose you're right. It's just hard when you lose a patient like that.'

'It must be.' She stood up. 'How about a cup of tea? Or something stronger? I've a bottle of wine if you'd like a glass.'

'I'd love one but I'm driving.'

'You can always leave your car here and call a cab,' she suggested, trying not to think about the other alternative. Inviting him to spend the night on her sofa would be asking for trouble.

'I could, couldn't I?' He smiled up at her. 'All right, you've talked me into it. I would love a glass of wine, please.'

'Coming right up.'

Mia hurried into the kitchen, refusing to think about what she had seen in his eyes. There was no point wondering if the same thought had occurred to him as had occurred to her. She poured them both some wine and took the glasses back to the sitting room. Leo had his eyes closed when she went in; he looked exhausted and her heart filled with tenderness. Maybe he did present a detached front to the world but there was no doubt in her mind that he genuinely cared about his patients.

'Is that the wine?' He opened one eye a crack and peered up at her. 'Would you mind putting it on the table? I'm not sure if I have the energy to drink it just yet.'

'Just try a sip,' she said persuasively, offering him the glass. 'It might give you the boost you need.'

'You could be right.' He sat up and went to

take the glass from her. Mia wasn't sure what happened but the next second the glass tipped over, showering red wine all down the front of his sweatshirt.

Leo shot to his feet. 'What a mess! At least it didn't go on your sofa, Mia.'

'I don't think there was much left after you had a soaking,' she observed ruefully.

'Hmm, I did seem to get most of it,' he agreed, staring down at his sweatshirt.

'Here, let me have it.' She held out her hand. 'If you let it dry, you'll never get the stain out. I'll pop it in the washer for you.'

'There's no need to go to all that trouble. It's only a sweatshirt.'

'It's no trouble,' she insisted.

Leo shrugged as he dragged it over his head and handed it to her. 'Then thank you.'

'No problem.' Mia summoned a smile but it was an effort. Maybe it didn't bother him that he was standing there naked to the waist but it most certainly bothered her.

She took the sweatshirt into the kitchen and filled the sink with cold water, deciding to wash out some of the wine before she put it into the machine. She heard footsteps behind her but didn't look round, not sure if she could maintain her composure if she was treated to another glimpse of that broad tanned chest with its dusting of crisp black hair...

'Is it coming out?'

Leo's voice rumbled softly in her ear as he peered over her shoulder and Mia felt a wave of desire wash over her. She nodded, keeping her eyes on the water, which was slowly turning pink.

'Looks like it. I'll let it soak for a few minutes before I put it in the machine.' She took a deep breath then turned, trying not to look at him as she picked up the wine bottle. 'How about a top-up seeing as you never got chance to taste the first glass?'

'If you think I can be trusted not to cause more mayhem I'd love one.'

His tone was light but she could hear the undercurrent it held and the feelings inside her intensified. Her hand was shaking as she took a clean glass off the shelf and poured some wine into it. It was harder than ever to deal with how she felt when it was obvious that Leo felt the same way, but she had to try. Maybe she did want him and maybe he wanted her too but they both knew it would be wrong to act upon their feelings. They had to think about the effect it could have on the boys when their relationship ended, as it undoubtedly would.

Mia picked up the glass and took it into the sitting room, putting it down carefully on the table. Leo had followed her and she glanced at him as she made for the door. 'I'll find you something to wear.'

'Thank you.' He stepped aside, making sure she had room to pass. He knew as well as she did how dangerous it would be if they touched one another.

Mia ran upstairs and opened one of the bags she had filled to take to the charity shop. Although Chris had been a lot smaller than Leo, there were a couple of his T-shirts that might fit him. She felt her breath catch as she imagined how Leo would look wearing them, his muscular body filling out the fabric in a way that Chris's had never done.

Tears sprang to her eyes because it felt wrong to think such thoughts, *wrong* to compare the two men this way. She had loved Chris and he had loved her. He had given her so much, taught her to trust and made her see how good life could be if you had the right person to share it with. Their marriage had been a success despite the problems they had faced and she didn't regret a minute of the time they had spent together. However, she couldn't pretend that she had wanted Chris the way she wanted Leo.

Leo sat down on the sofa. If he hadn't been half-naked he would have left. It would have been the sensible thing to do, far more sensible than sitting here and waiting for Mia to come back. What was the point of torturing himself? He and Mia could never be anything more than Harry's and Noah's parents. He understood that so why did he find it so hard to do the right thing? Was he really so weak-willed that he could no longer take charge of his actions, even for the sake of his son?

He stood up abruptly and went to the door, stopping when he saw Mia coming down the stairs. She paused when she spotted him stand-ing in the doorway.

'Everything all right?'

'Fine.' He drummed up a laugh, his heart pounding when he realised he had missed his chance. Now he would have to stay and simply pray that he didn't make a complete hash of things. 'I've managed not to spill the wine again, you'll be pleased to hear.'

'Good. One soaking per night is enough for anyone.' She came the rest of the way down the stairs and showed him the T-shirts. 'These might fit, although they're bound to be on the snug side. Chris wasn't as big as you.'

'Thanks.' Leo reluctantly took them from her. He went back into the sitting room, wondering why he hated the idea of wearing her late husband's clothes so much. Picking up one of the T-shirts, he dragged it over his head. It was a tight fit, as she'd said, but it was better than nothing.

'I can try to find something else if you prefer,' she said softly.

Leo grimaced when he realised that he had made his distaste rather too obvious. 'No, this is fine. I only need to wear it to get home after all.'

'Well, if you're sure?' She left the question open and he shook his head, feeling worse when he saw the hurt in her eyes. It wasn't her fault that he felt this way after all.

'Quite sure.'

He picked up his glass, calling himself all kinds of unflattering names. He had never considered himself to be the male equivalent of a prima donna. Having been sent away to boarding school at a very early age, he had learned to ignore his finer feelings. However, the thought of wearing the other man's clothes made him feel very odd. It was as though he was trying to step into his shoes: first he'd laid claim to his son; now he was wearing his clothes; and, to cap it all, he wanted his wife!

A little wine shot down the wrong way and he coughed. Mia looked at him in concern. 'Are you all right?'

'Uh-huh,' Leo grunted. His lungs had gone into spasm and all he could do was grunt.

Mia hurried over and patted him on the back. 'Try to relax, that's it.'

She patted his back again and Leo felt all sorts of things happen inside him as his lungs started functioning again. He sucked in a much-needed breath of air, trying to ignore the fact that his pulse was racing, his heart was beating out a tattoo, whilst other bits of him were reacting in time-honoured fashion. It was as though every cell was firing out signals, telling him what to do, and all of a sudden he couldn't hold out any longer.

Turning, he pulled her into his arms and kissed her, kissed her as he had been longing to do for what seemed like an eternity. He knew it was madness, knew he would regret it, *knew* he shouldn't be doing it, but it didn't make any difference. As soon as he felt her mouth under his, he was lost.

CHAPTER TWELVE

MIA COULD HEAR the blood drumming in her ears. Leo's mouth was so hot, so hungry as it plundered hers that there was no way she could resist. Closing her eyes, she gave herself up to the sensations that were flooding through her. It was as though every cell was on fire, burning up, consuming her, and she groaned. Desire was even more powerful than she had imagined.

He drew back at last, his grey eyes pinning her with a look that made her tremble. 'I won't apologise, Mia. It was what we both wanted.'

His arrogance would have annoyed her at any other time but she knew it was true. She had wanted his kiss as much as he had wanted to kiss her. She bit her lip, feeling a shiver run through her when she discovered how tender her mouth felt. Leo hadn't held back. He had kissed her with a raw, unchecked passion and her mouth bore the evidence of it.

'I don't want you to apologise,' she said quietly, stepping out of his arms. She picked up her glass, hoping the wine would help her focus on what needed to be done. Although she had wanted his kiss, she couldn't afford to see it as the start of something more. She had to think about Harry and Noah, and how it could impact on them. They had enough to face in the coming months without her and Leo disrupting their lives any further. She also needed to think about herself. She didn't want to end up with her heart broken when their affair had run its course.

'We both know it was merely a matter of time before something happened,' she said flatly. 'However, now that it has, we can forget about it and focus on the main issue.'

'Namely the boys.'

His tone was cool, far cooler than hers, and Mia felt pain pierce her heart. It had been hard for her to strike the right note but Leo didn't appear to find it nearly as difficult.

'Exactly.' She dredged up a smile, refusing to let him see how hurt she felt. So what if kissing her hadn't been the mind-blowing experience for him that it had been for her? He was a lot more experienced and it was only to be expected that he could deal with his emotions better than she could do. Leo definitely wasn't going to feel as though the bottom had dropped out of his world just because of a kiss!

'We can't afford to do anything that might upset them, Leo. The situation is difficult enough without the added complication of us getting involved.'

'I agree. It will only confuse them even more and that's the last thing we want.'

He shrugged, his broad shoulders rising and falling beneath the overly tight T-shirt. Mia looked away, not proof against the feelings that flooded through her. It would be only too easy to change her mind and tell him that they *could* have a relationship so long as they made sure the boys didn't find out. Whilst she didn't doubt that Leo would be able to handle it, could she? Could she live a double life, pretend that she and Leo were merely friends in front of the boys and be his lover the rest of the time? She didn't think so. Desire was still so new to her that she would never be able to hide her feelings; somehow they would slip out. It was a risk she couldn't take and not only for the sake of the children either. She didn't want Leo to know how vulnerable she was where he was concerned.

'Precisely.' She shrugged. 'I suggest we forget what happened. After all, it hasn't been the best of evenings for you, has it?'

'Definitely not.' He smiled thinly. 'Despite what my colleagues think, losing a patient does affect me.'

It was on the tip of her tongue to assure him that it wasn't what she thought but she managed to hold back. Maybe most people viewed him as a very cold fish, but she didn't, not after tonight. Heat flowed through her again. There had been nothing cold about the way Leo had kissed her.

'I'd better go.' He went to the door, pausing briefly to look at her. 'Thanks for the drink, Mia, and for having Noah. I really appreciate it.'

'It's my pleasure,' she murmured as she followed him out of the room. 'Do you want me to call a taxi for you?'

'There's no need. I only managed a sip or two of the wine after I poured the first glass all over me.'

He laughed and Mia did her best to join in,

knowing it was expected. Leo was as keen as she was to put what had happened behind them. She saw him out then went back inside, trying not to think about the fact that he probably regretted it. After all, he could have his pick of women, women who were far more beautiful and socially acceptable than her. Maybe he had wanted to kiss her but it hadn't meant anything to him. Not really. Certainly not as much as it had meant to her.

The next week flew past. Between his NHS commitments and his private work, Leo was hard pressed to keep up. Normally, he had no difficulty fitting everything in but, for some reason, he found himself struggling. Maybe it was the fact that he wanted to spend as much time as possible with Noah before he had to tell him about the mix-up, but there didn't seem to be enough hours in a day. He knew that he was fast reaching a point where he would have to do something about it but he kept putting it off. Too much was happening in his private life without him making changes to the way he worked as well.

Mia was no longer covering the cardiology unit. Sister Thomas was back, briskly efficient as she took charge once more. Leo had always valued her no-nonsense approach yet he found himself missing Mia's gentle kindness. Ward rounds were back to being slickly efficient affairs, carried out with the minimum fuss and the maximum speed, and he reacted accordingly. He could feel himself slipping back into his old ways, becoming cold and distant once more with the patients and the staff, and he hated it. However, without Mia there to strike the right balance, there was little he could do.

The fact that Mia had such power over him was very hard to accept. Although he longed to see her, he didn't make any attempt to contact her. He needed time to get over what had happened, time to allow the memory of that kiss to fade. What he mustn't do was put himself in the same position again. Mia had made it clear how she felt about them becoming involved and he agreed with her.

The weekend rolled around and Noah seemed particularly restless. It was the start of the half-term holiday and Leo had managed to book a week off work so he could spend some time with him. He had been planning to take Noah to their cottage in Sussex. Noah loved it there, although they hadn't been able to go very often because of the pressure of work. Leo decided to make it a surprise and tell him on the Saturday morning but the child woke several times on Friday night, screaming after he'd had a nightmare.

Although Leo did his best to find out what was wrong, Noah refused to tell him. He was tired and listless on Saturday morning, and shook his head when Leo mentioned going to the cottage. After the recent improvement in his behaviour, it was extremely worrying, so much so that he set aside his misgivings and phoned Mia. If she could suggest a way to help Noah, that was all that mattered.

She listened carefully as he explained what had gone on. 'And nothing's upset him at school?'

'Not as far as I know.' Leo heard the concern in her voice and immediately felt better. Knowing that he could share his anxieties with her helped. 'The problem is that Noah won't tell me what's wrong. He just shakes his head when I ask him.'

'It must be very difficult for you,' she said softly, and he allowed himself the rare luxury of basking in her sympathy for a moment.

'It's not me who matters, it's Noah,' he said shortly, guiltily aware that he was doing what he had sworn he wouldn't do. This wasn't about him and how he felt: it was about Noah.

'Of course. But you're bound to be upset, Leo. I would be if it was Harry having nightmares and I had no idea what was causing them.'

Leo sighed, realising that it was pointless trying to present an indifferent front. Mia understood him far better than anyone else had ever done. 'You're right, of course,' he admitted, trying not to dwell on that unsettling thought. 'I hate it that he's upset and that I can't do anything about it.'

'Would it help if he spent some time with Harry, do you think?'

'It might do, although it doesn't seem fair to land you with this problem, Mia.'

'Rubbish! I want to help and not just because of who Noah is. He's such a lovely little boy and it's a real shame that he's having to go through something like this.'

'That's what hurts so much, the thought that he's unhappy and yet I have no idea what's causing it.'

'Then let's make arrangements for him and Harry to get together. They get on so well, don't they, and it might help to take Noah's mind off whatever's troubling him. When would suit you best? I'm off work next week because it's the half-term holiday so you choose whichever day is best for you. I take it that Noah's off school as well?'

'He is,' Leo said, his mind racing. Mia was right because the two boys did get on extremely well. It was rather surprising really as Noah hadn't made any friends since he'd started school. However, there seemed to be a definite connection between him and Harry.

He came to a swift decision, pushing aside any doubts he had about the wisdom of what he was about to suggest. This wasn't about him but Noah, he reminded himself. And he would do anything to help him.

'Actually, I was planning to take Noah to our cottage in Sussex. It's right next to a farm and he loves seeing the animals. I mentioned it to him this morning but he shook his head. However, I'm sure he'd change his mind if Harry came as well.'

'Oh. I'm not sure…' Mia tailed off and Leo immediately realised what the problem was.

'Obviously, you're invited too, Mia! Sorry. I should have made that clear.'

He took a deep breath, trying to control the thunderous beating of his heart. This was all completely above board, he told himself firmly. He had invited Harry purely because having him around might help Noah. It certainly wasn't some sort of cunning plan to spend time with Mia! He hurried on, not wanting to examine his motives too closely in case he discovered they were flawed.

'It's got three bedrooms. One for you, one for me and the boys can share. Please say you'll come, Mia. It'll make the world of difference to Noah to spend some time with you and Harry.'

The cottage was chocolate-box-perfect. Tiny mullioned windows, a thatched roof, roses—or rather the remains of roses—around the door. Mia sighed with pleasure as Leo drew up outside.

'It's beautiful. I didn't think places like this actually existed.'

'It belonged to my godmother. She left it to

me in her will.' Leo switched off the engine and turned to smile at her. 'I used to love coming here when I was a child. My parents travelled a lot and I spent a lot of school holidays here with Deborah.'

'It must have helped make up for the fact that you couldn't spend them with your parents,' Mia suggested, and he shrugged.

'It never bothered me, to be honest. I was sent away to school when I was seven so I was used to not seeing very much of them.'

He got out of the car and after a moment's hesitation Mia followed him. She helped Noah and Harry out of the back, thinking about what he had said. She couldn't imagine sending Harry away to school and not seeing him every day, although Leo seemed to think it was completely normal. It worried her that their views were diametrically opposed. There was no way that she would agree if Leo planned to send either Harry *or* Noah away to boarding school.

Mia squared her shoulders as she herded the children up the path. This was something they obviously needed to discuss, although there was no way that she would change her mind. Harry and Noah were not going to be sent away to school, no matter what Leo said.

Leo unlocked the door, ducking his head as he passed beneath the lintel. Mia stepped inside and looked around, loving the inside as much as she loved the outside.

A tiny vestibule led straight into a sitting room packed with original features. A low ceiling complete with old oak beams, a huge fireplace set with logs. The floor was made from what she assumed was local stone, softened by an eclectic mix of rugs in shades of red, green and gold. A huge squashy sofa and a couple of armchairs bore the hallmarks of many years of use but that merely added to the charm of the place and she smiled in delight.

'It's absolutely gorgeous, Leo! If I owned a place like this I couldn't bear not to live here permanently.'

'It is lovely,' he agreed, looking around. 'I haven't changed anything since Deborah died. I suppose it's silly but I wanted Noah to be able to enjoy the cottage the way it was when I was a child.'

'It's not silly at all,' Mia said, touched by the

sentiment. She ran her hand over a faded chintz cushion. 'If you'd bought new furniture you might have been tempted to nag Noah about not damaging things.'

'That's it exactly.' He smiled at her, his grey eyes holding a warmth that made her heart race. 'I was always getting told off for doing something or other when I was at home—spilling a drink on some priceless rug or scuffing an antique chair-leg. However, life here was far more relaxed.'

'It sounds as though it was a real haven for you,' Mia said quietly, and he sighed.

'It was. This was the one place where I always felt completely happy.'

It was such a sad thing to say that tears came to her eyes. She blinked them away but not quickly enough to stop Leo noticing.

'What's wrong?' he said in concern, coming over to her.

'Nothing. I'm just being silly.' She turned to the boys and smiled. 'Why don't you two go on upstairs? Can you show Harry your bedroom, Noah? If it's big enough maybe you two can share it.'

The idea was met with whoops of delight. Mia

laughed as the two boys went thundering up the stairs. 'I hope you haven't spent a fortune re-decorating the bedrooms. That pair are obviously going to make the most of being here.'

'I haven't changed a thing upstairs or down,' Leo assured her, and she shivered when she heard the grating note in his voice. Had he guessed that her tears had been for him, because she hated to think that he had been unhappy as a child? Mia knew it was true, knew also that he was deeply moved by the idea. Maybe they had agreed to focus on the boys but they couldn't pretend that they didn't feel anything for one another.

'Good. Now, how about a cup of tea? I don't know about you but I'm parched.'

'Lovely. I'll leave you to make it while I bring in the bags,' he said smoothly.

Mia went into the kitchen and filled the kettle with water. She placed it on the hob then looked round, taking determined stock of the sunny yel-low-painted cupboards and blue and white crock-ery arranged on the old dresser, but no matter how hard she tried she couldn't blank out the thought that she and Leo had a lot in common. Her childhood had been less than perfect too and it seemed to forge an even stronger bond between them. She sighed. It was going to make it that much harder to keep her distance.

Leo took the cases upstairs, not allowing himself to linger as he closed the door to the room Mia would use. It was a pretty room with a wonderful view over the garden to the river but there was no point thinking about how much he would love to wake up and enjoy it with her. He and Mia weren't going to share the room. They weresn't going to be lovers. If he said it often enough then maybe—just maybe—the thought would imprint itself in his head.

Mia had the tea made by the time he went downstairs. She looked round as he went into the kitchen and he felt his heart give a funny little jolt. It was as though it had momentarily forgotten how to work properly, which would have been a worrying thought in other circumstances. However, Leo was aware that the temporary arrhythmia was due to something other than cardiac malfunction.

'I've left your case in your room,' he told her, sitting down at the table because his legs felt decidedly shaky all of a sudden. He cleared his throat, determined to get a grip on himself. 'I've given you the room at the back. You have a wonderful view down to the river from there.'

'It sounds lovely.' Mia poured the tea. She brought the cups over to the table and sat down. 'I couldn't remember if you took sugar.'

'Not for me, thanks.' He got up to fetch the sugar basin, pushing it towards her.

'No, thanks. I take sugar in coffee but not in tea.'

She took a sip of her tea and he looked away, not wanting to put his heart through any more workouts by watching her beautiful lips purse around the rim of the cup. He added a heaped spoonful of suger to his tea, almost gagging when he discovered how sweet it tasted. He pushed the cup aside, suddenly conscious of the silence. Normally, he wouldn't have given it a second thought; in truth, he would have relished the fact that he didn't have to make conversation. However, it was different when he was with Mia. He was afraid that if *he* didn't occupy his thoughts, they would find something to occupy themselves!

'Fingers crossed the weather forecast is wrong,'

he said hastily. 'It's supposed to rain for the next few days, heavily too.'

'Let's hope they've got it wrong,' she agreed, glancing out of the window.

Leo's hands clenched as he found himself admiring her profile. How had he ever thought she was ordinary looking? he wondered in amazement as his gaze travelled from the smooth sweep of her brow to the delicate curve of her chin. Although he had known many women who were far more noticeably beautiful, Mia's beauty stemmed not just from how she looked but from who she was. She was beautiful inside as well as out, and the combination touched something inside him, a part of him that he had never been aware of before.

'Still, if it does rain, we'll make the best of it. I expect your godmother kept a stock of board games to entertain you when you stayed with her.'

She turned and Leo hurriedly smoothed his face into what he hoped was a suitable expression, although he couldn't be sure he had hit the mark. 'She did. All the old favourites too—snakes and ladders, Ludo, tiddlywinks,' he said, his voice grating just a little because it was impossible to get every tiny bit of himself under control.

'Tiddlywinks? Oh, Harry will be pleased. He loves tiddlywinks. In fact, he's a bit of demon at it and usually wins!'

Her laughter was overly bright and Leo felt his heart lurch again. Could she feel it too, feel the tension that filled the air? He hoped she could yet also prayed she couldn't because it would only complicate matters. If he knew that Mia felt the same as he did then how would he stop himself doing what he wanted and take her to his bed?

His head began to pound at the thought so it was a relief when the boys reappeared. They were starving, they declared, and needed something to eat. Mia laughed as she got up and went to sort out some lunch for them. Leo watched them, listening to the interplay between her and the children as they helped her make a mound of sandwiches. Although Harry did most of the talking, Noah wasn't shy about making his views known. He looked so animated and happy, so different from how he had been at home that Leo felt his heart suddenly ache.

He loved Noah with every scrap of his being but he couldn't draw a response from him like Mia could. It made him wonder if he was right to hold onto him. Maybe Noah would be better off living with her. Not only would he be with his real mother but he'd have Harry too, the brother he would never have if he stayed with Leo.

Leo felt a knifing pain run through him. He had sworn he would do whatever it took to make Noah happy but could he keep that promise if it meant he would have to give him up?

CHAPTER THIRTEEN

'NOW, YOU ARE to stay well away from the river. Understand?'

Mia waited until both Harry and Noah had promised that they would do as she said then opened the back door, smiling as she watched them race down the garden. Although the day was very overcast, the promised rain hadn't materialised yet so the children may as well run off some steam. At least they'd have had some exercise if they did end up playing more board games later on.

She went back to the stove and added more bacon to the pan. From the sounds coming from upstairs, Leo was in the shower so she would get breakfast ready for him. He appeared a few minutes later, pausing in the doorway as though taken aback by the scene that met him. Mia felt a little colour run up her cheeks when it struck her that he might not appreciate her taking over.

After all, it was his cottage and she was merely a guest.

'I hope you don't mind,' she said quickly. 'The boys were hungry so I made them breakfast.' She shrugged. 'It seemed silly not to make some for you as well.'

'Of course I don't mind,' he declared, grinning at her. 'I may be a dab hand with a scalpel but I'm no great shakes when it comes to wielding a knife for the culinary arts. I'm truly grateful that I won't have to eat my own cooking!'

Mia laughed, feeling her unease melt away. 'Ah, so that's your one failing, is it? You can't cook?'

'One failing?' He crooked a brow as he helped himself to coffee. 'You're far too kind, Mia. I've a lot more failings than that, believe me.'

His grey eyes met hers and she looked away when she felt her heartbeat quicken. She busied herself with their breakfast, trying not to think about what other faults he could lay claim to. Even if she tried her hardest, she couldn't think of any herself and it was worrying to know that she held him in such esteem.

She finished cooking and took the plate over

to the table. 'I hope you're hungry. I may have overdone it on the bacon.'

'I'm famished,' he assured her, tucking in. He chewed and swallowed, rolling his eyes in pleasure. 'Delicious! My compliments to the chef.'

'Thank you.' Mia laughed as she poured herself a cup of coffee. She sat down and helped herself to a slice of toast. 'All compliments gratefully received. It's not often I get the chance to cook for someone who actually *notices* what he's eating.'

'It sounds as though Harry's view on food is much like Noah's. So long as it's something he likes, that's fine.'

He gave her a quick smile then carried on eating. He seemed to be really enjoying the meal and Mia couldn't help feeling a little glow of satisfaction spring up inside her. She was one of life's carers and enjoyed looking after the people she loved.

The thought hit home and she put down her toast, afraid that she would choke if she tried to eat it. She didn't love Leo. The idea was ridiculous...

Wasn't it?

Panic rose up inside her as she studied his downbent head. That she was attracted to him wasn't in question but it was a huge leap from attraction to love. She'd only ever loved one man and that had been Chris, and her feelings for Chris had been very different from how she felt about Leo. Her love for Chris had made her feel safe and secure. For the first time in her life she'd had someone to rely on, someone who wouldn't let her down.

It wasn't like that with Leo, though. There was an edginess to her feelings for him, an air of excitement and danger that sprang from the fact that she found him sexually attractive. She hadn't wanted Chris that way and she wouldn't demean their marriage by pretending that she had.

Maybe it was the fact that she had known from the outset that they couldn't have a full physical relationship that had tempered her feelings—she wasn't sure. However, the truth was that not once had she felt for Chris even a fraction of the desire she felt for Leo. She bit her lip. Adding it all up, what did it mean? Was it love? Or was it something far less demanding?

Leo wasn't sure what Mia was thinking. It was obviously something profound because she seemed to be lost in thought. He carried on eating even though his appetite had disappeared. There was no point speculating about what was going through her mind, definitely no point asking her either. He couldn't afford to go down that route, didn't dare try to find out anything more about how she thought or felt. It was far too risky, especially when they were both here in the cottage, the one place where he had always been able to relax and be himself.

He sighed. They had managed so well up to now too. Even though he had found it a strain being around her the previous evening, having the boys there had helped. However, the boys weren't here now and he was very aware that his emotions could easily get the better of him. He had sworn after his divorce that he wouldn't get involved again. Although he hadn't loved Amanda, their break-up had been taxing. He didn't intend to put himself through that experience again, especially now he had Noah and Harry to consider. He needed to concentrate on them and forget all these crazy ideas that kept invading his mind.

He forced down the last morsel of food and

placed his knife and fork neatly on the plate. 'That was delicious. Thanks again for making it, Mia, although I didn't invite you along so you could be chief cook and bottle-washer.'

The jocular note he'd been aiming for didn't quite ring true but she seemed not to notice. Leo felt his heart lurch when she looked up and he saw the awareness in her eyes. He knew then that whatever she'd been thinking had concerned him and it was both intriguing and scary to wonder how he had featured in her thoughts.

'I'm glad you enjoyed it.' She gave a little shrug and he had the distinct impression that she was trying to shrug off whatever had been bothering her. 'As for doing the cooking while we're here, well, it's no hardship. I'm more than happy to sort out the meals.'

'Careful! I may take you up on that offer,' he warned her in the same falsely jovial tone that filled him with impatience. Why on earth didn't he just ask her what was wrong and be done with it? It was on the tip of his tongue to do that when she pushed back her chair and he knew—he just knew!—that she had read his mind and taken steps to forestall him.

'The boys are in the garden. I think they're hoping you'll play football with them.'

'Ah, right. I suppose I'd better go and show willing, although after that breakfast I doubt I'll have much of a chance against the two of them.'

Leo drummed up a laugh as he went to fetch a sweater. Harry and Noah came rushing over when he went outside, demanding that he played with them. They formed a makeshift goal out of a couple of logs and Leo acted as goalkeeper, letting as many balls slip into the 'net' as he stopped. He didn't believe in being too hard on them, unlike his own father had been. On the rare occasions his father had played with him, he'd been treated as an adult and never allowed to win. His father believed it was character forming to make a child face up to the realities of life at an early age, but Leo could remember how dispiriting it had been and refused to adopt that approach with Noah and Harry. They would find out how difficult life could be all in good time.

He sighed as he glanced towards the cottage. He was only just discovering exactly how hard it was himself.

* * *

The rain started after lunch. Mia had packed a couple of Harry's favourite DVDs so once the boys were settled in front of the television, she went up to her room to find the book she had brought with her. Rain was beating against the bedroom window and she paused to watch the raindrops racing down the glass. Whilst she loved the cottage, she couldn't help hoping that it wouldn't rain the whole time they were here. The thought of being shut up inside with Leo was enough to cause her more than a few misgivings.

'Seems the forecast was spot on after all.'

She swung round, her heart lurching when she saw him standing in the doorway. He had changed out of his muddy clothes after the game of football and was wearing a black tracksuit with a pair of old trainers. It was the first time she had seen him wearing such casual clothing and she couldn't help thinking how much it suited him, the soft cotton top emphasising the width of his shoulders and his dark good looks.

'So it seems.' She dredged up a smile as she showed him the novel. 'Good job I brought this along, just in case.'

'Oh, there are plenty of things to entertain you,' he said softly, and her heart went into overdrive as she found herself picturing all the things she could do. With Leo.

'That's good to know.'

Her voice sounded more than a little husky and she cleared her throat. Had he said that deliberately or, rather, said it in *that* way? She hurried to the door, refusing to work out the answer because it was too dangerous. To allow herself even to *think* about all the things they could do to pass a rainy afternoon was asking for trouble!

'Deborah was a keen reader so there's a stack of books if you run out of reading matter.' Leo led the way along the landing, pausing when he reached his room. He swept a hand towards the open door. 'Here, have a look and see if there's anything you fancy.'

Mia hesitated, unsure why she was so loath to enter his bedroom. With the boys downstairs, Leo was unlikely to pounce on her even if he'd been the pouncing sort, which he wasn't. She poked her head round the door, taking rapid stock of the old oak furniture and half-tester bed, a bed that was definitely big enough for two people to enjoy…

'I've added to the collection over the last few years.' Leo went over to the bookcase. Lifting down a couple of paperbacks, he offered them to her. 'Have you read these? I really enjoyed them.'

'I…ehm… No. I don't think I have.' Mia reluctantly stepped into the room, realising how ridiculous it would appear if she remained hovering in the doorway like a nervous virgin. Colour rushed up her throat at the thought and she hastily took the books from him, making a great show of reading the back blurbs although she had no idea what they said.

'You should read this one first so you get a feel for the characters.'

He took one of the books from her and she froze when his fingers brushed against hers. There was a moment when neither of them moved, when even the air seemed to freeze, and then slowly, so very slowly, he placed the book on the bed and turned to her.

'I'm going to kiss you, Mia. If you don't want me to then say so.'

Mia tried her best. She really did. The refusal

was hovering in her throat, one tiny word that just needed to be forced out and yet somehow she couldn't seem to do it. She saw his eyes darken, watched the question in them melt away and be replaced by a hunger that awoke an answering hunger inside her. When he reached for her, she was already moving towards him so that it took minimal effort for their mouths to meet.

His lips settled over hers, softly, warmly and so familiarly that she sighed. It shouldn't feel so good to have him kiss her. It shouldn't feel so right when they both knew it was wrong. However, there was no point lying. She wanted his kiss. She wanted him.

Mia closed her eyes, giving herself up to the sensations that filled her. She'd had a taste of desire the last time they had kissed and this was just as potent. She could feel her breathing quicken, feel her body heat, feel all sorts of things she had never felt before, and it was all Leo's doing. He seemed to be able to tap into her emotions in a way that no man had ever done before.

He drew back, tilting her face so that he could look into her eyes and whatever he saw there obviously reassured him because his expression lightened. Bending, he rested his forehead against hers and Mia felt the tremor that passed through him.

'I don't know why this is happening, Mia. But I've never felt this way with anyone before.'

'Me neither,' she whispered, deeply moved by the confession. She cupped his cheek with her hand, shuddering when he turned his head and pressed his lips to her palm. 'I had no idea that desire felt like this.'

He drew her to him and enfolded her in his arms, and she knew that he was as affected by her admission as she'd been by his. When he bent and kissed her again there was a tenderness about the kiss that brought tears to her eyes. The fact that he was making allowances for her inexperience simply proved that she had been right about him. Beneath that cold hard exterior he presented to the world, there was someone very different. A man she could very easily love.

Mia wasn't sure what might have happened next. However, a sudden crash from the sitting room brought them both back down to earth. Leo sighed as he gently set her away from him.

'I'd better go and see what's happening.'

'Yes.' Mia dredged up a smile, wondering where they went from here. Although they had agreed to forget what had happened the last time they had kissed, it didn't seem feasible to do so again.

'It'll be fine, Mia. I promise you that.'

He tilted her face and she shivered when she saw the hunger in his eyes. That he wanted her as much as she wanted him was clear and it made the situation even more difficult. Could she do the right thing, the *sensible* thing, when she knew that Leo wanted her this much?

'Will it?' she whispered anxiously. 'Are you sure about that?'

'As sure as I can be.' He ran the pad of his thumb over her throbbing lips. 'We'll work something out, Mia. We have to.'

The desperation in his voice was an aphrodisiac in itself. Mia's heart was pounding as he let her go and hurried from the room. Sitting down on the bed, she took a shaky breath. Was it the fact that it was her first real taste of desire that made it so difficult to control her feelings? If she'd been more experienced then she might be able to deal with what was happening with equanimity, but there was no way that she could do that. Leo had awakened feelings she'd not known existed before and it was impossible to behave calmly and dispassionately.

She shivered as a rush of fear assailed her. If she weren't careful her feelings for Leo would take over and that was something she couldn't allow to happen. She had to think about the harm it could cause to Harry and Noah if she and Leo had an affair and it all went wrong. She also had to think about the harm it could do to her too. If she fell in love with Leo and lost him, she might never recover. She had to protect the children and herself, and if that meant steering clear of Leo, that was what she would have to do.

The day seemed never-ending. As Leo played one board game after another, he could barely contain his frustration. He didn't want to play snakes and ladders. He had far more adult games in mind, games that involved him and Mia and a bed. He could have happily passed the afternoon *and* the evening playing with her!

'Daddy! You've just gone *up* a snake!'

Leo dragged his mind back to what was happening when he heard the disgust in Noah's voice. 'Sorry. I wasn't concentrating.' He placed his counter on the correct square and handed the dice to Harry, trying not to look at Mia. He had a feeling that she knew only too well why he was so distracted.

His gaze slid sideways and he felt his heart leap when he saw the colour in her cheeks. It was rare that women in his circle blushed and he found Mia's propensity to do so all the more erotic. That she'd admitted to being an innocent had both surprised and touched him. Even though he had guessed that she and her husband hadn't been able to have a full physical relationship, most women her age had had love affairs and he had assumed she had too. However, from what she had said, her experience of lovemaking, of passion, was limited.

The thought struck deep. It was an effort to focus on the game rather than on the thoughts that filled his head, thoughts of how much he would enjoy teaching her about making love. Would she be as sweetly responsive in his bed as she'd been in his arms? he wondered, and groaned because the thought was too much to deal with. He took the dice from Harry, summoning up a suitable show of enthusiasm when he scored a six. However, he couldn't help thinking that if he did make love to Mia it would be like scoring a dozen sixes all in a row.

The game finally ended and Noah was declared the winner, much to his delight. As Leo watched him and Harry go racing out of the room, he realised that no matter what else happened this week, he had achieved his objective. Being here with Harry and Mia had made a huge difference to Noah. He seemed so much happier, more like he'd been before the accident. Once again the thought that he might have to let Noah go if it was in his best interests crossed his mind but he pushed it aside, not wanting it to ruin the day. He would deal with it if and when it became necessary, although, please, heaven it wouldn't come to that.

'Tea?'

Mia finished stowing the counters in the box and stood up. She smiled at him and Leo felt warmth envelop him. All of a sudden it struck him what had been missing from his life. Maybe he did have wealth and professional standing. He might even move in the highest social circles and be accepted by princes and lords, but none of that mattered. For the first time ever, he'd been accepted for who he was, not what he had. Mia saw him as a man first and everything else second. Reaching out, he caught hold of her hand and pulled her towards him.

'I can think of something I'd like more than tea,' he growled.

He kissed her swiftly on the lips then let her go, not wanting to run the risk of the boys bursting in on them. Mia didn't say anything as she hurried into the kitchen but he had felt her response and knew that she felt the same as he did. One kiss wasn't enough for her either. She needed more and not just more kisses either.

Leo closed his eyes, feeling excitement rippling along his veins. Tonight they were going to have everything they wanted.

CHAPTER FOURTEEN

IT WAS GONE nine before Harry and Noah finally fell asleep. Mia switched off the light and tiptoed from the room. With a bit of luck they would sleep through till morning so she and Leo could have some time on their own.

Colour rushed up her face as she found herself imagining how they would spend that time. That they would make love wasn't in question. They both knew it was going to happen and there was no point pretending that it wouldn't. She wanted Leo to make love to her and she wouldn't cheapen the experience by dissembling.

She wanted to lie in his arms and discover how it felt to be a woman. She wanted to feel the power of passion as it carried her away, allow her mind as well as her body to be consumed by desire. Although she'd had a child, the fact that Harry hadn't been conceived naturally had robbed her of that experience and she intended to make up for it. If she knew how desire felt, she would feel complete and not as though something was missing.

Mia frowned, surprised to discover she felt that way. After her one and only foray into a sexual relationship had turned out so badly, she had shied away from any more such experiences. Although Chris had fretted about the fact that they couldn't make love, she had been secretly relieved. Now she was going to put it all behind her and move on, and the fact that it was Leo—Harry's real father—who would help her make the transition seemed fitting. No matter what happened afterwards, she would never regret this night.

'I've opened a bottle of wine.' Leo was waiting for her when she went downstairs. He held out his hand and smiled. 'Can I tempt you to a glass?'

'You can.' Mia slid her hand into his, feeling her skin tingle as his fingers closed around hers. Her skin seemed unusually sensitive and the slightly abrasive touch of his fingertips made her shiver.

'You're shivering. Are you cold?'

He paused to look at her, a frown drawing his elegant brows together, and she shivered again. Did he have any idea how sexy he was? Did he realise that a look or even a frown could set light to her feelings? Even now she could feel the tingles spreading to other parts of her, places she had never been aware of before she had met him. She bit her lip, wondering if it was normal to be so responsive. Did all women feel this way prior to making love or was there something wrong with her?

'Stop it.'

The order was softly given but it brought her up short. Mia's eyes refocused and she saw him shake his head. 'Whatever crazy thoughts you're harbouring, forget them, Mia. There's nothing to be frightened of. You and I are going to make love but only if you want to. OK?'

His bluntness might have embarrassed her before but not now. Not tonight. Mia nodded. 'All right.'

'Good.' He squeezed her hand then let her go so he could pour the wine. Mia was a little surprised that he hadn't kissed her, although she didn't say anything. Leo knew what he was doing and she would be guided by him.

The thought set loose another volley of thoughts and she took a gulp of the wine in the hope that it would calm her. She mustn't spoil things by panicking. It would be such a shame. Leo dropped down onto the sofa and raised his glass aloft.

'A toast. To the boys and us. May we all get what we want.'

'To the boys and us,' Mia repeated, wondering if it was possible for all of them to get what they wanted. Harry and Noah took priority, of course; she would do whatever was necessary to make sure they were happy. If it meant that she and Leo couldn't have a proper relationship, she would accept it. It meant that tonight would be even more special. Precious. This one night might be all she had.

It was a sobering thought but she refused to dwell on it. She drank a little more wine then put her glass on the table. 'I've had enough wine,' she said quietly.

'Me too.' Leo put his glass next to hers and stood up. His eyes were very dark as he searched her face. 'Are you sure this is what you want, Mia?'

'Yes.'

Mia turned and headed from the room. She made her way upstairs, hearing the soft tread of

Leo's footsteps behind her. The landing floor-boards creaked and she paused, half expecting that Harry or Noah would wake up, but there was no sound from their bedroom and she carried on to her room. She had left the bedside lamp on and it cast a soft glow over the room. When Leo followed her inside and closed the door, it felt as though they were the only two people in the world. Whatever happened in this room tonight was between them, no one else.

'Mia.'

He said her name softly and with great ten-derness. Mia turned to him, feeling the last tiny doubt melt away when she saw the expression on his face. That he wanted this as much as she did was clear. She moved towards him, emboldened by the thought. She had never initiated physical contact before, yet it was *her* arms that reached for him, *her* hands that drew his head down so *she* could kiss him. Their mouths met and she sighed as she felt his lips immediately shape themselves to hers. This was even easier than she had hoped it would be.

They kissed for a long time, a kiss that was filled with so many emotions that she felt dizzy when they broke apart. When Leo had kissed her before, he had kissed her with hunger and with passion, but this kiss had been very different. It was as though he had stripped himself bare, allowed his real self to shine through, and the thought made her feel very humble. He had lowered his defences because he trusted her and now she must trust him too.

She sank down onto the bed and held out her hand. 'Make love with me, Leo. It's what I want more than anything.'

He didn't say a word as he took her hand and sat down beside her but she had seen the flare of emotion in his eyes and knew how much it had meant to him to hear her say that. When he bent and kissed her again, she closed her eyes, savouring the feel of his mouth on hers. This was just the beginning and there would be so much more to come, so many new experiences to enjoy and treasure. If they were to have just this one night, it would be a night to remember.

Leo could feel his heart pounding. The taste of Mia's lips was pure seduction and he was more than willing to be seduced. He gathered her into his arms, groaning when he felt her breasts pressing against his chest. Her nipples were already hard but he didn't intend to rush her. She'd admitted how inexperienced she was and he couldn't bear it if he ruined things by going too fast. He had to take his time no matter how difficult it was. Mia needed to be loved gently, slowly, and with the utmost care.

Tenderness washed over him as he kissed her again, letting his tongue slide between her lips this time. His heart jerked when he felt her respond but he managed to control the desire that surged through him. Lifting his hand, he smoothed her hair away from her face, his fingers tangling in the silky fine threads at her temple. Her hair smelled of lemons, clean and fresh, and he drank in its scent, amazed that such a simple aroma could be so erotic. Forget all the expensive perfumes, he thought. This was far more seductive!

His hand moved from her hair to her cheek, his fingers exploring the velvet softness of her skin. It felt so warm to the touch, so smooth, that he could have sat there and stroked it all night long, only he knew there were more delights to enjoy. His fingers glided down her cheek and across her jaw then moved to her neck, following the line of her throat until they reached the tiny pulse that was beating so frantically at its base. He could feel it tapping away, feel its rhythm imprinting itself on his flesh and shuddered. If he needed proof that she wanted him then here it was, here where this tiny reflection of her feelings was making itself known.

Bending, he pressed his mouth to the spot, letting the tip of his tongue rest on the tiny pulse point as though in some way he could absorb the evidence of her desire for him. She gave a soft little moan as she tipped back her head to allow him easier access and he felt his own desire spiral out of control.

He wanted her so much! Wanted to lie her down on the bed and cover her body with kisses, seek out the source of her heat and kiss her there as well. He had made love to many women over the years but he knew that making love to Mia would be unlike anything he had experienced before. In that respect they were very much alike. All his experience amounted to nothing when it came to loving her.

The thought was just too much to deal with, way too much to soothe and calm him as he needed to be calmed. He knew he shouldn't rush her yet his hands seemed to possess a life of their own as they stripped off her clothes. Mia helped him, wriggling out of her jeans, shrugging off her shirt, and he realised that she was as eager as him to take things to the next stage. It stopped him feeling so guilty. Maybe it wasn't wrong to allow passion to dictate the speed of their love-making after all.

He stood up and stripped off his own clothes, feeling her eyes on him as he stood naked beside the bed. Did she like what she saw? he wondered in a rare fit of self-doubt. He had never worried about his appearance before and it shocked him to discover how vulnerable he was. He cared what she thought, cared far more than he had ever cared about anyone's opinion.

'You're beautiful.'

Her voice was husky, filled with a wonder that swept away his fears. Leo laughed as he lay down on the bed and gathered her to him. 'I don't think men can be classed as beautiful, sweetheart.'

'Well, you can.' She drew back and looked

at him and he could see the desire in her eyes smouldering away, and shuddered again. Maybe she lacked experience but by heaven she turned him on! 'You're beautiful, Leo, and there's no other word to describe you.'

'Then thank you.'

He kissed her hungrily, unable to hold back a second longer, but there again he didn't need to. Mia was as eager for him as he was for her. Her heart was racing as he let his lips glide down her body, following the full, lush curves of her breasts, the dip of her waist, the gentle swell of her hips. She had never felt more like a woman than she did right then as Leo paid homage to her.

Everywhere his mouth touched, it seemed that he discovered a fresh delight to explore, a new discovery to savour, like the tiny mole on the top of her hip bone or the dusting of freckles on her arms. She ran her hands down his back, feeling the smoothness of his skin, the hardness of his muscles as they slid beneath her palms. She had never felt so aroused before, wouldn't have believed that just the feel of his body could set light to her desire like this. Every inch of him was so perfect that she was overcome with greed. She wanted to stroke and caress him for the rest of her life!

The thought pushed her to the edge and beyond. 'Make love to me, Leo,' she said urgently. 'Now!'

There was a moment when he paused, the tiniest hesitation, and then he entered her in one strong, fluid thrust. Mia felt her body resist for a second and then it opened to him, warm and eager as it welcomed him inside. Mia felt the blood start to drum along her veins, felt her passion gather momentum until she was totally consumed by its heat and Leo's desire for her. Then all of a sudden she was crying out and clinging to him and he was clinging to her as the world dissolved around them. Nothing existed any more. Nothing except her and Leo and the magic they were creating together.

It was after midnight when Mia awoke. She stared at the ceiling, listening to the steady sound of Leo's breathing as he lay beside her. Reaching out, she ran her hand down his arm, shivering when she felt the silky dark hair slide beneath her palm. Making love with him had been so much more than she had hoped it would be. Not only had he shown her how passion felt, he had proved that she was capable of arousing passion in someone else. His need for her had been every bit as consuming as hers had been for him.

'Are you all right?'

His voice was soft and deep but she heard the concern it held and felt warmed to her core. That he cared how she felt, cared about *her*, wasn't in doubt. Rolling onto her side, she smiled at him, surprised and yet unsurprised by how comfortable she felt. Maybe she should feel awkward or ill at ease but she didn't. It had felt right to make love to him, just as it felt right to wake up beside him.

'Fine. In fact, I feel better than I've felt in ages.'

'Really?' His brows quirked as he propped himself up on one elbow. 'And why is that, do you think?'

'Oh, I'm not sure. It could be the nice little nap I've had. Or maybe it's being here at the cottage and having some time to myself for a change.' She grinned wickedly. 'What do you think?'

'Hmm, I'm not sure either. Maybe it's a combination of the two.' He trailed the tip of his finger across her mouth, smiling smugly when she gasped. 'It may even have something to do with the fact that we just made love.'

'Th-that's another theory,' she murmured because it was hard to form the words when her lips felt as though they were on fire.

'It is, isn't it? And like all theories it needs testing.' He bent and kissed her, drawing back before she could respond, and she could see the mischief in his eyes. 'Although it's rather late to be carrying out a proper scientific experiment, don't you think?'

He kissed her again, his mouth lingering a fraction longer this time before he pulled away. Mia sucked in her breath, determined that she wasn't going to beg. He either kissed her properly or he didn't…

Her resolve lasted no longer than a heartbeat. Leaning forward, she pressed her mouth to his, sighing in pleasure when he immediately took charge, kissing her with a hunger that allowed no room for any more questions. If this was an experiment, she thought in the moment before passion swept her away, it would prove one thing: she now understood *exactly* how desire felt!

They made love again and it was so beautiful that she cried afterwards. Leo drew her into his arms and held her, not asking her what was wrong because he knew. Her tears weren't a sign of unhappiness but of joy. She had found the last bit of herself that had been missing, discovered how it really felt to be a woman. It was a moment she would remember all her life, a moment she would treasure no matter what happened.

It was a sobering thought because it brought all the old doubts flooding back. Mia sighed as she reached for a tissue and wiped her eyes. There was no point pretending when Leo knew how volatile the situation was.

'Tonight has been everything I dreamt it would be, Leo, but I'm terrified in case it causes complications.'

'Me too.' He sat up, packing a pillow behind his back. Drawing her into his arms, he cradled her against his bare chest. 'Tonight was wonderful for me as well, Mia. There's no point lying—I've had a lot more experience than you, but tonight was special. I only wish we could make this a permanent arrangement, but at the moment it would be wrong.'

'It would,' she agreed, her heart aching with

a mixture of pleasure and pain. The fact that it had meant so much to him thrilled her; however, what he'd said merely confirmed her own view. They couldn't get involved because of the harm it might cause to the boys.

'So I suppose what we're really saying is that this has to be a one-off.' He tilted her face and looked into her eyes. 'It's not what I want and I don't think it's what you want either but our feelings have to come second to Harry's and Noah's. They'd find it too confusing if we started seeing one another and then they found out we aren't their real parents.'

'They would. It'll be difficult enough for them to understand the situation without that as well.' She bit her lip, determined that she wasn't going to cry. She didn't want to put any pressure on him, didn't want to try to change his mind. They knew what had to be done and they must do it.

Leo didn't try to stop her as she got out of bed. Taking her robe off the chair, she slipped it on and made her way to the bathroom. She switched on the light then stood and stared at her reflection in the mirror over the basin. Although it was the same face she saw every day, she looked different. Making love with Leo had left its mark; she looked more aware, more alive even. However, it was the changes she couldn't see that she would have to live with.

Closing her eyes, she allowed herself to recall the passion that had swept her away, the hunger that had filled her, the feeling of peace and completion that had enveloped her afterwards. She had discovered who she was at last, found the last link that had been missing, and she was a different person because of it. Because of Leo. Because she loved him.

Mia opened her eyes and stared at the face that was staring back at her. She could see the truth in her eyes, see it so clearly that there was no point pretending any more. She was in love with Leo.

CHAPTER FIFTEEN

THE RAIN HAD stopped the following morning so Mia sent the boys outside to play. Going over to the stove, she turned on the gas so she could make a start on breakfast. Although she wasn't hungry, it would help to take her mind off the events of the night. She sighed as she cracked eggs into a bowl. It was doubtful if scrambling eggs would alleviate this sadness she felt.

'Good morning.'

She hadn't heard Leo coming in and jumped so that some of the egg mixture slopped over the side of the bowl. He frowned as he picked up a dishcloth and mopped up the mess.

'Sorry. I didn't mean to startle you.'

'It wasn't your fault. I didn't hear you,' she countered politely, picking up a fork and beating the eggs to within an inch of their life. Reaching over, he took the fork off her and tossed it into the sink.

'Don't, Mia. I couldn't bear it if we started pussyfooting around one another. The situation is difficult enough without that.'

'You're right, it is.'

She turned to him, seeing the shadows under his eyes, proof that he too had had a sleepless night. It was a small sop to her feelings to know that he was suffering as well. By the time she had got back from the bathroom, Leo had gone. Maybe he had wanted to make it easier for her, but she wished he had stayed. Although she doubted if they would have made love again, at least he could have held her in his arms, made her feel less lonely, less lost. Now she dredged up a smile, knowing she was being unreasonable. Leo had done what he had to do and she should be grateful.

'Scrambled eggs all right? We've run out of bacon, I'm afraid.'

'Nothing for me, thanks. I'm not hungry.'

He poured himself a cup of coffee and took it over to the window. Mia looked at the bowl then tipped the eggs down the sink. There was no point cooking them when she wasn't hungry either. She filled a mug with coffee and sat down, wondering what to do. Would it be better if she and Harry left or would Leo think she was abandoning him and Noah? After all, this break had been arranged for Noah's sake, so surely she should stay.

'What do you want me to do?' she said, deciding it was simpler to ask him. 'If you want me and Harry to leave then say so.'

'Do you want to leave?'

He swung round and her heart ached when she saw the misery in his eyes. It was all she could do to sit there and not go to him but it would wrong to start something they both knew could only end in more confusion for the boys.

'I'm not sure. That's the honest answer.' She shrugged. 'I love it here and it's obvious that Harry loves being here too, but...'

'But it will be a strain,' he finished for her.

'Yes.' She sighed. 'It might be better if we left, Leo.'

'Maybe.' He drank some coffee then put the cup on the window sill. 'It's up to you, Mia. You must do whatever you think is best.'

He opened the back door but there was no way

she was letting him toss the ball into her court. She stood up and glared at him.

'It isn't up to me, though. This is something we both need to decide, the same as we need to decide how we intend to handle things from here on. Harry and Noah need to see one another when we get home...*we* need to see *them*! Which means that whether we like the idea or not, we're going to have to see each other.'

'I realise that. However, you'll have to forgive me if I don't feel up to working out the practicalities at the moment.' He pinned her with a cold-eyed stare. 'What happened last night is still very much on my mind even if you've managed to dismiss it.'

It was so unfair to accuse her of doing that that she couldn't speak. He was halfway out of the door before she found her voice. 'How dare you say that? Just because I'm trying to be sensible, it doesn't mean that I've forgotten what happened.'

'No? I'm flattered.' His smile was sardonic. 'It's good to know that I'm not instantly forgettable.'

'Why are you saying these things?' she demanded, bitterly hurt by the way he was behaving. 'We both agreed that we had to call a halt, Leo. It isn't what I want, but it's not my feelings that matter.'

'Are you sure about that? Sure you don't regret what we did?' He shrugged. 'From the length of time you spent in the bathroom last night, I got the distinct impression that you were having serious doubts.'

'Then you were wrong. Yes, I was thinking about what had happened, but I wasn't regretting it.' Her voice caught. 'The only thing I regret is that we can't risk being together again.'

'I got it wrong, didn't I?' His voice echoed with pain. 'When you took so long to come back I assumed it was because you were having second thoughts and couldn't face me.'

'And that's why you left?'

'Yes. I thought it would be less embarrassing for you if I wasn't there when you came back.' He sighed. 'Obviously, I was mistaken.'

'You were. If you want the truth, I wish you'd stayed. I could have done with a hug.'

'Oh, sweetheart!'

He took a step towards her then stopped when there was a scream from the garden. Mia was hard on his heels as he raced out of the door, her heart turning over when she saw Noah standing on the far side of the fence next to the river. There was no sign of Harry and she could barely contain her fear as she ran across the grass.

Leo scooped Noah up and swung him back over the fence. 'Where's Harry, Noah? Tell me!'

The little boy pointed to the river and Mia went cold as she turned and stared at the water rushing past the end of the garden. With all the rain they'd had, the water level was extremely high, lapping at the bank as it swirled past.

'He went to fetch the ball and fell into the water,' Noah choked out through his sobs.

Leo didn't hesitate as he vaulted over the fence. Kicking off his shoes, he waded into the water. 'I can see him! He's caught up in some bushes.'

Mia clapped a hand to her mouth as he dived into the river. The current was very strong and within seconds he was swept away. She could just make out his head bobbing above the water, although she couldn't see Harry from where she was standing. Noah was shivering with cold and fright so she put her arms around him and hugged him. She wanted to jump into the river herself and help but she knew it was the wrong thing to do. If Leo couldn't reach Harry, she would have to summon help.

The next few minutes were a nightmare. Leaving Noah safely on the far side of the fence, she made her way to the edge of the bank. She could see Harry's red jumper snagged on some bushes and just make out the dark shape of Leo's head as he struggled to reach him. When he finally managed to grab hold of Harry and lifted him out of the water, she felt tears pour down her face. She'd been so terrified that she would lose them both.

Leo made his way back along the river bank. He was carrying Harry, who was shivering violently. 'I don't think he's hurt, just very cold and scared. Let's get him inside and see how he is then.'

Mia hurried on ahead with Noah while he carried Harry back to the house. He took him straight into the sitting room, setting him down in front of the fire and stripping off his sodden clothes. Mia ran upstairs to fetch a towel and wrapped Harry in it. His teeth were chattering and he was crying but he didn't appear to be injured.

'Are you hurt anywhere, darling?' she asked, cuddling him close.

'I've hurt my hand,' Harry told her, holding up his hand so she could see the angry red scratch on his palm.

'I'll put a plaster on it,' she assured him, giving him a kiss. She gave Noah a kiss as well then stood up. Recriminations could wait till later; for now all that mattered was that Harry was safe thanks to Leo. She turned to him, overcome with gratitude. He had risked his own life to save Harry.

'Thank you. I don't know how I can ever repay you for what you've done.'

'It doesn't matter. The only thing that matters is that Harry is safe. I don't know what I'd have done if anything had happened to him.'

His voice grated and Mia felt tears fill her eyes once more. That Leo cared about Harry was obvious. Harry was his son after all, and he must love him just as much as she loved Noah.

It was the first time that she had admitted how she felt about Noah and it filled her with warmth. Holding out her hand, she drew him to her and hugged him, her heart overflowing with love for this child she and Chris had created. Noah was her son just as Harry was Leo's, and somehow they had to make this situation work for all of them. No matter how hard it was, or what sacrifices it took, she and Leo would make sure the boys didn't suffer.

Leo made his way upstairs, aware that what had happened had brought the situation into sharp focus. He shuddered as he recalled his fear as he had tried to get to Harry. He'd been terrified that the child would be swept away before he could reach him. Harry's life had been hanging, quite literally, by a thread and those endless minutes he had spent struggling to reach him were imprinted on his mind. He didn't know how he would have been able to bear it if he had lost Harry.

He sank down onto the bed, uncaring that his wet clothes were soaking the quilt. Finding out that Noah wasn't his child had been the worst thing that had ever happened to him but if he had lost Harry today, it would have been equally as bad. He loved the boy, loved him not only because Harry was his biological son but because of Mia. She had given birth to Harry, brought him up, loved and cared for him, and it was thanks to her that Harry had turned out the way he had. He loved Harry and he loved Mia. They were both unassailable facts.

'Are you all right?'

He looked up, his heart racing when he saw Mia standing in the doorway. Her face was very pale thanks to the shock she'd had but she was still the most beautiful woman he had ever known. If he could be granted just one wish, it would be the chance to spend his life with her but he couldn't see it happening. Mia may have enjoyed making love with him but she didn't see him as a permanent part of her future.

'Fine. Just a bit shocked, I suppose.' He summoned a smile, refusing to let her see how devastated the thought made him feel. 'Kids certainly know how to put you through the mill, don't they?'

'They do indeed.'

She returned his smile but he could see the sadness in her eyes and realised that she found the situation as difficult as he did. Maybe she was waiting for him to make the first move, he mused, needed his assurances that it could work, as indeed it could. After all, Harry and Noah got on extremely well; surely they would be thrilled at the idea of them all living together as a family?

Leo's head reeled as the full impact of that thought hit him. He didn't just want to have an affair with Mia. He wanted to spend his life with her. But was he *sure* it was what he wanted? Or was it merely the result of all the emotional turmoil he'd been through that day? Although he loved her, he had no idea if his feelings would last.

How long *did* love last? A lifetime? A couple of years? He had never been in love before and had nothing to measure it by, so what if it was like desire and faded with time? How would it affect Noah and Harry if he discovered that he no longer loved her? He could end up doing the very thing he had wanted to avoid and ruin the boys' lives.

Mia could see a range of emotions racing across Leo's face and she frowned. She had no idea what he was thinking but it was clear that there was something troubling him. She was on the point of asking him when she heard Harry shouting for her.

'I'd better go and see what he wants,' she said, turning away. 'I've put the kettle on so come down once you've changed and have a hot drink. You must need it after the soaking you've had.'

'Thanks. I won't be long.' Leo smiled but there was a reserve about it that made her heart ache. She had a feeling that he was deliberately distancing himself and it hurt after their closeness of the previous night.

She didn't say anything, however. She merely returned his smile and went downstairs. Harry wanted to know if he and Noah could watch a DVD and she immediately agreed. It was good to know that Harry seemed to have got over his fright, she thought as she went into the kitchen to make them a drink. He was a resilient little boy and seemed to cope with most things. It made her wonder if she was being too cautious. Maybe Harry would cope better than she feared if she told him the truth about Leo being his father?

Mia sighed as she poured milk into a pan. It was far too soon to tell Harry the truth, especially when it would mean them having to tell Noah as well. She had to wait until she and Leo had worked out all the details and what it would entail. There would need to be a lot of changes made if they were to amalgamate the two families, always assuming that was what Leo wanted, of course. Just for a second the thought of them all living together as a proper family filled her head before she dismissed it. Maybe she and Leo were sexually compatible but he had given no indication that he wanted anything more from her than that.

The boys were fast asleep by seven o'clock that night. Maybe it was all the excitement they'd had but neither of them objected when Leo suggested they go to bed. He gave them a bath and read them a story, thinking how much he enjoyed doing it. He made a point of being home in time to put Noah to bed and having Harry there simply doubled his pleasure. As he made his way downstairs, he found himself imagining how it would be if it became a permanent part of his nightly routine. Tucking the boys up in bed each night would be a joy, especially when Mia would be waiting for him afterwards.

He sighed as he made his way to the kitchen, where Mia was cooking dinner for them. He needed to take off the rose-tinted spectacles and see the situation in its true light. Family life wasn't all baths and stories—it was so much more. It might be fine for a while but how long would it last? When would the daily routine become a chore? When would the thought of Mia waiting for him become boring rather than exciting? Although he couldn't imagine it happening at this moment, it could do. It happened to lots of people and there was no guarantee that it wouldn't happen to them too.

'All settled?'

Mia looked round when he went in and Leo did his best to respond in a fitting manner. He didn't want to upset her, especially not after last night. The thought of what had happened the previous night made him go hot and cold and he shook his head to clear it of the images that had invaded it. Mia frowned in concern.

'Why? What's wrong? Is Harry upset about falling into the river?' She put down the spoon she'd been using to stir the gravy and hurried to the door. 'I'd better go up and see him.'

'There's no need. He's fine.'

Leo laid his hand on her arm, flinching when

he felt every cell in his body fire off a veritable volley of signals. He could feel his skin tingling where his hand rested on her arm and quickly removed it. Last night had been a one-off and there wasn't going to be a repeat tonight despite what his libido hoped.

'Oh. I thought something had happened,' she said, sounding confused, which was understandable.

'No. Everything's fine. They're both fast asleep.' Leo treated her to another smile because it was impossible to explain. Admitting that he'd been trying to clear his head, and of what, wouldn't help. 'Something smells good,' he said, changing the subject to a less stressful topic.

'Lamb chops and new potatoes,' she said briskly, going back to the stove.

'Lovely. How about a glass of wine? I've a rather good red that I've been saving. Let's open it tonight, shall we?'

Leo gritted his teeth when he realised that he had adopted his 'social' tone, the one he used when dealing with a particularly difficult guest. That Mia had noticed it too was obvious from her clipped reply.

'Don't open it for me. Save it for something special.'

'I can't think of anything more special than having you and Harry here,' he said quietly as he went to fetch the bottle.

He sighed as he lifted it off the rack. He was out of his depth and it was worrying to know that he had no idea what to do. He was used to making difficult decisions but he couldn't decide what to do in this instance.

He loved Mia and he wanted to be with her with all that it entailed, but would it work? Or would it turn out to be a disaster? He had sworn he wouldn't get involved again after Amanda yet here he was, thinking about doing that very thing. If it were only him who might suffer, he wouldn't hesitate; he would tell Mia how he felt and be done with it. However, it wasn't only him, it was the boys too. How could he do what he so desperately wanted when it could impact badly on Harry and Noah?

CHAPTER SIXTEEN

DINNER WAS A stilted affair. Although they talked, Mia sensed that Leo was merely going through the motions for the sake of politeness. She wasn't sure what was wrong and didn't want to ask him either. However, the thought that he was no longer interested in her now that they had made love refused to go away. It was a relief when they finished. She shook her head when he offered to do the washing up.

'I'll do it. You go and relax. You deserve a rest after what you did this morning.'

He didn't argue, simply turned and left, and that in itself seemed to prove her suspicions were correct. Leo had got what he wanted and now he had no more use for her. Tears filled her eyes and she dashed them away. She wouldn't cry, wouldn't embarrass herself or him. Within the circles Leo frequented affairs must be commonplace and she refused to make a fool of herself by letting him see how upset she felt.

Once the dishes were done, she went up to bed, unable to face making any more stilted conversation. She checked on the boys, who were fast asleep, then went to her room. She heard Leo come upstairs a short time later and held her breath but he passed by her door without pausing. One night had obviously been enough for him, she thought bitterly.

She must have drifted off to sleep only to be woken by the sound of screaming. Leaping out of bed, she ran along the landing, fully expecting it to be Harry after what had happened that morning. However, when she went into the boys' room she discovered it was Noah screaming. Rushing over to the bed, she gathered him into her arms.

'It's all right, darling. You're quite safe. You've had a bad dream, that's all,' she said, rocking him to and fro. She looked up when Leo appeared at her side, feeling her heart turn over when she was presented by the sight of his naked torso. Her mind swooped back to the previous night before she brought it back to the present. There was no point thinking about that, no point at all.

'Is he all right?' Leo crouched down beside her and stroked Noah's hair. 'Hey, what's wrong, tiger? Did you have a bad dream?'

'Go 'way!' Noah pushed Leo's hand away and buried his face in Mia's shoulder.

Leo drew back, an expression of pain crossing his face. 'He obviously doesn't want me so will you try and find out what's wrong with him?'

'Of course.' Mia felt a wave of sympathy rise up inside her. She knew how she would have felt if Harry had reacted that way when she'd tried to comfort him. 'He doesn't really know what he's saying right now. Give him a few minutes to calm down.'

'Of course.' Leo stood up and glanced over at Harry's bed, forcing a smile when he saw that the little boy was watching them. 'Noah's had a bad dream and your mummy's going to give him a cuddle. Shall we go downstairs and have a drink until Noah feels better?'

Harry shot out of bed, obviously excited at the thought of getting up in the middle of the night. Leo took hold of his hand and led him to the door, pausing briefly to glance back.

'Noah will be fine,' Mia said, knowing how hard it must be for him to leave the child with her.

'I know he will. He couldn't be in better hands,' he replied roughly.

Mia bit her lip as he and Harry left the room. Had she been wrong to assume that he had tired of her so quickly? There had been something in his voice just now that seemed to disprove that idea.

Noah gave a little moan and she cuddled him close. What Leo did or didn't feel wasn't the issue. It was Noah who mattered. She needed to find out what had upset him.

She stroked his hair and gradually the tension started to leave him. A wave of motherly love washed over her as she felt the thinness of his little body pressing against her. She loved him so much even though she had never expected to feel this way. He was her son and no matter what happened between her and Leo, she intended to play a role in his life. Once his sobs had abated, she gently set him away from her.

'Can you tell me what frightened you, sweetheart? Was it a bad dream?'

'Yes,' he whispered. He looked so solemn that

she was tempted to tell him that it didn't matter, only she knew that she had to get to the bottom of this.

'Do you remember what you dreamt about?' she asked softly, and felt him stiffen. 'If you tell me then it might make it less scary.'

'I was dreaming about Harry falling into the water,' he muttered.

'Oh, that was scary,' she said, giving him another cuddle. She smiled at him. 'But Harry's fine now. Your daddy got him out of the water and he's promised not to go near it ever again.'

'It was my fault he fell in,' Noah said in a rush. 'I didn't catch the ball and it landed in the water and Harry had to get it.'

'It wasn't your fault,' she said firmly. 'Harry knew he shouldn't go near the river.'

Noah considered that for a second. 'It was my fault that Mummy crashed her car.'

Mia managed to hide her surprise, although she had a feeling that this was the real root of the problem. 'I'm sure that isn't true, darling. It was an accident.'

'No, it was my fault. I started crying and Mummy got angry and didn't see the bus coming.' Tears filled his eyes. 'I don't want a new daddy. You won't let Mummy make me live with her and my new daddy, will you, Mia? She said that my old daddy doesn't want me any more so can I live with you and Harry?'

Mia didn't know what to say. It was worse than she had imagined, far, far worse, and not just because of what Noah must have been going through for all these months. All of a sudden she was overwhelmed by doubts, by thoughts so dark that she felt sick. Had Leo known that his ex-wife had been planning to take Noah away from him? Was that why once he'd discovered that Noah wasn't his real son, he had set out to find the child who was? Was Harry to be some sort of trade-off, offered in Noah's place?

She didn't want to believe that Leo would do such a terrible thing but she knew how much he loved Noah and how desperate he was to keep him. He had been so ambiguous about his ex-wife's involvement, too. She had put it down to the fact that he had little time for Amanda after the way she had abandoned Noah as a baby, but maybe there was another explanation. Had he deliberately played down Amanda's involvement so that she wouldn't become suspicious?

Mia's head reeled as thoughts rushed this way and that. It was only the fact that Noah needed reassuring that helped her hold it together. She tilted his face and looked into his eyes so that he would see that she meant every word.

'No one is going to take you away from your daddy, my love. Mummy was wrong when she said that Daddy doesn't want you any more because he does. He loves you an awful lot and he'll do everything he can to make sure you stay with him. Do you understand?'

Noah nodded, his face relaxing into a smile as he put his arms around her and hugged her. Mia hugged him back, although her heart felt like lead. Was she right to suspect that Leo had had an ulterior motive all along? Had he been lulling her into a false sense of security, playing on her emotions to get what he wanted, which was Noah living with him? Even sleeping with her could have been part of his plan and that was the worst thought of all, to wonder if he had used her that way too.

Mia took a deep breath, forcing back the tears

that threatened to overwhelm her. She didn't want to believe that Leo could have done such a thing but after everything that had happened to her as a child, she couldn't rule it out. The fact that she might have put Harry at risk by her gullibility was very hard to accept but she had to face it. Even if Leo hadn't planned this, there was still Amanda to consider.

Although Amanda hadn't wanted Noah initially, people changed and she could have changed too. Maybe she had found it difficult to bond with him, somehow sensing that he wasn't hers.

Mia's heart filled with dread. It would definitely explain Amanda's past behaviour. She'd always found it hard to believe that any woman could reject her own child but there may have been a reason for it, a good one too. Now, if Amanda was so desperate for a child, she could very well try to claim Harry, her real son. And Leo might help her if it meant he could retain custody of Noah.

Leo could barely contain his anxiety. Mia seemed to be taking an inordinately long time, he thought as he made Harry a mug of hot chocolate. He added cold milk to cool it down then placed it on the table, forcing himself to smile. He didn't want Harry to know how worried he felt.

'Here you go. Drink this up and then we'll see if Noah is feeling better.'

Harry buried his face in the mug, gulping down the treat with obvious pleasure. When he asked if he could have a biscuit, Leo nodded. He found the tin and let the child choose what he wanted, glancing at the clock while Harry debated. How much longer was Mia going to be?

He put the tin away, looking round in relief when he heard her footsteps. She smiled as she came into the kitchen but Leo could see the strain in her eyes and his heart turned over. It was obvious that something had happened. However, with Harry there he couldn't ask her what it was. It was another ten minutes before Mia took Harry back to bed. Leo waited with mounting impatience for her to return. He needed to know what was going on and needed to know it soon! She came in and sat down, her face set as she looked at him.

'I expect you're anxious to know what was wrong with Noah,' she said in a cold little voice he had never heard her use before. It struck fear into his heart so that he had to sit down as well.

'Obviously,' he replied equally coldly, because he didn't want her to know how scared he felt.

'It appears that Noah believed he was responsible for that accident he and his mother had.'

She didn't try to dress it up and Leo realised that there was more to it than that. It was an effort to reply calmly when it felt as though his insides were churning.

'That's ridiculous. It wasn't Noah's fault and I'll make sure he understands that.'

'Good. And while you're doing that, I suggest you make sure he understands that you still want him.' She shrugged, ignoring his stunned gasp. 'It appears that your ex-wife told him he was going to live with her and his new daddy because you no longer wanted him. When he started crying, she got angry and crashed into the bus.'

'I don't believe it!' Leo leapt to his feet, unable to sit there and listen to such rubbish. 'Amanda actually told him that I didn't want him?'

'So it seems.' She shrugged again. 'Are you saying you didn't know?'

'Of course I didn't know!' he exploded, stunned

that she would think he'd had any inkling. 'If I'd known Amanda had told him that, I'd have done something about it.'

'Maybe you did.' Her expression was glacial. It matched her tone and Leo felt his blood run cold.

'And what's that supposed to mean? Come on, spit it out. Something is obviously bothering you.'

'You're right. It is.'

She stood up as well and he realised that she was trembling. It was hard to stand there and not go to her, but he knew that it wasn't what she wanted. Leo steeled himself because he also knew that whatever she said was going to hurt. A lot.

'You found out what your ex-wife was planning and took steps to avoid it. That's why you were so keen to find Harry, Amanda's *real* son.' She gave a broken laugh. 'What was the plan, Leo? Was Harry to be a trade-off—you'd get to keep Noah while she had Harry, and both of you would be happy?

'Maybe you two planned it together—who knows? Well, even if you did, I'm sorry to have to tell you that it isn't going to happen. I shall fight you through every court in the land if either of you tries to take Harry away from me. He's my son and he always will be mine!'

She spun round but Leo didn't move. He couldn't. He was so stunned by the accusation that he couldn't move a muscle. Did Mia honestly believe he would do that? Sink so low as to take her child so he could give him to another woman? He couldn't begin to explain how it made him feel to know that she thought him capable of that kind of deception.

He sank down onto a chair and put his head in his hands. Last night he had reached previously unknown heights of pleasure, of happiness, of joy. And tonight he had sunk to the very depths of despair.

It was raining again the following morning. Mia carried her case downstairs and placed it by the door. The taxi was due shortly and she wanted to be ready to leave as soon as it arrived. Harry trailed after her, looking mutinous as he placed his bag next to hers.

'Why do we have to go, Mummy? Noah's staying so why can't I stay with him?'

'It's just not possible, sweetie.' Mia tried to

smile but her lips refused to obey her. 'Noah and his daddy want to spend some time on their own.'

'Don't they want me to stay with them?' Harry asked, looking puzzled.

'Yes, we'd love you to stay, Harry. But your mummy has things to do and that's why you have to go home.'

Mia glanced round when Leo came to join them. His face was set and it was impossible to guess how he was feeling. He smiled at Harry and her heart filled with pain when she realised what a good actor he was. Nobody could tell from looking at him how devastated he must feel that his plans had been scuppered. It made her wonder if his so-called delight in their lovemaking had been an act too. If it had, it had certainly convinced her.

Her eyes swam with tears so it was a relief when the taxi sounded its horn. Picking up her case, she shooed Harry out of the door. Leo followed her out, laying a detaining hand on her shoulder.

'I'll be in touch as soon as I get back, Mia.'

Mia didn't say a word as she shook him off. She helped Harry into the cab and fastened his seat belt then fastened her own. She didn't look back as the driver pulled away and had no idea if Leo was waiting to wave them off. Whatever they'd had…whatever she'd *thought* they'd had… was over.

Mia was relieved when the half-term holiday ended and Harry went back to school. He'd been sulky and out of sorts ever since they'd got back from the cottage, obviously blaming her for cutting short the treat. He cheered up on the Monday morning, though, waving happily as she saw him into his classroom, and she breathed a sigh of relief. Although the worst certainly wasn't over, at least Harry was back to his old self and that was something to be grateful for.

She went into work to find that Penny had put her down for the cardiology unit again. Sister Thomas had booked a week's leave and Penny wanted her to cover. Mia shook her head.

'No, I'm sorry. You'll have to find someone else.'

'There isn't anyone else, or at least no one who can handle the redoubtable Leo Forester,' Penny told her with a grin. 'All the staff agree that he's a changed person when you're on the unit, Mia. Obviously, you know how to bring him to heel!'

It was just too much on top of all the sleepless nights she'd spent worrying about what Leo intended to do about Harry. Tears poured down her face and Penny leapt up in alarm.

'Hey, what's the matter, love? If it was what I said, then I'm sorry. I was only teasing.'

'It isn't that. It's everything. Leo and Noah and Harry and me.'

Mia knew she wasn't making sense but there was nothing she could do. When Penny sat her down, she didn't protest. What if Leo used his vast resources to take Harry from her; what would she do?

'Come on, tell me what's wrong.' Penny patted her shoulder. 'I'm the soul of discretion and I won't repeat a word of what you say.'

It was too tempting. Mia let it all pour out, all her fears, her hopes and her devastation. It was good to be able to tell someone and she felt much better afterwards, although Penny was open-mouthed with shock.

'I don't know what to say. I had no idea...' Penny stopped and gulped. 'What a mess, Mia.

But are you sure that Leo was planning to take Harry off you so he could trade him for Noah?'

'No. But it's possible and that's enough.' Mia dried her eyes. 'I won't risk anything happening to Harry.'

'I understand, really I do. But I can't see any judge countenancing such an action.'

'Not even if he was to be handed over to his real mother?'

'With her track record?' Penny shook her head. 'No, I honestly can't see it happening.'

'But what if Leo and Amanda got back to-gether? They might do, even on a temporary basis if it meant they would get what they wanted.'

'Highly unlikely.' Penny dismissed the idea. 'Anyway, the papers are always banging on about the fact that courts try to keep a child with its mother even when they should be removed for their own safety.'

'But that's just it. I'm not Harry's mother. Harry is Leo and Amanda's son. Noah is mine and Chris's.'

'Then you'd have equal rights, I imagine, to sue for custody of Noah.' Penny held up her hand when Mia went to speak. 'I'm not saying you should do it, merely pointing out that you're in the same position as Leo.'

'Except I don't have his money so I can't hire a fancy lawyer to fight my case.'

'There's help available. Anyway, it's not all down to money. Harry loves you. You're his mum. Noah loves Leo. He's his dad. There has to be a way to work this out and the only way to do that is by talking to Leo.'

Mia summoned a watery smile. 'Which is your very clever way of getting me to cover Cardiology.'

'Yep!' Penny gave her a hug. 'You can do this, Mia. You can sort it out. I'm sure of that.'

Mia hoped her friend was right, although she doubted it. She couldn't imagine that Leo would want to invest too much time talking after the way they'd parted. She made her way to the cardio unit and started work, checking the theatre list to see who was scheduled for surgery that day. Leo's name wasn't on the list as one of the attending surgeons and she breathed a sigh of relief. At least she wouldn't have to face him just yet.

* * *

Leo had spent the remainder of the week trying to get in contact with Amanda. She had changed her mobile number and he had to phone everyone he knew to find out where she was. In the end he tracked her down to a villa in the south of France where she was staying with friends. He kept it brief, explaining that Noah had told him about her plans and that if she thought she was going to take Noah from him, she could think again.

He didn't mention Mia or Harry; he couldn't bear to. He simply made it clear that Amanda would regret it if she attempted to put her plan into action. Although it might not be the last he heard from her, at least she knew that she'd have a fight on her hands, and if there was one thing Amanda loathed it was doing anything that would upset her pampered life.

With one problem if not solved at least addressed, he realised that he had to deal with an even bigger one. He still hadn't got over his hurt and anger at Mia's accusations but he knew he couldn't leave it as it was. He was going to have to speak to her, assuming she would speak to him, of course.

He drove to her house first thing on Monday morning, wanting to talk to her without Harry being there, but there was no reply when he knocked on the door. She must have gone into work, he decided, turning the car round. Although it wasn't ideal to have an in-depth discussion in working time, he needed to get this sorted out. He couldn't bear it if they were at loggerheads, couldn't bear to imagine how worried she must be. He had to reassure her that he didn't intend to take Harry away from her, no matter what happened.

Maybe it was the fact that he was so distracted but he didn't notice the van that suddenly pulled out of a side road until it was right in front of him. He slammed on the brakes but there was no way he could avoid it. There was a horrible crunching sound of metal striking metal and a roar as the airbag deployed and then silence, broken by the anxious voices of passers-by.

Leo sat in the driving seat, feeling breathless and disorientated from the force of the airbag hitting his chest. He knew the car was quite badly damaged but that didn't matter. What mattered more was that it would delay him speaking to Mia.

* * *

Mia was getting into the lift after accompanying a patient to Theatre when she heard a couple of nurses talking. They were saying something about one of the consultants being brought into ED following an RTA but it was only when she heard Leo's name that she started listening.

'Excuse me, but did you say that Mr Forester was in ED?' she asked, feeling a trickle of fear run down her spine.

'Yes. Seems he crashed into a van,' one of the nurses explained. Both women got out at the next floor so she didn't have time to question them further but she knew that she couldn't leave it at that. If Leo was injured she needed to know how bad he was.

Her heart contracted as she pressed the button again, bypassing the cardio unit and heading to ED. There was a queue at the reception desk and she waited with mounting impatience for her turn. 'I believe you have Mr Forester here?' she said, trying to sound as cool and composed as possible, no mean feat when her heart was hammering away.

'That's right.' The receptionist took note of her

badge and grinned. 'Checking to see if we'll be keeping him here so you can have an easy ride today?'

'Something like that,' Mia agreed, dredging up a smile.

'I don't blame you. Anyway, Rob's looking after him—he's over there, the tall guy with the bald head.'

Mia nodded her thanks and hurried over to the registrar. He shrugged when she asked him if Leo was badly injured.

'We're still running tests—CT scan, X-rays, bloods—so I can't give you a definite answer. However, from the fuss he's making, I doubt he's on his way to meet the Grim Reaper today.'

'Oh, right. Thank you,' Mia murmured, feeling faint with relief. She went and sat down on a chair, wondering what to do.

Despite the registrar's assurances, she would have liked to see for herself that Leo was all right but would that be wise? She could be playing into his hands by showing her vulnerability, couldn't she? For all she knew, he could have been plotting away, working with his ex-wife to take Harry off her…only she didn't really believe that, did she? Not in her heart. Not where it truly mattered.

Mia stood up, her legs trembling as she went over to the desk where the registrar was talking to one of the nurses. It was a question of trust, wasn't it? Quite simply: did she trust Leo enough to believe that he would never try to hurt her and Harry?

'Excuse me,' she said, feeling a rush of warmth run through her and chase away the chill that had invaded her for the past few days. She did trust him, trusted him to do what was right for Harry, trusted him to do what was right for her too. It was hard to speak when there were so many emotions welling up inside her. 'C-can I see Mr Forester?'

'If you want to, although I warn you he's not in the best of tempers, although I expect you're used to that.' The registrar grinned. 'I never believed the stories about him before but I do now. I'm only glad I don't work for him!'

Mia didn't say anything as he led her to the end cubicle and left her there. The curtains were drawn and she took a quick breath before pushing them aside. She was probably the last person Leo wanted to see but tough. She needed to make sure he was all right and then…

What?

What did she intend to do? Talk to him? But would he want to talk to her? Leo would be well within his rights to refuse to have anything to do with her after what she'd said to him. She could, in fact, make the situation worse by attempting to discuss what had happened and that was the last thing she wanted. Although she wasn't foolish enough to think that they could pick up where they had left off, she wanted them to be friends at the very least. But would Leo want to be her friend? That was the big question.

Mia stood there, gripping the curtain as she debated the idea. Could a man and a woman ever be just friends after they'd been lovers?

Leo swung his legs over the side of the bed. He'd had enough of hanging around. Maybe that young registrar was only following procedure but *he* knew he was fine.

He slipped his feet into his shoes, groaning when his ribs gave him gyp. No doubt he'd have a mass of bruises from the combined force of the seat belt locking and the airbag deploying but what was a bit of physical discomfort compared to this inner agony he felt? He had to see Mia and convince her that she could trust him!

He thrust back the curtain and came to a dead stop when he was confronted by the very person he longed to see. Whether it was shock or relief, he had no idea, but there was no way that he could play it cool. That was the old him, the man he'd been pre-Mia, and he was a completely different person now.

He hauled her into his arms and kissed her right there in the middle of ED, uncaring that there were people watching them. He loved her, he wanted her, and by heaven he was going to make her understand that if he had to stand here all day and kiss her!

There was a moment's hesitation and then she was kissing him back and Leo knew it was going to be all right, that miraculously they could sort out this whole stupid mess. Mia loved him as much as he loved her and they could take on the world and win so long as they took it on together.

He drew back, his breath coming in spurts that were only partly the result of his bruised ribs. 'I had no idea what Amanda was planning. You have to believe me, my darling. I would never have tried to trick you and take Harry from you.'

'I know you wouldn't.' Her breathing sounded strained too and he smiled as some much-needed confidence came roaring back.

'Good.' He rewarded her with another kiss then looked round, grimacing as he realised the attention they were attracting. 'Shall we take this somewhere a little more private?'

'Please.'

She didn't protest as he caught hold of her hand and led her from ED. They passed Rob on the way out but he was too stunned to object when Leo informed him that he would come back later for the results of the tests. It took just a few minutes to reach the consultants' lounge, which was mercifully empty. Leo closed the door and leant against it.

'So where do we go from here?'

'Where do you want to go?' she countered, looking at him with so much love in her eyes that he trembled.

'Nowhere that you won't be,' he growled, pulling her into his arms and kissing her with undisguised hunger. He leant his forehead against hers, feeling uncharacteristically bashful about revealing the true depth of his feelings, although maybe it was understandable. After all, it would be the first time he had told a woman that he loved her.

'I love you, Mia. I want to spend my life with you and build a future for us and the boys, if it's what you want too. Do you?'

'Yes. It's what I want more than anything. If we can do it and not harm the boys in any way.'

He stroked her cheek, understanding her fear. 'There's no reason to think they'll be unhappy about it. We've seen how well they get on and I'm sure they'll be thrilled to be part of a family.' He looked into her eyes. 'But we'll take it slowly, make sure they're completely comfortable with all that we have to tell them, make sure they understand how much we love them too. OK?'

'Yes. It's more than OK,' she murmured, reaching up on tiptoe to kiss him.

The kiss lasted several minutes and only ended when Leo's pager bleeped. He sighed as he checked the display. 'Theatre's paging me. I'll have to phone and cancel. It wouldn't be a good idea to operate at the moment.'

'Because of your accident?' she said anxiously.

'No, because admitting how much I love you has left me with very shaky hands.'

He held them out for her inspection and she laughed, loving the fact that he could admit to his vulnerability, simply loving *him*. He made the call then arranged to go back to ED and meet her later, once all the results were back, not that he expected there to be a problem, he assured her.

Mia went back to the cardio unit and spent the rest of the morning feeling as though she was floating several inches above the ground. Leo loved her and, in time, they would be together: him, her and their boys. Maybe a mistake had brought them together, but the result couldn't be more perfect.

Two years later...

'Now take turns. And don't push the swing too high. We don't want Grace falling off.'

Leo waited until he was sure that Harry and Noah understood then went and sat down on the grass. They were spending a week at the cottage and the weather had been perfect. Long sunny days followed by gloriously warm nights. Taking hold of Mia's hand, he sighed in contentment. Life was wonderful and it was all thanks to her. Raising her hand to his lips, he smiled up at her.

'Have I told you lately how much I love you?'

'Oh, not since about eight o'clock this morning.'

'Very remiss of me. It's enough to make you instigate divorce proceedings.'

He laughed as he kissed the inside of her wrist, sure enough of their relationship to joke about it. They had married a year ago, as soon as they had discovered that she was expecting Grace. It had been right for many reasons, the main one being that Harry and Noah were comfortable with their relationship.

The DNA tests had confirmed what they had already known, that Harry was his child and Noah was Mia's, so once the time had felt right they had sat the boys down and explained what had happened, answered their questions and assured them that even though they had different mums and dads than they'd thought, it made no difference. He and Mia loved them both and amazingly the boys had accepted it.

It had been so much simpler than he'd feared, but then most things were simpler now that he had Mia there, loving and supporting him. When little Grace had been born some eight months later it had been the icing on the cake and the boys had been as thrilled as them. Harry and Noah loved their little sister to bits.

As for Amanda, either she had taken his warning to heart or, more likely, changed her mind again about being a mother. Rumour had it that she had split up from the man who she had been hoping would become Noah's new daddy. Apparently, he'd been very keen to be a father and Amanda had hoped that providing him with a ready-made son would satisfy his longings.

Leo had no idea what had really happened and didn't care. He was simply glad that he hadn't heard from her, although as a precaution he had taken legal advice if she did try to sue for custody of Harry or Noah in the future and he was confident that she wouldn't win if it came to a court case. Now he lay back on the grass, feeling the warmth of the sun seeping into his pores.

This was how his life felt every day, filled with warmth and love. He had Mia and their family. He had it all.

* * * * *

Mills & Boon® Large Print
Medical

May

June

July